WHY ME? WHY US?

WHY ME? WHY US?

Why This, Lord?

ANTHONY MCMARYION

Library of Congress Control Number:		2015901453
ISBN:	Hardcover	978-1-5035-3947-1
	Softcover	978-1-5035-3948-8
	eBook	978-1-5035-3949-5

To order additional copies of this book, contact:
Xlibris
1-888-795-4274
www.Xlibris.com
Orders@Xlibris.com
699971

CONTENTS

INTRODUCTION

This Is Why

I am writing this book to help those like myself who have got into relationship for what you believe, feel, and know is for all of the right reasons and seemingly all of and a lot of all of the wrong things happen to them, with them and to the other person. The other thing that happens is while they are in that relationship the wrong things happen in that relationship. I truly believe that every person who says their wedding vows really take them seriously. When they say "until death do us part," they literally mean it. Every person who makes a commitment in a relationship do so for what they feel is and will be everlasting.

Please take this insightful journey with me as I take you on a behind-the-scene look at and into the behind-the-scene reasons why relationships fail and end up in divorce. At one time or another we all have to sit down and take a look at where we are in our relationships and where we are when we get out of a relationship. We all, in our own way, ask our family, friends, those we confide in, and God the same question, which is, "Lord, Why me, Why us, Why this, Lord?" We want to know why those negative, hurtful, and painful things happen to us while we are in that relationship. We want to know why those negative painful events that we didn't plan for and we were not really prepared for, just showed up in our relationship seemingly on their own. And finally, we want to know why did that which happened had to happen to you and that person.

We cry out from the deepest depths of our hurt, pain, and place of brokenness, "Lord, why did this have to happen to me? Why did this type of circumstance, situation, confrontation, and end result to our relationship have to happen? Lord, why did this have to happen to us?" In this book, I will provide you with a behind-the-scene look into Satan's masterfully and systematic attempt to assault, attack, and finally assassinate your relationship long before you meet and the relationship start to connect, grow, develop, and mature. I pray that as I do so, God will enlighten the eyes of your understanding, and he will open the eyes of your heart so that your heart will receive his divine help and healing.

What I'm about to tell you right not is a fact, a truth and it must be your reality; Satan wants to assault, attack, assassinate, kill, steal, and destroy a relationship, your relationship, and the people in them. This is especially true if a relationship have any type of biblical or spiritual grounds, backing, or foundation. I also will provide a behind-the-scene look into the unseen, unexpected, unplanned, unknown, unfair, unaware, unsure, unforgettable, unexplainable, unthinkable, and unbelievable of relationships. I also will share with you, in a way that you can and will clearly see it and them, along with some of the wiles, trickeries, schemes, devices, deceptions, and delusions that Satan uses to assault and then attack and then finally assassinate relationships.

The devil's assaults, attacks, and assassinations directed at and upon every relationship are consistent and strategic. It is masterfully orchestrated and carried out by his core of demon spirits. Whatever weapons he formed against our relationship, he fires with the intensity and with the pinpoint accuracy of a skilled marksman assassin. He know if you do not have the right relationship with yourself you cannot and will not have the right relationship with God and with others. He also knows if you do not have a relationship with God you will never have a prosperous, productive and successful relationship with yourself and with others. Every negative feeling and emotion you have about yourself and about your life is the Satan's way of keeping you distracted and keeping you from having a healthy and whole relationship with God and with others.

As you take this journey with me into the behind-the-scene dark places and low points that relationships so often get into, I pray, believe, and know the Holy Spirit of the only true and living God will illuminate your relationship awareness light, your relationship sensitivity, and in the end, God will reveal and then expose what the devil see, think, and feel and what is the vision he and all of his demons and imps have for our relationship.

I will, through the power of the Holy Spirit, prepare and present to you the devil's perspective view on your relationship. Yes, it is true—the devil have a plan, purpose, destiny, and a vision for your relationship. When you have finished this book, you will, with clarity and with a blessed assured conviction, end up being able to say this is why all of this has happened to you, me, us, and to our relationship. Take in my message and listen to my music. Welcome to the journey!

CHAPTER ONE

Fairy-Tale Relationship

We all have had them at one time in our life, those fantasies, and we all have dreamed them and had, one time in our life, believed in them—yes, fairy tales. I'm talking about fairy tales and fantasies, those things that we were taught to believe in and those things we learned to desire. We all want to live a life that is different from the one we had when we were growing up if it wasn't to our liking. There also are those who wanted to live the life and have the lifestyle their parents had or someone they knew and looked up to had. No matter which, the bottom line is we all want to live a life that is filled with the fairy tales we had and filled with fantasies we made our secret hiding and dwelling place.

From the time we came into this world and begin to learn about life, love, and living, we had those who read us fairy tales and gave us the okay and the approval to believe in them. Some of the fairy tales we heard was just for our amusement, and there was those that actually inspired, encouraged, and motivated us to believe something or someone would happen in our life that would lead us into living a life that would be filled with happiness and fulfillment. For every fairy tale we held on to believe in and make our own, there was a fantasy we had that kept us connected to that fairy tale. A fairy tale is defined as a story that is often too unbelievable to be true, or it's a story that is totally untrue where magic deeds happen to those who dare to believe, dare to dream, and dare to put forth the effort in helping making them happen.

When it comes to our relationships, we all once had and still do, to some degree, have and hold dear to our hearts a fairy-tale romance, a fairy-tale relationship, or a fairy-tale romantic relationship idea that excel and exceed that of those individuals we are close to and share all or pieces of our life with. When it comes to a fairy-tale relationship, it is made up of, consist of, or have as its two main ingredients, magical moments and magical memories. Our fairy tales are good when they are realistic and obtainable through honest means. Fairy tales often provide a much-needed spark to our imagination, human spirit, and set fire to the human soul and the human will.

Can you remember the first real fairy tale you had and how you would do your best to align and set the course of your day and life with that fairy tale? No matter who we are, we all want to believe in something and someone that is good. We all want to have the fairy-tale faith or faith in a fairy tale that turns the unbelievable into the believable and the untrue into being true. Holding on to and believing that our fairy tales will someday or one day become our reality often help us to feel good about our lives, who we are, what we are, where we are, what we have been through, and where we are going. To have fairy tale faith is to have complete trust, confidence, and unquestionable belief in the unbelievable being made believable and the untrue being turned into truth because of the visible manifestations that prove otherwise.

If you are to see the visible manifestation of your fairy tale, you are going to have to demonstrate that you can be loyal to it no matter what happens from the time you believe in it and until you see the visible manifestation of it. You are going to have to exercise complete, unfailing trust, confidence, and an unquestionable belief that is so strong that fate and faithless people cannot hinder, kill, steal, destroy, distract, detour, delay, or deny you the fulfillment of your fairy tale. All around you, me and us, there are those whose life has been so traumatic, beaten, battered, and messed up that they have lost and do not believe in fairy tales.

They are the ones who specialize in saying, "real talk now." There has been something or someone that has stolen their power to believe that fairy tales can, will, and still do happen. Why are they like that? As their life begins to unfold, it also began to unravel right before their eyes. Their life was plagued with or had been consistently hit with unseen, unexpected, unplanned, unknown, unfair, unaware, uncertain, unsure, and unheard of rounds and doses of hurt, pain, brokenness, being abused, battered, neglected, rejected, ostracized, labeled, targeted for bad words, acts, action and deeds, being victimized, tormented, and tortured, etc., that they do not and cannot find the willpower, the power within themselves to revive, restore, and relive their fairy tale and to believe in it again.

I do believe all of our fairy-tale faith believing should be rooted and grounded in truth and reality, but not so much to the place or point where when it seem like, feel like, and look like our fairy tales can't and won't become a reality. We can't and shouldn't allow ourselves to give in to the negatives and hopelessness and give up fighting for the fulfillment of our fairy-tale faith believing. Fairy tales do come true, and they happen every day. There are everyday people just like you and me, living or have lived in an odds-stacked-heavily-against-them life who still fight through all of the unseen, the unexpected, the unplanned, the unknown, the unfair, the unaware, the uncertain, the unsure, and the unheard of things that has happened to them and remain loyal to their belief in their fairy-tale happening.

There are good and right fairy tales, and there are bad and wrong fairy tales. As long as the fairy tales we have, hold on to, believe in, and is working to help see come to fruition do not violate or contaminate our human will nor our human spirit and our drive, motivation, ambition, senses, sensibility, sensitivity, creativity, etc., or hurt and hinder, distract, detour, delay, and deny other's the power to believe in and see the fulfillment of their fairy tale, then the fairy tale they have and we have is good, real, and right. You have to consistently fight a good fight and a good warfare on the behalf of your fairy tale if you want to see it fulfilled.

All of us have had hurtful and painful things that has happened to us while and when we were on the road to the fulfillment of our fairy tale, and all of us had, at one time or another, failed at seeing the fulfillment, but we didn't and don't give up. We just *get up*, learn from our failed fairy-tale fulfillment attempt, regroup and get back into the fight for the fulfillment of it. You can and you will see the right fairy-tale fruit you desire to see if you remain loyal to the fairy tale, demonstrate a tenacious, persistent patience, perseverance, and consistent unquestionable belief in it, and demonstrate you possess, know how to, and when to release and apply complete trust and confidence in your fairy tale's fulfillment.

Fairy-Tale Relationships

A person who is in a fairy-tale relationship is quite often someone that is similar in a lot of ways, often see things alike, think alike, feel alike, and they have a special bond, association, involvement, and emotional connection because they do not look at things just as they appear or what they look like. They have the ability to see beyond what is unbelievable or untrue. Most of the people who enter into a covenant fairy-tale relationship do so because the fairy-tale relationship to them and to the person they are in it with are believable and true, and both have a tenacious belief and confidence that their fairy-tale relationship will take place or happen.

To the others, their fairy-tale belief seems crazy and filled with nothing but failures; but to the persons who have the fairy-tale faith, belief, hope, and confidence, their fairy tale can end up being their reality. Therefore, they do not care nor seek the approval and validation of others. There are those who are not patient enough to wait for their fairy-tale relationship, as a result they end up making a relationship choice and decision that come out of being "halt between two opinions", deceived, fear-driven and motivated. They end up allowing their fear impacted feelings, emotions and desires to be the power and force that lead them into making the relationship choices and decisions they make. They jump into a relationship and make what I call a fairy-tale relationship compromise.

Split-Decision Relationship Makers

When a person make a fairy-tale relationship compromise, what this mean is the person they entered into the relationship with is someone who had or have some traces or traits of, some features and characteristics of, in some ways looked like, conducted themselves like, and sounded like, reminded them of, was similar to, or was close to their ideal fairy-tale relationship and person, so they compromised or reached or settle for the bare minimum that is close to and what look like their ideal fairy-tale person, agreement within themselves, and with their fairy-tale relationship expectations.

And they made a concession or made a conceded agreement with their own fairy-tale expectations that basically declared, decreed, and stated: "this fairy-tale relationship I am getting into is not the real fairy-tale relationship I want to be in nor does it have all of the fairy-tale ingredients that I have been waiting patiently to see the fruits of, what I dreamed of, hoped for, prayed for, anticipated and expected in my fairy-tale relationship; but I am willing to get into the relationship and meet this relationship that have my kind of fairy-tale implications, possibilities, aura, scent, appearance, etc., at a midway point and place and get into it anyway."

They never really took the time to count up the cost for being in such relationship. I call people who make quick, fast, and in-a-hurry relationship choices and decisions *split-decision* relationship people. They quickly make up their mind on whether to get into a relationship without really thinking things out, and they basically really are relationship risk-takers. They often make fearful, haphazard, irresponsible, immature and dangerous, deadly, self-destructive, and damaging relationship choices and decisions. The main reason they do so is because they

> ➤ are so afraid of not being in a relationship;
> ➤ are afraid of being alone;
> ➤ feel their fairy-tale relationship biological clock is ticking real fast, and they will run out of fairy-tale relationship time;
> ➤ are fearful of not really finding someone who can and will give them and meet all or a majority of their fairy-tale relationship wants, needs, and desires;
> ➤ Have allowed themselves to get into some type of relationship circumstance, situation, or confrontation, and they need a refuge person.

Split-decision fairy-tale relationship seekers and makers are people who are willing to ignore all of the new relationship red flags they see, ignore all of the character, conduct, conversation, communication, and cultural differences, barriers, boundaries, breakdowns, hindrances, and limitations that they obviously do and can see and know of and they know can, will, and do exist, and they get into the relationship anyway.

A lot of times they do so because they feel like they have something to prove to the person they just got out of a relationship with, feeling like that person wasn't going to make a fairy-tale relationship commitment with them, and they also feel they have to prove something to themselves and to others when it comes to relationships. When that split decision is made and the person get into that relationship, they will still end up with an empty feeling inside of themselves.

Why? The person they got into the split-decision relationship with may meet and fulfill few areas in their life, but the areas or places within them that they need, want, and desire the real fulfillment still goes unfulfilled. For example, they may have needed financial security, but what they really wanted more than anything is the one thing they never had and that was someone who had/has a strong, stable, safe, secure, consistent, deep, personal relationship with God, and they have their directions clear and straight. The person basically has everything they ever needed, wanted, and desired spiritually, physically, mentally, emotionally, etc., that they had never possessed before.

But the person got impatient, listened to the wrong voice, and started opening themselves up to deceptive and deceiving relationship information. From that point, they started to make a lot of or started to demonstrate irrational behavior and behavior patterns. Satan slipped in and blinded their heart and mind to the relationship truth, and they alienated themselves from the real relationship truth. A split decision, what look like, etc., might one day kind of be like my fairy-tale guy and relationship was made, and the decision maker is still running on empty fulfillment. They allowed themselves to get caught up in blind ambition.

Creative Compromise Choices

When a person makes this kind of fairy-tale relationship compromise, they are opening themselves up for the unseen, the unexpected, the unplanned, the unknown, the unfair, the uncertain, the unaware, the unsure, the uncertain, and the unheard of negatives concerning the person they have made the fairy-tale relationship compromise with. The person who made the fairy-tale relationship compromise in most cases did not see or know or did know of and had seen at the beginning of the relationship what type of compromises they were making. The what-looked-like-felt-like-and-sounded-like-a-part-or-piece-of-my-fairy-tale-relationship negatives started to show as the relationship begins to unfold. And in most cases, the wrong things started to show up when the person who made the original fairy-tale relationship choice and decision began to place fairy-tale relationship expectations on that new relationship person, and that new person could not, did not, and was not able to meet nor match their fairy-tale relationship expectations.

Looking through the Windows

As we look through the windows of relationships, what we will see are people who are making what I call creative fairy-tale compromised choices or creative fairy-tale relationship compromises and choices over and over again. Basically, what happens is, the person out of reasons they feel is right allow their mind, thoughts, train of thought, thinking and way of thinking to be seduced, tricked, deceived, pulled, pushed, persuaded, drawn, driven, forced, enticed, entangled, and entrapped into having a misled and misguided quality or power of originality of thought and expression they are led to believe and feel is originative, productive and have the right imaginative ingenuity that can and will cause, create the atmosphere for and contribute to a fairy tale relationship settlement by mutual concessions.

In all actuality the only thing that's happened is it end up being a fairy-tale relationship agreement reached by or within the fairy tale holder's mental state of mind, mental condition/conditioning, and within their mental frame of mind that produce, prepare, and present a fairy-tale relationship adjustment of conflicting or opposing fairy-tale relationship claims, principles, etc., by reciprocal fairy-tale relationship modification of demands that is immediately made within. Those same relationship modifications of demands that were immediately made within will also become the mind-set and the mentality of the fairy-tale relationship beholder. Out of those creative compromises that's made will come creative compromise choices or creative compromise selections.

The fairy-tale relationship beholder is giving and allowing their imaginative and the originality of thought, the power and the freedom to function, flow, and follow in the path of and pursue after reciprocal fairy-tale relationship modifications and demands that open the door for that person to exercise their power of choice and give them their power and train of thought, thinking, and way of thinking suggestions and influences they will feel and think gives them the right, power, opportunity, and the option to make split-decision relationship selections. The problem with all of this is the wrong power and force is behind this dead and unprofitable fairy-tale relationship deductive reasoning.

One of the most important things that you have to be aware of and remember is whatever there are fairy-tale relationship expectations, desires, dreams, hopes, etc., they are ones your unconscious state know of that can and will bring you the fairy-tale fulfillment you need and want. Our fairy-tale expectations fulfill a part or parts of us. That is why we choose the fairy-tale qualities, characteristics, and features we choose because we know the fairy-tale expectations will benefit us. Those fairy-tale expectations or requirements we place on or seek out in our relationships will also meet and satisfy a human relationship flaw, a place of weakness that is within us. The main reason(s) why we often abandon our fairy-tale relationship faith and belief is because we trust and place our fairy-tale faith in the hands of family and friends that we think, feel, and believe will support us and encourage us in our fairy-tale relationship desire.

What those who do so, can count on is running into family and friends who do not believe in fairy tales and in fairy-tale relationships, because they have had their fairy-tale faith killed, stolen, destroyed, or severely handicapped to the point where they have given up on believing, expecting, and anticipating, any type or kind of fairy tale experience or encounter and they don't know if they can and will believe again nor do they know if they still know how to believe again. People who have had this happen to them have so much negative relationship and fairy-tale relationship feelings, emotions, images, information, instructions, insights, and energy flowing inside of themselves that the end result is they end up being fairy-tale naysayers, what I call fairy-tale faith, fairy-tale relationship swagger jackers.

Fairy-Tale Swagger Jackers

A fairy-tale swagger jacker is someone who cannot believe again, will not believe in, have not believed in, don't know how to believe in fairy-tale relationships; and as a result, they will say and do anything they can to distract, detour, delay, deny, discourage, and draw you away from being confident that you will see the fulfillment of and steal the flow of your fairy-tale relationship, steal your fairy-tale relationship confidence, steal your fairy-tale faith, and steal your fairy-tale hope and belief. Not only will they say and do anything, but they will also handle a matter that can bless, break, help, or hinder your fairy-tale relationship from coming forth in a way that it can do nothing but fail. Fairy-tale swagger jackers will also take it upon themselves to make wrong and bad choices and decisions on your behalf and without you knowing it if and when they see even the most remote possibility of your fairy-tale relationship being made visible.

A swagger jacker is someone who wants to kill, steal, destroy, block, sabotage, derail, etc., your fairy-tale walk that is bold, confident and has given you the confidence you have that your fairy tale is surely going to happen. Swagger jackers want to take away your faith filled fairy tale faith stride by using sneaky, dirty underhanded, unnoticeable, undetected, and hidden selfish, self centered, self righteous, self justified jealous motives and methods. The trick they use is to find ways to gain your total trust and then swindle, bamboozle, trick, and deceive you into believing what they are saying about your fairy-tale relationship faith. And the moment when you let your fairy-tale relationship faith guard down, they will hit you from the blind side, stealing your fairy-tale relationship faith with the smoothness of a smooth criminal.

Fairy-tale relationship faith swagger jackers are always on the alert for fairy-tale people whom they can get to entrust them with praying for them and their fairy tale. Swagger jackers know how to, know when to, know where to look for and bring about ways to incite, excite, initiate, cause, create the atmosphere for, and contribute to fairy-tale expectations, fairy-tale realities, fairy-tale fulfillment fillers, fairy-tale friends and family members, fairy-tale flow, fairy-tale functioning, fairy-tale fellowships, fairy-tale feelings, fairy-tale features showing up that can and will hinder, hold up, stop, and lead to a fairy-tale relationship not occurring.

Fairy-tale relationship swagger jackers usually will or always will show up just when you have finally got past or you are close to getting past your past and all of its negativities, and you are finally working hard at believing your fairy-tale relationship will happen.

Fairy-tale relationship swagger jackers can show up in all types of shapes and sizes, and they can come from any and all races, colors, creeds, nationalities, nonreligious belief and from various religions. They can be tall or short, thick or thin, and have different features. From the time you were a kid growing up in the city, state, town, community, neighborhood, housing project, province, etc., that you were in, at some place, point, and time, you too had a fairy-tale relationship dream, hope, and desire that you held on to and protected, visited, and revisited on the occasions that you deemed important. Every day you looked for and prepared yourself for the moment when that fairy-tale relationship person's arrival in your life.

At times you could feel that fairy-tale relationship person's spirit and presence close to you. At times in your day and in your life you dreamed and had daydreams about when, where, and how the visible manifestation of your fairy-tale relationship person would take place and what you would say and do, how you would act, react, and respond, what kind of atmosphere would be surrounding that moment, who would or wouldn't be there and what would take place in that meeting and what the end results would be. All of your personal anticipated expectations of that fairy tale persons moment of arrival into your life and into your day were to your personal liking, for your good, in your favor and the meeting would meet or exceed your every expectation.

A fairy-tale swagger jacker is someone who is so jealous and envious and even fearful of the relationship that you could have or can have that they will intentionally try to ruin, block, stand in the way, hinder, handicap, be a stumbling block in the way, be a bearer of bad news when it comes to the possibility of your fairy-tale relationship coming into fruition and then they will intentionally try to steal the flow of that magic deed filled unbelievable fairy tale relationship moment. They want to make sure the unbelievable part becomes true and the untrue part stays that way. A swagger jacker is also someone who always has something bad or negative to say about your fairy-tale relationship or always see something wrong with it.

Fairy-tale relationship swag: When your fairy-tale relationship have a swag, it is a magic deed filled with unbelievable relationship aura that have caused the person(s) in that relationship to walk, strut, stride, and behave in a very confident and typically arrogant or aggressive way. Your fairy-tale relationship has so much confidence powering it that it gives off an arrogant and aggressive aura, making the relationship so strong that it has a presence of its own. The people who are in a fairy-tale relationship or is really feeling and seeing evidence that they are about to walk right into the reality of their prayed for, prophesied, purpose-filled fairy-tale relationship will walk in a flow that is confident, arrogant, and aggressive. The aggressiveness is needed to help overpower and overtake the negatives that try to fight against the swagger a fairy-tale relationship can have, and the aggressiveness will also give the person or persons in that relationship what they need.

Fairy-Tale Moments

With every God-sent, God-caused, created, and destiny-fulfilled fairy-tale relationship moment that takes place, there are also fairy-tale memories that are made. Fairy-tale moments happen or show up when we least expect them, and they happen with little to no effort(s) at our hands. For the most part, we end up showing up at a place, point, event, circumstance, situation, and even at a confrontation; and without you knowing it and without you really trying to get or be noticed, that fairy-tale relationship person is there. Both of your paths cross, making it impossible for either one of you to avoid seeing, talking, listening, hearing, helping, or having some kind of contact.

Both of you may try to deny, reject, resist, and refuse what you know is there. It may be something, but you don't know what that something is that has brought you both together and what you are to do next. At that moment, Satan usually and more than likely will try to disguise fate as faith and he will in a deceiving way try to suggest and influence you and that person into accepting, making, and using the excuses and explanations and explaining why the fairy-tale relationship can't and won't work. No matter what you and that person experience in your decision making when it comes to that fairy-tale relationship a fairy-tale relationship moment has happened.

It's a fairy-tale relationship moment that you didn't make or help bring about. You were just there at the moment when it was made manifest. It is then up to you and that person to decide what you will do with that fairy-tale relationship moment. You can run it through your abused, neglected, rejection-filled, battered and violated past, mind, mind-set, thinking, mental state of mind, mental frame of mind, and you can let that moment draw a reference and referral for that manifested fairy-tale relationship from your hurt, painful, broken past. It's all up to you.

Those fairy-tale moments have a magic of their own, and they end up making memories that are unforgettable, and they have so much destiny empowering them that they don't just linger around, but they last forever. You have but one life to live. Why not live your life in the fairy-tale relationship you desire and deserve? Satan have been and is using your past hurt, pain, brokenness, abuse, being neglected, being abandoned, being violated, being battered, rejected, low self-esteem, lack of confidence, and all of the other negative feelings, emotions, and thoughts, etc., you have or had as a weapon formed against you. He wants to keep you out of your fairy tale magic moment and memory fulfillment. Yes, I know you say life happened. Things you never expected happened to you. Yes, I know you may not think and feel the way you once felt about yourself and your fairy-tale relationship dream, hope, and desire.

I know it's been downright hard, and the bad and negative relationships you have been in have all but ruined the reality that you once felt when it came to your fairy-tale relationship becoming visible. Life didn't happen. The bad and negative spirit that was upon the people you got into a relationship(s) with happened, and Satan made sure the spirit that was upon them and the person(s) you got into a wrong relationship with and the wrong people with the wrong motives, with bad and negative hidden agendas, with the wrong heart, wrong spirit upon them, those with a bad mind, bad and negative attitude, feelings, and thoughts about themselves, bad and negative feelings, emotions, desires, and had family generational curses alive and active in them have, did, would, couldn't, and wouldn't miss meeting them. That's what happened in your life.

A fairy-tale moment manifests itself for an indefinite brief period. It has a definite point in time and a brief time of importance before the magic deeds and what others have said is an unbelievable or untrue story or relationship actually happens. When a fairy-tale moment happens, it is an instant and important something that happens that is beyond and out of our control. It happens with or without you or me being the cause, creating the atmosphere for, nor contributing to it happening. It is divinely designed, and it has a divinely designed destiny delivery date assigned feature attached to it.

We are at the right place, at the right time, and in the right moment, and the right fairy-tale things and fairy-tale-participating people happen.

When a fairy-tale moment happens, it is positive, good, an attention getter, can and will catch you when you are not expecting nor looking for it. It's inspirational, encouraging, motivational, heartfelt, heart-warming, touching, and it can cause all of the right, sincere feelings and emotions to show up in you and be expressed.

I love being in the flow of and at the right place, at the right time, when the right circumstance, situation and even a right confrontation is taking place and it turns into a fairy-tale moment. It is indescribable, awesome, incredible, unforgettable and non-repeatable. Every unexpected fairy-tale moment seemingly comes out of a place that we couldn't and wouldn't and didn't see coming with our human eyes. We were there in the midst of the moment when it would just show up out of seemingly the unseen, the unexpected, the unplanned, the unknown, the unfair, the unaware, and the unsure. It is an invaluable, priceless, and a breathtaking experience that is encountered for an indefinite brief period and for a definite point "in" time, of importance.

Nothing can compare to you being blessed and afforded the opportunity to be in the flow of an unbelievable, indescribable, fun, and exciting fairy-tale moment when it is being created by angels of good tidings living in the unseen. Those angels love to wow us and catch us off guard. They love to deliver the unexpected, the unplanned, and the unknown fairy-tale moments. Fairy-tale moments are never unfair moments, but they do catch and show up when we are unaware, and they will never keep us living in the unsure.

Can you imagine for just a moment there, being those majestic angels who are there waiting for the opportunity, their opportunity to bring into the visible a relationship, a romantic relationship, that is an unforgettable, undeniable, undisputable fairy tale that lasts for an indefinite brief period, that is for a definite point in time, and have a brief time of importance that no one that happen to be around at that time or was close to or near the moment when it was made manifest was knowingly involved in or the real, actual recipient(s) and beneficiary(ies) of it all.

Function and Flow

Those fairy-tale moments and the assigned majestic angels who are the designated visible manifestation deliverers are there waiting for us to release them with our faith and release them from fate and from our painful past, hurt, brokenness, past feelings and emotions that are associated, connected, tied, yoked, in bondage, enslaved, held captive, a hostage, being bound and limited, linked, is a direct reaction, and due to your past abuse, neglect, being battered, rejected, abandoned, brutalized, and victimized.

We have to release our fairy-tale moments so it can flow freely, and we, in turn, can function in and out of it or them. When we are able to flow and function, function and flow in agreement with, in harmony with, in accordance with a free-flowing, faith-filled fairy-tale moment that has been majestically handmade and tailored to fit the designated relationship recipient(s) or relationship beneficiary, the windows of heaven are open, our prayer closets are being cleared out, and blessings and benefits are being poured out. Dreams, hopes, and right and good desires are easily being made a reality when we are in the flow and functioning in alignment with faith-filled fair-tale moments.

We cannot humanly plan, prepare, nor position ourselves for the moment when we can and will function and flow under the blessings and benefits of a fairy-tale moment. You and I will have to be spiritually, physically, mentally, emotionally free from the past so we can sense, perceive, be aware, and recognize that you

A. have been/is being set up to function and flow in a fairy-tale moment and receive its blessings and benefits
B. have been highly favored so that you can function and flow in a fairy-tale moment and receive its blessings and benefits and
C. you are, have been and will be in the flow of a moment that is faith-filled fairy tale

It is so important that you free your plans, heart, mind, and soul from any ties to your past—old things, people, places, events, matters, negativities, pain, hurt, and broken moments that can take away, distract, detour, delay, and deny you from being in the flow and functioning freely when a moment that is fairy tale flavored is trying to come forth.

Fairy-Tale Memories

Whenever there is a fairy-tale moment being made, there will be fairy-tale memories that are also being made. Fairy-tale moments and fairy-tale memories flow at the same time, and they function in tune and in harmony with each other. One will not outdo nor outshine the other. There are faith-filled fairy-tale moments and memories, and there are fate-filled moments and memories. You have to know and be clearly able to recognize the difference. A fairy-tale memory is the power or act of remembering or being mindful of an indefinite, brief period, a definite point in time, and a brief time of importance when a magic deed or something that was unbelievable or untrue took place or happened.

When you are involved in a fairy tale memory you have allowed and you have given your mind, thoughts, train of thought, thinking, way of thinking, your mental state of mind and your mental frame of mind the freedom, the right, the power and the authority to engage in:

(a) the power to bring to mind, b) the power to think of again, (c) the power to bring back to mind with an effort, (d) the power to recall, (e) the power to be careful and not forget, (f) the power to bear something in your mind, (g) the power to call something back to mind and (h) the power to mention to another.

The exact details concerning what kind of and what was the positive and powerful experiences, images, instructions, and information that came out of an unforgettable, unseen, unexpected, unplanned, unknown, unaware, and unsure, circumstance, situation, confrontation, and matter that they end up causing, creating the atmosphere for and contributing to a story or stories about magic deeds that took place in a relationship, and in a story or stories about unbelievable relationships or untrue relationships.

Memory and Moment Think Tank

Let's take a break from the flow that we were in, and let us focus on a fairy-tale relationship that you wanted to be in, had been in, or came close to being in. Answer the questions below based on that fairy-tale relationship experience:

1. Can you remember the first fairy-tale memory you had? () yes
   () no
2. What was it?_____

   _____

3. Can you remember the first fairy-tale moment you had? () yes
   () no
4. What was it?_____

   _____

5. Can you remember when you were in the flow of a fairy-tale
   moment? () yes () no
6. Describe the moment._____

   _____

7. Can you remember when you were in the flow of a fairy-tale
   memory? () yes () no
8. Describe the moment._____
9. Can you remember when you were functioning in and out of
   with a fairy-tale memory?
   () yes () no
10. Describe that functioning memory._____
11. Can you remember when you were functioning in and out of
    with a fairy-tale moment?
    () yes () no
12. Describe that functioning moment._____

It's amazing how easy it is for us to tutor, teach, and train our mind, thoughts, train of thought, thinking, way of thinking, and our mentality to flow and function in alignment, in accordance, and in agreement with moments and memories where we experienced and encountered past hurt, past pain, and past brokenness. And when we do so, we are also tutoring, teaching, and training our mind-set, mentality, mental state of mind, mental frame of mind, and our mental condition to accept, adopt, flow, and function within the boundaries and limitations of confined thoughts, train of thought, thinking and way of thinking that had to do with memories and moments where you had to endure through past abusiveness, abandonments, battering, rejections, moments, and memories where you were victimized and belittled.

Check Yourself

The question I have for you is why are you so quick to be defensive and so quick to defend and protect the moments when there were memories of your past hurt, pain, brokenness, and mistakes? You automatically do so without procrastinating, hesitating, questioning, and second-guessing when someone who loves and cares about you confront and challenge you to change.

The foul spirits that have you locked, yoked, enslaved, bound, limited, held hostage, in bondage, in a stronghold is a nasty, violating trespasser that is using you to defend and protect the very past that is hurting and hindering you and not helping you.

Do you really love what you had to suffer and endure through in your past so much that you don't and won't to let it go but continue to live in and out of it, make your choices and decisions out of it, handle matters, moments, and memories out of it, and see everything and everyone through it and continue to have feelings, emotions, desires, low self-esteem, a lack of confidence, and everything else you secretly deal with and go through that no one or a select few know?

Do you love those low-class, no-class, rude, disrespectful, dominating, manipulating, controlling, and deceiving demons that is trying to keep you entangled and entrapped to your past so much that you really get and feel offended when someone is reaching out to you and want to help you get the deliverance, cleansing and purging, healing and being made whole that you need? But instead of accepting the help, you get hostile and defend and protect your *deceived, dangerous, destructive,* and *distorted* right to get angry, mad, and upset when your past is brought up and is being checked.

Do you really love the abuse, neglect, beatings, rejection, being raped, molestation, vicious attack, prostitution, etc., and feeling like someone's doormat so much that you want to keep protecting, defending, flowing, and functioning under the suggestive influence of them? You are not defending and protecting the right you have to be free of all of it. Why are you defending and protecting a satanic and demonic damaging past? Yes, you are! In fact, you get hostile and very defensive when the truth about the parts, pieces, memories, and moments from your past you are holding on to is the subject and center of attention.

Why are you protecting those demon spirits that is troubling, tormenting and torturing you with past driven and motivated memories and moments that is associated with and keep you connected to what happened to you in your past; and in turn bring back the moment and memory when you first felt those past feelings and emotions, relived the thoughts, and with a defensive and protective attitude your raised your voice, flowed and functioned under and in the spirit of the past as if it were happening to you all over again?

You raise your voice, use profanity, say and do things you wouldn't normally say and do, etc., if you did not have the past you have. You even threaten and refuse to talk about your past as if it is a priceless, precious past. Why are you protecting and defending your past memories and moments that have kept you suicidal, depressed, downtrodden, feeling low, addicted, strung out, taking from others, not trustworthy, weak in the flesh, etc., and you don't want to talk about what is hurting, hindering and stopping you from letting go of the past? You want to protect and defend your right to relive your past and judge others out of what happened to you because of your past. You are now using your past and being selfish, self-centered, self-righteous, and self-justified as your defensive and protective walls and weapons. Why are you protecting and defending the very past memories, moments, flow and functioning that is and has caused you deep-rooted hurt, pain, and brokenness?

Nothing that has happened to you in your past is your friend. Do you really like and love how your past make you feel, how, when relived, it trick, seduce, entice, drive, force, push, persuade, get you to live in fear and treat others the wrong way? It makes you do evil and think the wrong thoughts. You say you are not protecting and defending the past that is hurting and hindering you, deceiving you, lying to you, but you won't let it go. Do you love what your past and the pressure it put and keep you under, how it keep pushing you into the wrong things and into the wrong direction, choices, and decisions, and how it consistently persuade you into saying and doing the wrong things and handling things and matters the wrong way?

My Mind Is Playing Tricks on Me

Past pain protectors are people who are so hurt and filled with so much brokenness to the point where they cannot handle and hear you trying to bring out the best in them. When you are trying to do so, even when it is through the use of constructive criticism that is accurate and true, the receiver is so pain-filled because of their past, thoughts, mental state of mind, mental frame of mind, and mental interpretation or perception of what you are saying or have spoken as words that are negative.

So you are trying to bring out the best in that person and they take what you are saying and doing the wrong way, and your efforts end up bringing out the worst in them. Their mind-set won't let them believe, react, and respond in a positive way, adopt and accept words spoken to them by you and anyone that could and would be good and encouraging. Any positive words you speak are perceived and interpreted in and through their mentality that is yoked, in bondage to, and is under a past stronghold. What the person's mind, mind-set, and mentality basically have the person pulling out and isolating anything you say that could be interpreted as negative or bad, even though what you said was good and positive.

In other words, you can say a thousand words and things that are positive, helpful, encouraging, a blessing, etc., and the one or two words that you say that are constructive criticism, the person who is in a perceptive past mode can and will only hear those two constructive criticism words, isolate them, and twist how you spoke them so that they have a totally different meaning. The context in which you spoke the constructive criticism words will not be interpreted and used in the context you spoke them.

As a matter of fact, they will use what you said that was in a positive, insightful, and helpful way. They will use what you said in a negative way and make it sound like you were intentionally trying to tear them down, and they will turn around what you say to make it look like and sound like you were using your constructive criticism as a weapon formed against their already-low self-esteem. They will make sure they give you the credit for them using the two isolated constructive sentences and words they chose to hold on to. Out of thousands of positive words you have spoken, they will consistently repeat, "you said" and you in turn will say, "yes, I said that but not in the way you interpreted it or not in the way you are using what I said". You will also say to them, "You are twisting my words, and you are taking out all of the other positive things I said about you, and you are focusing only on those two words, sentences, or constructive criticism statements. Is that all you heard?"

The bottom line is, when your moments and memories, how you flow and function is entangled and entrapped because of the hurt, pain, and brokenness that has been in your past, fate have a hold on your fairy-tale ending and fairy-tale relationship. Fate will dominate, manipulate, and control what type of memories and moments that are made, and fate will ultimately dictate, decide, and determine what type and kind of and when and how your fairy-tale relationship will function and flow and how your fairy-tale relationship ending will function and flow into its unbelievable, unforgettable, unseen, unexpected, unplanned, unknown, unfair, unaware, and unsure ending.

Teachers and Teachings

When a person's mind-set have had their thoughts, train of thought, thinking, way of thinking, mental state of mind, mental frame of mind, and mental condition tutored, trained, and taught by the teachers that are known and recognized and is received and best known as past hurt, pain, brokenness, abuse, neglect, being battered, being victimized, being abandoned, and being rejected, those same teachers will end up seducing, enticing, persuading, influencing, suggesting, leading, and opening up that persons mentality to vicious cycles of past hurt, pain, brokenness, abuse, neglect, being battered, being victimized, being abandoned, and being rejected teachings.

All of the process that I have described is taking place in the unseen, unexpected, unplanned, unknown, unfair, unaware, and the unsure in an unbelievable manner and in an unforgettable method that we cannot humanly see. The end results of what I just described is the memories and moments, and the function and flow of that person's mind while they are in a fairy-tale relationship experience or encounter end up playing tricks on them.

It is really dangerous to have or let the negatives from your past be, become, and end up being the teacher for your present and the teacher for your future. Your past can and will only teach past negative experienced reactions, responses, realities, negative experienced choice and decision-making process and procedures, negative-experience-filled urges, tendencies, inclinations, intuitions and instincts, and negative experienced images, instructions, information and perceptions. All of which will end up being stored in your mind and all of its capabilities and abilities and easily recalled or replayed. As your mind begins to play tricks on you, without you knowing it, you will begin to defend and protect your past and end up being a bodyguard for it.

The only thing your negative, damaged, fear-driven past can teach your fairy-tale relationship expectations and anticipation and dictate to your present and your future is how to bow down to the negative, tormenting, and torturing thoughts, feelings, and emotions that you once was or you are still holding on to because of and from your past until you have a mental meltdown or a mental breakdown.

The other reason why you cannot and do not expect and anticipate and believe in fairy-tale relationships is due to you being impatient and anxious, and you have adopted and accepted the world's concept, view, and perception of what a fairy-tale relationship is. That image is always dipped deeply in self-deception. It's delusional, distorted, lust-filled, selfish-driven, ego-craved, and the fairy-tale relationship has happened because of self-effort and because of self-will influences and suggestions. Every self-effort, self-willed-created fairy-tale relationship will always have a fleshy or carnal-minded motive and hidden agenda as an underlying basis or foundation.

CHAPTER TWO

Fantasy and Fantasies

It's true: men and women are different. They think and feel different and place importance on things and matters that are totally the opposite from each other most of the time. Women look for and want fairy-tale experiences and encounters, and men look for fantasy experiences and encounters. Both are different from each other, but in the end, they are expected to bring about the same end result, and that is relationship. We all have different qualities and features we look for in a relationship, and none that we prefer is neither wrong nor right because we have the right to make those type of relationship choices and decisions.

His friends would laugh at him every time he was nice, kind, and caring to the women who were in his life. Why? Because he wasn't like they were, and he didn't have the heart to mistreat them and take advantage of them. He was one of those guys that was raised and taught to treat people with respect and to treat every little girl like they were a princess and treat every woman just like the queens they were. His friends were the opposite, and they didn't think and feel the way he did. He's what you would call a gentleman, and that often made him stand out in a crowd.

Every time he saw her, she brought about something in his mind and in his heart that he had never seen or felt before. And when he was alone and sometimes when he was with others, his mind and thoughts would drift off into another world. He could see himself spending the rest of his life with the person he had felt like he had some kind of connection to. The person he had his eyes on was someone that he felt could and would be the one who would be able to walk with him and help him fulfill the highest calling that was upon his life. He could see himself living with and being with her for the rest of his life.

When a man finds that special person that he feel is the right person for him, and he really want to be with her, he often will have fantasies about her. A fantasy is defined as something that is produced by the imagination, an idea about doing something that is far removed from normal reality. It is the free play of creative imagination, a creation of the imaginative faculty expressed or merely conceived as.

Men don't have fairy tales; they have a fantasy or fantasies. Most people think having a fantasy is always an event that has some type of sexual content or overtones involved, and that is not the truth. A fantasy for a guy is the way he opens himself up for relationship. A guy's way of thinking when it comes to relationship is if he can't and don't see and feel it first, he won't get involved. For a female, her way of thinking is if she don't feel it first and then see herself in a relationship with him, she more than likely won't get involved.

Women have their fairy-tale relationships, and they have their fairy-tale romance that they envision. Most men have fantasy relationships and fantasy romances in which they can see themselves being able to trust the person he is having a fantasy over with his feelings, emotions, and desires. He sees her as someone he can share his sensitivity with and not have to worry about her violating and betraying him. It takes a lot for most men to open up all of himself to a woman because that man knows if he do so with the wrong woman, she can end up really damaging him and hinder or stop him from accomplishing, achieving, and acquiring his destiny dreams, hopes, and desires.

She can also hinder and stop him from accumulating all of the things that he feels is important to him. If a woman is some man's fantasy, he has already had a vision for having a relationship with her, and he can see himself with her. That is how the relationship choice and decision work with most men, and they have to have a vision for their relationship before they will open the doors of his heart. When a man have a clean, pure, and right fantasy about a woman, he have made her the center of his attention, and he have already decided and determined within himself that she would be the one who would bring out the best in him.

That is the ultimate fulfillment that a man expects out of a woman he has made his fantasy. He really expected her to bring out the best in him always. Most women have a knack for bringing out the worst in a man. They say and do things he really don't like nor appreciate. Not only so, but most woman are also not willing to change things about themselves so that they can help that man who has made her his fantasy. Her number 1 priority should be to help him become and end up being prosperous, productive, and successful.

Another fact that I must state is if she is really his good and right fantasy, he have already decided he is going to open up his heart to her and for her, and he will love her to the limit. A woman starts out making a man her fairy tale, and he eventually will become her fairy-tale fantasy man. As the man decides to make her his fantasy, she will eventually become his fantasy fairy-tale woman. This is where the mystery and the magic is when it comes to her being his fantasy. The truth is a man doesn't want to spend forever looking for something better.

When she is his fantasy, he has already decided she is the one he really desire and want to love, live with, need, want, and spend the rest of his life with. Her next move is to prove he did not make a mistake by opening up and giving himself to her. And that is usually where she falls out of being his fantasy. He expects her to go one on one with him and not include anyone else in their relationship. He expect her to learn for herself how he need and want her to love him, need him, want him, live with him, and help him be the man he know he can be.

A fantasy man is what is known as a choosy lover. He does his very best to be very precise in selecting whom he will open himself up to. There are some specific criteria that he is looking for in her, and there is no compromising. The one thing is for sure: she has his attention, and he is already into her, and she doesn't even know it. Without even knowing it, she has already sparked something in his imagination that no other woman have ever done. And he is willing to step out in a place he's never been when it comes to a relationship. She have to prove to him she is really his fantasy woman by showing him he can trust her with himself and with his dreams. If she is really his fantasy woman, then she will know how to and when to inspire him into opening up to her.

Fantasy Function

In order for a fantasy to be fulfilling and rewarding, it must have a function. A fantasy function is described as something that is produced by the imagination, an idea about doing something that is far removed from normal reality that work or operate in a proper and particular way. Did you get that? A fantasy that is pure, clean, and wholesome is on that work or operates in a proper and particular way, meaning it stays on the right path so that it can arrive at the right place and point on time.

The person's imagination work and operate in a proper and particular way. What is being produced work and operate in a proper and particular way. What is being produced by the person's imagination when it comes to the woman that is the center of his attraction and attention works and operates in a proper and particular way. Everything that his mind, thoughts, train of thought, thinking, and way of thinking came up with and can come up with will work and operate in a proper way and not in an improper way and it will work in a particular way.

To have what is being produced when you are imagining, when it comes to another person, working and operating in a proper and particular way is to have what you are imagining under control and directed toward the right destination target. None of your thoughts, feelings, emotions, and desires is out of order. Why? Because that which is being produced in your imagination and by your imagination was conceived the right way and for all of the right reasons, and the moment when what have been produced in/by your imagination is birthed into the natural realm, it works, it operates, it's proper, and it has a particular way that it has an effect and affect on the recipient.

If and when a man have an idea about doing something that is far removed from normal reality that work or operate in a proper and particular way, this means she has inspired his creativity and his creative images, ideas, inspirations, insights, and ingenuity. He is then locked into wanting to say or do something for her that no man has ever done for her. It may also be something that he has never said or done for any woman. The woman who is the focus of his fantasy has brought that out of him.

He knows she have brought out his creative urges, tendencies, inclinations, intuitions, and instincts for all of the right reasons, and they are working and operating in a proper and particular way so that they can end up producing, preparing, and presenting the right end results. She did not do so for selfish, self-centered, self-righteous, or self-justified reasons. All of the right things and the good things are being produced out of his imagination, and they work right, operate right, and his imaginations are proper and they have a particular way in which they can and will connect to the right fulfilled fantasy processes, procedures, and principles.

As long as his fantasy work or operate in a proper and particular way that is honest, pure, and right, it will always cause, create the atmosphere for, and contribute to him having a consistent, established, strengthened, and settled behavior and behavior patterns that his fantasy woman will feel safe, strong, stable, and secure in. They both will begin to experience something that is produced by his, her, and their imagination and encounter an idea about doing something that is far removed from normal reality that they both will enjoy.

Fantasy Flow

Every fantasy must have the right flow if it is to produce, prepare, and present the right end results that are a blessing and a benefit to the person that is the center attraction. A fantasy that is in the right flow is something that is produced by the imagination, an idea about doing something that is far removed from normal reality that go from one place to another or move continuously in one direction in a steady and smooth way.

A real, true, good, pure, and fulfilling fantasy is not wild and all over the place. It will have a continuous, steady path that it travels in so that it can hit its intended targeted place and point at the right time. That good something (a feeling, an emotion, and a desire) that is produced by and in the man's imagination moves continuously in one direction in a steady and smooth way, and it is not distracted, detoured, delayed, and denied access to reaching and touching her heart, mind, and soul.

As his mind, thoughts, train of thought, thinking, and way of thinking is consistently tutored, trained, and taught to have an idea about doing something (for her) that is far removed from normal reality, his mental state of mind, mental condition, and mental frame of mind will move continuously in one direction in a steady and smooth way, and his mind-set and mentality will grow, develop, and mature in the art of fantasy fulfillment

His fantasy must flow and move continuously in one direction in a steady and smooth way out of him and move continuously in one direction in a steady and smooth way into her at the right place, point, and time and in the right manner so that it will ignite, draw, drive, pull, push, persuade, and force the twin flame and twin fire spirit that is within her to get linked, tied, and connected to attracting, adopting, and applying fantasy-met expectations.

If she is his real, true destiny fantasy, then she is definitely his twin flame, and she has the same passionate-driven fire that is within him. She has the same twin fire, and if, when, and as long as they function and move continuously in one direction in a steady and smooth way, they will place themselves, their life, and their relationship on the right path and position themselves and their relationship where they can and will begin to accomplish, achieve, acquire, and accumulate super abundantly, far over and above all that they dare ask or think, infinitely beyond their highest prayers, desires, thoughts, hopes, or dreams.

Fantasy Mode

Men are more visual than women. We are driven and inspired by our ability to dream dreams and see visions. If a man can't see the need for a person, place, or thing, more than likely, he will walk away from them or turn them into something that he just play with. Women, as I said earlier, are driven by their feelings, emotions, and desires. The only way a pure and right fantasy can become a fulfilled reality has to do with what type of mode that man is in.

A fantasy mode is defined as something that is produced by the imagination, an idea about doing something that is far removed from normal reality that is customary or preferred way of doing something. A man who is in the right, good, and pure fantasy mode is a man who can stand and face the impossible that come in his life with the strength and courage of David when he volunteered to stand face-to-face and toe-to-toe with a giant that was bigger, taller, worse, and a lot more stronger than he was. But David had a vision and a dream that showed the demise of the giant Goliath. And it was his belief in the fulfillment of that dream and vision that gave him the courage to do what other men his size had dared to do. His belief gave and produced a fiery faith, and that fiery faith produced a confidence or ego, as some may say, that took the giant down.

Standing with a Fantasy Man

If a man is surrounded with the right supporting cast for the dreams and visions that he is having, his faith and his ability, drive, and motivation will soar like an eagle flying radiantly in the sky. He will demonstrate a relentless faith that is second to none. She can be the beautiful, wonderful person in the entire world, but if she does not inspire him to dream dreams and have visions, she cannot motivate him, and she has lost him. A woman have to know what to say to that dreamer and visionary have to know what to say, what to do, when, where, and how if she is to stay in his life. Most women have the knack for saying and doing the wrong thing when it comes to being with a dreamer and a visionary.

They say and do things they think or feel is right or their right when in all actuality they are completely wrong, or the most common occurrence is a woman will take the advice of another person listening to, hearing and paying close attention to what that person is saying and how they feel when it comes to what have worked for their relationship man and the listener will try to apply the same "heard my friend, associate" tell me to say and do instructions. That is tainted information, and if accepted, adopted, and applied to your relationship with a man who is good, right, and pure fantasy dreamer-visionary, you are basically setting you, the fantasy man that you are with, and your relationship up for a fall to fail and to experience and encounter failure.

Advice number 1 to a woman: You have to take the time to listen to the fantasy man you are with. Hear him, function, flow, and follow the faith that is leading him in his quest for fantasy fulfillment, and more important, you must always be awake, cautious, active, give strict attention, and watch and pray that you may not come into temptation, selfish, self-centered, self-righteous, and self-justified temptation. The spirit, your spirit, indeed, is willing; but the flesh, your flesh, is weak (Matthew 26:41). You must guard and protect the fantasy dreamer-visionary man that you are with, and you must guard and protect the good, right, and pure fantasy dreams and visions that he is having.

Advice number 2 to a woman: Don't share his fantasy dreams and visions with anyone else, and don't open what is happening in your relationship with him to just anyone. Be cautious and careful, and handle all with a lot of tender, loving kindness. The one thing you as a woman don't want to be a victim of is causing, creating an atmosphere, and contributing to the same thing that cause man and mankind to fall and fail in the Garden of Eden. Don't be so zealous of your own womanly needs and wants that you forget the man, your fantasy dreamer-visionary guy. Don't forget it was man that God originally gave the instructions to and the vision for his relationship in the garden.

Advice number 3 to a woman: Don't be guilty of opening up your relationship with that right and good, pure fantasy dreamer-visionary to satanic and demonic suggestions and influences just as Eve did in the garden. When God brought Eve to Adam (Genesis 2:21–22), in that moment, he had a godly, good, right, and pure revelation, fantasy dream, and vision of who she was and whom she was and would be to him; and out of that place, deep down within himself, he said, "The creature, creation, woman creation is now bone of my bones and flesh of my flesh. He said she shall be called Woman, my woman, my wife, my helpmate, my companion, my twin flame, my twin fire because she was taken out of a man."

Adam gave a significant and a very important name to what God had brought before him. You can have all of that fantasy dreamer-visionary man's heart and be the center of his attention if you say and do the right and non-selfish things to him and for him and if you concentrate on finding and implementing ways in which you can and will *continuously* bring out the best in him. The key words are you have to be constant and consistent and be in a continuous mode, mind-set, and mentality. I hear you. You are saying, "But what about my dreams and the things I want to accomplish and achieve?" You are thinking and saying, "I work just as hard as he do and... and... and..."

Another Perspective

Well, hello, Eve. Yes, you have the Eve syndrome and spirit! God told Adam what the plan was. Adam saw the dream, and he caught the vision. Satan, who was more subtle and crafty than any living creature of the field that the Lord God had made, came into the garden, and he appealed to Eve and her selfish feelings, emotions, and desires that she probably didn't even know she had, but the serpent knew. Why and how did he know? He is and was the master over thrower of all times. He got the angels in heaven on his side, and he led a rebellion in heaven; and he and those angels were kicked out of heaven, and they were kicked out of their heavenly inheritance.

Satan knows how to suggest and influence you, woman, into getting over into selfish pursuits, self-willed, self-performance, and into self-effort acts, actions, and deeds. He knows how to get you to rebel against being submissive and against authority. When God gives a man a good, right, and pure revelation fantasy dream and vision it is purposed by divine design, and it will make his relationship(s), home, family, life and his wife's life prosperous, productive, and successful. That revelation fantasy dream-vision should take precedent over anything and everything that goes on in that relationship, and it should become and end up being the center in which everything in those persons' life revolve around if and as long as it is God-given.

When a woman interferes with the fulfillment of that revealed good, right, and pure fantasy dream-vision, she is hindering herself, and she is opening up the door for more negative, bad, and wrong relationship vicious cycles. The other thing that happens is when that God-given revealed, good, right, and pure fantasy dream-vision is hindered in any way whatsoever by her, Satan can then step in and turn that same good, right, and pure fantasy into a fantasy lust. And that is what is happening more today in relationships than ever before.

God's perspective number 1: This is what grieves the heart of God when it comes to our relationships. We have opened up our relationships to the suggestive and influencing advice of people who are the major cause and creators of the wrong relationship atmosphere, and they are the major contributors of failing relationships. God's heart is grieved. Over and over we seek out relationship advice from those who, for the most part, are not listening to God. Nor are they seeking out and is following God-given, God-inspired, God-conceived, and birthed revelation relationship wisdom, knowledge, and understanding.

The serpent knew who to talk to, and he knew Eve didn't even know she had those selfish, self-centered, self-righteous, and self-justified feelings, emotions, desires, urges, tendencies, inclinations, intuitions, and instincts within herself, but Satan did. He knew how to do the opposite of what God created relationship people to do, and that was to get them to bring out the worst in each other.

God's perspective number 2: The serpent knew God didn't tell Eve the dream, and he didn't give her the vision he gave Adam, so he stepped to her and said, "What about you? You are important to Eve." It was a test and a trick, and she fell for it. That is the vicious cycle that Satan keeps using us to open the door in our relationships. Society has and is still working to overthrow God's relationship system, standards, principles, processes, and procedures. The decision makers of this world have basically taken all relationship power, authority, revelation fantasy dreams, and fantasy visions out of the hands of man, and they have given it to women.

God's perspective number 3: Men today as a whole have been made to be subject to the woman's relationship reign, relationship rule, and relationship rules. Women are being given power and authority over men, and the rights of woman are more protected than those of a man. The workforce is filled with women who get promotions over men not because the man is not qualified, but most employers feel they can dominate, manipulate, and control a woman more than they can a man. The other thing that is happening is some employers will hire minority women and use them to keep a minority man from being hired, getting a promotion, or for other reasons that are unethical.

This in not to suggest all women get promotions, and they are hired for the reasons I just stated above; but for the most part, that is some employer's reasons. That is not to say that there are women who are not just as qualified for positions as men are, but we have to look at the spirit that is behind such workforce practices. Look at this from another perspective and not from that of a man or a woman. Try looking at this from a relationship perspective.

God's perspective number 4: Take for instance when a domestic call is made to the 911 operator, when the responding officers arrive, their first line of thought is go get the man and detain him because he is guilty. That may not be what they say, but their actions when they respond says this. The man is being subjected to all kinds of interrogation, and basically, he have to prove he is innocent, while the woman engage in some type of emotional outburst and make unproven accusations. She can injure herself intentionally or unintentionally, and the mere fact that there are noticeable injuries, the man is taken into custody.

In America, a man/person is supposed to be considered *innocent* until proven guilty and not *guilty* until proven innocent. My point is the woman can make up some type of emotional scene and make up all kinds of lies and accusations, and the man is hauled off to jail. The they will find out later that she was mad at him and she wanted to get back at him, or she was mad because she could not and did not have control over him. The laws protect a woman before they will protect a man. This is Satan's way to dominate, manipulate, and control a man and to keep him from being in the place and in the mode Adam was in when he was in the garden. He was in a place of power, authority, and he reigned and ruled.

God's perspective number 5: The serpent didn't like that nor did he want that, so he had to find someone whom he knew will do anything that he suggest as long as it appealed to her carnal mind, carnal feelings, emotions, desires, and appealed to her selfishness and, if she took the bait, partake of what he was suggesting. He knew she would open up herself and the relationship she had with Adam to his influences. And it worked. He had her in the relationship mode he wanted her in. Satan have tricked, trapped, and deceived a lot of women into being in the mode of thinking where they feel it is their responsibility and their duty to tutor, teach, and train a man how to be a man or the kind of man they selfishly want and need.

They also feel like they know how a man should be a man, and some women feel it is their duty to tell a man how to be a man. A woman who is in this type of mode is one that Satan will consistently use to try and influence her into believing and thinking she have to teach a man how to be what she think and feel a man is, and she is to have authority over him. This way of thinking is deceptive thinking at its highest level.

Man in the Mode

As I stated before, a fantasy mode is defined as something that is produced by the imagination, an idea about doing something that is far removed from normal reality that is customary or the preferred way of doing something. A man who is in the revealed, good, right, and pure fantasy dream-vision mode is not lust-driven or motivated, but he possesses a dream and a vision for his relationship. He is always being drawn, driven, pulled, pushed, persuaded, and forced into saying and doing something, handling matters, and making choices and decisions for his fantasy woman that is customary or the preferred way of doing things for her. He does not struggle, procrastinate, hesitate, question, nor does he second-guess, and he does not seek after nor need the advice and opinions of others.

A revealed, good, right, and pure fantasy dream-vision man is someone who possesses something that is good, real, and right, being produced by his imagination that is constant and consistent, and it is a customary mind-set and mentality for him. And what his imagination have produced, prepared, and presented for him when it comes to her is an idea about doing something for her that is far removed from his selfish, self-centered, self-righteous, and self-justified feelings, emotions, and desires, and it is far removed from his normal reality. It is customary for him to say and do the things he engages in.

Not only is he in a customary mode, but he is also in a preferred way of doing something for her mode that bring her happiness, joy, satisfaction, and fulfillment. Whenever he is with her, near her, or he is just thinking about his fantasy woman, it is customary for him to cause, create the atmosphere, and contribute to her wanting and needing to be close to him. He is her fairy-tale man, and he has discovered what his fantasy woman need and want that no man in her life have ever discovered, and he delivers that which she have never had. And in doing so, he have become her fairy-tale man's preferred way of doing things.

If he is in a *customary mode*, he is conducting himself according to what's in his thoughts, train of thought, thinking, and in his way of thinking when it comes to her that is according to the customs or usual practices associated with a particular society, place, or set of circumstances as a way or manner in which something occurs or is experienced, expressed, or done. Those customs or usual practices he have accepted, adopted, and applied are associated, connected, and tied to a God-inspired, God-led, and God-created relationship society that function, flow, and follow the right fantasy relationship principles, processes, and procedures, a way and the manner in which he want to see things occur or experienced, expressed, or done.

As he do so, his relationship will always end up at the right place for all of the right things to happen or occur in his relationship and the right set of relationship circumstances will always show up and prevail in a way or manner that will in turn lead to the right something's occurring in his relationship and those right something's are experienced, expressed, and carried out.

And if he is in a *preferred-way mode*, he is in a mind-set, mental state of mind, mental condition, and mental frame of mind and have a mentality where he like one thing or person better than another or others. And that which he like he tend to choose as his method, style, or manner of doing something that is and have become the way or manner in which something occurs or is experienced, expressed, or done.

When he see her, and he is with her, and he thinks about her. He is so inspired that he have ideas and images that drive and motivate him to want to be open and honest with her because he like that one special, different, and unique thing about her that is better than what he have had or seen in his other relationships, that which she has inspired, bring out of him, drive, and motivate him. He tend to choose as his method, style, or manner because he knows it can and will eventually dictate, decide, and determine what will occur in his relationship, what is experienced, expressed, and is done.

A mode is a way or manner in which something
occurs or is experienced, expressed, or done.

Remember, a good, right, and a pure fantasy is not a feeling, emotion, or a desire. It is a strong, stable, safe, and secure mind, mind-set, thinking, way of thinking, thought, train of thought, mental state of mind, mental condition, mental frame of mind, and mentality and mode that is established, strengthened, and settled when there is a healthy heart, soul, spirit, and consciousness.

If the person is still harboring and hanging on to or has any residue, hurt, pain, bitterness, resentment, negatives, and brokenness within them, their fantasy will be tainted and defiled. They will end up being in the wrong mode, and their relationship will not end up being prosperous, productive, and successful. What mode are you in? What mode have you allowed Satan to draw, drive, pull, push, persuade, and force you, your life, your love, and your relationship into? Look at the fruit that your relationship is producing.

Examine what is constant and is consistently manifesting and occurring in your relationship that you are always having to experience and is always being expressed. Examine what is continually taking place in your relationships and examine what is being done in your relationships that you really don't like nor care for. If you are to really be her revealed, good, right, and pure fantasy dream-vision man, it is important that you find and stay in the right mode and produce the right relationship way or manner in which everything in your fantasy relationship occurs or is experienced, expressed, or done. Be consistent! A man who is in his good, right, and pure fantasy mode is one of the most dangerous men on the planet. God will use him and his relationship in so many ways to help tear down the kingdom of relationship darkness.

Fantasy PPPM

The fantasy dreamer and fantasy visions man must be in the right mode in order for the right memories, moments, moods, processes, principles, and procedures to grow, develop, and mature and manifest themselves. If he is not in the right mode, then his mind and all of its capabilities, abilities, and capacities will end up being easily tainted, tricked, trapped, entertained, enticed, and entangled into the wrong kind and type of fantasy or fantasies.

This is dangerous in that it can open the door for wrong fantasy vicious cycles that are deadly, damaging, and destructive not only to the people who are in that relationship but also to the relationship itself and to the type of fantasy foundation that the fantasy relationship is supposed to automatically build. Once again, when we are talking about the mode that the fantasy holder possess, we are talking about the way or manner in which his fantasy relationship occurs or is experienced, expressed, or done.

Mode Facts

In order for his fantasy to have and be in the right fantasy principles, processes, and procedures mode (PPPM), listed below are some very important fantasy mode facts that must be in place so that his fantasy for her can grow, develop, mature, land, and have the right fantasy foundation to build upon.

1) His fantasy for her must grow, develop, and mature the correct way so when it is unveiled and it begins to unfold, it is done so in a way or manner that it can occur in the right way, be experienced in a right way, be expressed in a right way, and done in a right way and all at the right place, point, and time.

2) His fantasy for her must grow, develop, and mature in the right way *or* in the right method or system so that his fantasy for her can be powerful enough to produce, prepare, and present the type or kind of, what would be, become, and end up being his usual fantasy habits, qualities, and actions and the usual way he behaves, appears, feels, etc., when it comes to her.

3) His fantasy for her must grow, develop, and mature in the right manner *or* in the right way in which his fantasy is done or happen so that he can behave himself in a normal way while he is with her and with other people.

4) His fantasy for her must grow, develop, mature, and occur in the right way *or* happen, take place, exist, or be found to be present in a place or under a particular set of conditions in the right way and at the right point, place, and time.

5) His fantasy for her must grow, develop, and mature in the right way so when his fantasy for her is unveiled and it began to unfold before her and before all of those who know her and witness the unveiling and unfolding, it, his fantasy for her can be experienced *or* observed, lived through, and learned from at the right point, place, time, and at the right moment.

6) His fantasy for her must grow, develop, and mature in the right way so when time comes for her fantasy to be unveiled and unfolded, it can be expressed *or* put into words, stated, revealed, shown, said in a clear way, directly, firmly, and explicitly stated at the right point, place, and time, causing, creating the

atmosphere for, and contributing to her knowing and feeling she is safe, stable, and secure in his fantasy for her.

7) His fantasy for her must grow, develop, and mature in the right way so that it can be unveiled and unfolded and done or completed in the right function and in the right flow at the right point, place, and time so that the right fantasy principles, processes, and procedures can follow.

Every thought or idea that comes into the mind of the fantasy holder is conceived and birthed so that they can establish, strengthen, and settle his fantasy for her in good, right, and pure purposes, plans, and pursuits that will help give their fantasy dreams and visions the right leading, guidance, direction, and destiny.

Mode in the Mood

His fantasy mode will set the tone for his/her/their relationship mood or relationship conscious state of mind or predominant emotion. Once the fantasy relationship mood is set, then your fantasy relationship is ready to be instrumental in causing, creating the atmosphere for, and contributing to the right fantasy, dreams, visions, fantasy dream-vision moments, and fantasy dream-vision memories manifesting themselves. If the fantasy mode is right, then it will

- Produce the right fantasy mind, thoughts, train of thought, thinking, and way of thinking;
- Prepare the right fantasy mental state of mind, mental condition/ conditioning, and right fantasy mental frame of mind;
- Present the right fantasy mind-set and mentality.

To have your fantasy mode in the right fantasy mood is to have a way or manner in which your fantasy for her occur or is experienced, expressed, or done so that it can dictate to, decide, and determine what will be the conscious state of mind or predominant emotion that your fantasy relationship can and will function, flow, follow, and have as its fantasy relationship standards, fantasy relationship rules, and fantasy relationship guidelines.

The Final Fantasy Ingredients

With that being said, the final ingredients that a revealed, good, right, and pure fantasy dream-vision relationship will need in order for the fantasy relationship to have the deeply rooted and grounded, safe, strong, stable, and secure fantasy relationship roots that have authority, power, and presence when the fantasy relationship dreams and fantasy relationship visions is unveiled and unfolded are the following:

(1) *Fantasy principles*: A fantasy relationship that have the right fantasy principles is described as a fantasy relationship that is produced by the imagination and an idea about doing something for her that is far removed from normal reality of what he would do for anyone that end up becoming a fundamental truth or proposition that serves as the foundation for his system of fantasy relationship beliefs or fantasy relationship behavior or for a chain of fantasy relationship reasoning. A fantasy principle is also the established moral rule of a relationship belief that helps you know what in your relationship is "fantasy relationship right" and what is fantasy relationship wrong that in turn influences your fantasy relationship actions.

(2) *Fantasy processes*: A relationship that have the right fantasy processes is described as a fantasy relationship that is produced by the imagination and idea about doing something new, different, unique, and special that is far removed from normal reality and is something that he has never done before and she has never had done for her that cause, create the atmosphere, and contribute to a series of actions that consistently produce the same positive reactions, and responses or that lead to a consistent positive particular result—a series of constant correct changes that happen naturally.

(3) *Fantasy procedures*: A relationship that have the right fantasy procedures is described as a fantasy relationship that is produced by the imagination, a fantasy relationship idea about doing something that is far removed from his normal reality that brings about a series of fantasy relationship actions that are done in a certain fantasy relationship way or fantasy relationship order, a fantasy relationship established or accepted way of doing fantasy relationship things.

All of the stated above must be grown, developed, and matured in the right way, in the right manner, and for all of the right reasons so that the fantasy relationship can be built upon and stand on a strong, solid, stable, safe, and secure fantasy relationship dreams and fantasy relationship visions foundation.

Fantasy Foundation

Once that fantasy relationship is in its right mode, the mood is set, and there are the right fantasy relationship principles, processes, and procedures that are alive and actively bringing about the right fantasy relationship, Christ centered fantasy relationship connection, right fantasy relationship things in common and the right fantasy relationship compatibility components; the right fantasy relationship creative images, ideas, instructions, inspirations, information, insights and ingenuity will also end up being produced, prepared and presented. This fantasy relationship can and will have everything that is needed in order to establish a strong, safe, solid, secure, and stable fantasy foundation.

When a fantasy relationship has a strong, safe, solid, secure, and stable fantasy foundation, it has a strong, safe, solid, secure, and stable fantasy facts, modes, mood, ideas, principles, processes, and procedures that provides support or an underlying basis for that fantasy relationship to establish, strengthen, settle, balance, brace, and be built upon. To have this happen or occur in a fantasy relationship and in a relationship in general will bring about some of the most powerfully profound moments and things that can take place in a relationship.

Most of the relationships that we see people in do not have a strong, safe, solid, secure, or stable foundation, and most of those relationships are based and built upon the wrong things. Much of which is something that is tangible, physical, or financial. Both a fairy-tale and a fantasy relationship that is in their right functioning modes can and will have the power to flow into its right fantasy relationship mood, and both will have the authority to follow the right fantasy relationship principles, processes, and procedures.

When these aspects and dynamics are powerfully present in a fairy-tale or fantasy relationship, they will be constant and consistent in dominating, manipulating, controlling, and dismantling any and all types of negative unseen, unexpected, unplanned, unknown, unfair, uncertain, unaware, and unsure satanic and demonic generational cursed assaults, attacks, and assassinations attempts. Not only so, but this type or kind of fairy-tale and fantasy dreamer-visions will also be consistent in rejecting, resisting, rebuking, refusing, and refuting any and all negative fairy-tale and fantasy dreamer-vision arguments and theories and reasoning and every proud and lofty things that sets itself up against the true knowledge, presence, power, and authority that empowers a good, right, and pure fairy-tale and fantasy relationship.

When this happens, both of these relationships will have the freedom to function in agreement with and flow in in the path of good, right, and pure fairy-tale and fantasy relationship images, ideas, instructions, inspirations, information, insights, and ingenuity that tutor, train, teach, and then draw, drive, pull, push, persuade, force, dictate, decide, and determine what kind and to what degree the individuals who are in a fairy-tale and fantasy relationship will conduct themselves, converse, and communicate.

Another powerful dynamic that happens and occurs when a fairy-tale and fantasy relationship that is functioning in its right modes, flowing in its right moods and is following the right fairy-tale and fantasy dreamer-visions principles, processes and procedures is, both relationships will not only be established and built upon the right foundation but the persons in those relationship will have the power and the authority to lead every negative fairy-tale and fantasy relationship thought and purpose away captive into or unto the obedience of Christ, the messiah, the anointed one.

Which would strongly suggest that the persons who are in such relationships have been consistently tutored, trained, and taught safe, stable, secure, solid, and strong fairy-tale and fantasy relationship behavior and behavior patterns. These two kinds of relationships are powered by a presence that Satan and all of his demon spirits cannot take down, take over, take out, kill, steal, destroy, distract, detour, delay, deny, deceive, entice, entangle, entrap, etc., and the relationships and the people in them are consistent in challenging, confronting, contending, and warring a good, strong, and consistent warfare against any and all visible and invisible, seen and unseen satanic-sent fairy-tale and fantasy dreamer-vision relationship despotisms, fairy-tale and fantasy relationship powers, master fairy-tale and fantasy relationship spirits who are the world rulers of this present darkness, the fairy-tale and fantasy relationship spirit forces of wickedness in the heavenly or supernatural sphere.

Fantastic Voyage

I can go on and on pointing out the strong aspects and dynamics of this kind of well-established relationships because it is an endless list of what is accomplished, achieved, acquired, accumulated, and the positives in a fairy-tale and fantasy relationship that is functioning in its right modes, flowing in its right mood, and is following the right fairy-tale and fantasy dreamer-visions principles, processes, and procedures is endless. I want to just point out a few more important something's that happen and occur when you have a fairy-tale and fantasy relationship that is:

❖ Functioning in its right modes
❖ Flowing in its right mood
❖ Following the right fairy-tale and fantasy dreamer-visions principles, processes, and procedures and the
❖ Foundation for the relationship is safe, solid, stable, secure, and strong

Both relationships will be driven and motivated by the power of God and by the vision that God have for the relationships. That vision that God have for their relationship will be clear to both of them, and they will live purposefully and worthily and accurately as wise, sensible, and intelligent people.

She will respect and reverence, notice, prefer, regard, honor, venerate, and esteem him. She will defer to, praise, love, and admire him exceedingly. She will conduct herself in a pure and modest way, feel for him, appreciate him, prize him in the human sense, adore him, admire him, be devoted to, and deeply love and enjoy him because she know he is her fairy-tale Boaz, guy, man. She does not procrastinate, hesitate, question, nor second-guess when she does those things of her own free will, accept, adopt, apply, and adapt to being submissive as a service unto the Lord.

He will strip himself of his former tutored, trained, and taught relationship "man up", "be a man nature" and he will become eager to love her as Christ loved the church, and he want to make sure he is clearly able to correctly and rightly discern, recognize and receive, react, respond, and have the correct and right reactionary response to their fairy-tale and fantasy relationship being cleaned and washed by water with the precise, true, and accurate relationship Word.

She is his fantasy woman, and he want to make sure he have placed and positioned their relationship in a place and at the point where it is presented consistently to God for himself in glorious relationship splendor, a relationship that is without carnal or selfish spot or wrinkle. His daily objective and goal is to make sure their relationship is holy and faultless. In order for that to happen, he knows he is accountable and responsible for his fantasy relationship and helping her with her fairy-tale relationships standards and success.

And with that in mind, he loves his fantasy relationship woman/wife as being, in a sense, his own body. He has clarity in knowing he who loves his own fantasy woman/wife loves himself. He does not procrastinate, hesitate, question, nor second-guess loving his fantasy woman/wife as being, in a sense, his very own self. He is her fairy-tale man, and he have disconnected and discontinued following his family and friends' relationship advice and following his old tutored, trained, and taught relationship feelings, emotions, desires, urges, tendencies, inclinations, and instincts. He is sensitive, affectionate, and sympathetic with her, and he is not harsh or bitter or resentful toward her. He is drawn, driven, pulled, pushed, persuaded, and allows himself to be willingly forced into living considerately with his fantasy woman/wife with an intelligent recognition of their fantasy relationship and of the marriage relationship. He is consistent in honoring his fantasy woman as physically the weaker vessel, but he, with clarity, will realize, recognize, receive, release, put in motion, and put into effect the truth and reality, the fact that her fairy-tale relationship and his fantasy dream-vision relationship and themselves are joint heirs of the grace, God's unmerited favor of life.

He knows she has made him her fairy-tale man, and he does not want his prayers to be hindered and cut off to the point where he cannot pray effectively, so he sees his fantasy woman through God's eyes. He conducts himself properly, honorably, and righteously, making sure she sees and knows that she is a partaker of his good deeds. He makes sure he is circumspect and temperate and spiritually, physically, mentally, and emotionally self-controlled.

He is willingly and humbly yoked, in bondage, enslaved, in a stronghold of the Holy Ghost to being sensible, well-behaved, and dignified. He leads an orderly, disciplined life. He is not distracted, detoured, denied, nor delayed from delivering a good reputation and in being well thought of by those who see him and know he is with his fantasy woman. He is not shifty nor is he a double-talker, but he is sincere in what he says. He is not given too much wine, nor is he greedy for base gain, craving wealth, and restoring to ignoble and dishonest methods of getting it.

He is her fairy-tale man, and she is his fantasy woman, and both of them will willingly strip themselves of their old relationship nature and their old tutored, trained, and taught carnal relationship mode, mood, principles, processes, procedures, and foundation. They will put off and discard their old relationship self, which have always been characterized by their former manner of relationship life and had became corrupt through lusts and desires that spring from relationship delusions. Both will totally yield, submit, and surrender to being constantly renewed in the spirit of their relationship mind, having a fresh mental relationship, and spiritual relationship attitude.

As long as and because both have went through this relationship process and procedure, they will have a relationship that is established, strong, and settled. Neither person will ever get complacent, contented in their relationship, or in a comfort zone, and neither will engage and get involved with/in unhealthy, having a form of godlikeness, carnal and selfish, self-centered, self-righteous, and self-justified relationship instructions and information and driven and motivated relationship compromises.

They are on a fairy-tale fantasy dream-vision-filled fantastic voyage because they have an unfailing love for each another. They make sure that they constantly and consistently yield, submit, and surrender, allowing their mind, mind-set, thoughts, train of thought, thinking, way of thinking, mental state of mind, mental condition/conditioning, mental frame of mind, and their mentality to be linked, connected, tied, entangled, and entrapped into sharing and demonstrating a love that covers a multitude of sins. They forgive and disregard the offenses of each another.

When people see their relationship and see the both of them, they will see, experience, and encounter people who are in a fairy-tale and fantasy relationship who have put on the new relationship nature, the regenerate self and the regenerate relationship self, all because their relationship is and have been created in God's image, and is Godlike in true righteousness and holiness.

When you have all of the right ingredients in a fairy-tale and fantasy relationship, get ready for a fantastic fairy-tale fantasy dream-vision-filled fantastic voyage. You can expect there will be a consistent flow of wonderful super abundance, far over and above all that you and that person can dare ask or think, infinitely beyond your highest prayers, desires, thoughts, hopes, or dreams. Why? It's all because all of the right ingredients are in the relationship. The foundation is right, and God's powers is at work within the both of you, keeping you both consistently yielded, submitted, and surrendered to what you both know can and will make your fairy-tale and fantasy relationships be prosperous, productive, and successful.

Both people in a fairy-tale and fantasy dream-vision relationship will begin to experience and encounter unforgettable, unexplainable, unthinkable, and unbelievable rewarding and fulfilling relationship moments and memories that they will and have been tutored, trained, and taught how to maximize. Both will also begin to experience and encounter a constant and continuous free flow of fairy-tale fantasy relationship entitlements that they will not ever get entangled nor entrapped into thinking nor feeling they have a selfish right to or deserve.

Neither person will take each other for granted, nor will they ever take nor mistake each other's fairy tale and fantasy loving, giving, caring, concerned, and compassionate heart for weakness. Their fantastic fairy-tale and fantasy relationship voyage will continue to sail into all of the relationship blessings that God have spoken, declared, and decreed upon it and them. God will be able to carry out his purpose for both of them and for their relationship.

My First Conclusion to This Matter

The first point that I want to make when it comes to what happens and occur in a fairy-tale and fantasy relationship that is functioning in its right modes, flowing in its right mood, and following the right fairy-tale and fantasy dreamer-visions principles, processes, and procedures and have been established and built upon the right fairy-tale and fantasy dream-vision foundation is both relationships are divinely protected. And because these two types of relationships are in divine order, God disarmed the demonic fairy-tale and fantasy dream-vision principalities. He disarmed the demonic fairy-tale and fantasy dream-vision relationship powers that were ranged against you, the person that you are in a fairy-tale and fantasy relationship with, and your relationship.

Jesus made a bold display and a public example of all deadly demonic damage, destruction, demoralizing fairy-tale and fantasy relationship demon spirits in triumphing over them, in him, and in it—the cross. Isn't that great relationship news? Everything that have been warring and rising up in your relationship, Jesus have already disarmed and dismantled. He disarmed and dismantled the demonic relationship despotisms.

He disarmed and dismantled the demonic relationship powers. He dismantled and disarmed the demonic-sent relationship master spirits who are the world relationship rulers of this present darkness. God, the creator of relationships, has dismantled and disarmed every relationship spirit forces of relationship wickedness in the heavenly, supernatural sphere. Jesus personally dismantled and disarmed every relationship demon spirit and all of their evil relationship strategies and deceits on your behalf and on behalf of your fairy-tale and fantasy dream-vision relationship long before you were thought of, conceived, and born into this world.

Jesus knew who and what was going to take place in your life, in your desire for relationship, and in your relationships long before you knew what a relationship was. And because he knew you, your life, and what would happen to you that would distract, detour, depress, delay, and deny you the right to be in a right, good, and pure fairy-tale or fantasy relationship, he dismantled and disarmed any and all demonic relationship-sent yokes, bondages, strongholds, enticements, entanglements, and entrapments. He triumphed over them.

Jesus knew when, what, how, and who Satan would use to get and send generational-inherited relationship curses into your life and relationships. He, the one who died on the cross for you and your relationships, disarmed and dismantled the wrong relationship feelings, emotions, desires, urges, tendencies, inclinations, intuitions, instincts, processes, principles, procedures, etc., that would cause, create the atmosphere, and contribute to you being hindered, held, tutored, trained, taught, functioning, flowing, following, linked, tied, connected, dominated, manipulated, and controlled. He made a bold display and public example of them, and he triumphed over them in him and in it—the cross.

Long before that, your demonic suggested and influenced relationship matter, moment, memory, circumstance, situation, confrontation, test, trial, tribulation, temptation, behavior, behavior patterns, wrong and bad relationship accusations, assumptions, relationship addiction, etc., was ever conceived, birthed, and born and became a reality, Jesus disarmed and dismantled their power over you their strategic and deceiving assaults, attacks, assassinations, restrictions, restraints, their dangerous, deadly, damaging, destructive, dominating manipulation and controlling reign and rule over your relationship(s), you, and your life. He disarmed and dismantled, and he made a bold display of them long before Satan had a chance to send them and assign and attach them to your relationship(s) and life.

He also made a public example of them all, and he triumphed over all along with any and all relationship selfishness, self-centeredness, self-righteousness, self-justification, pride, stubbornness, unseen, unknown, uncertain, unfair, unaware, unplanned, unsure, unexplained, unforgettable, unimaginable hurt, pain, brokenness, etc. He personally disarmed and dismantled the demon spirits that was assigned to your relationship and your life and all of the negative and woeful strategies and deceits in himself and in it—the cross.

And because Jesus did all of this for you and your relationships and even more, you have a right to believe, trust, have faith, hope, and confidence and see your fairy-tale and fantasy relationship becoming and being a visible fulfilled reality. Never let Satan and all of the negativities he send and place in your pathway in your life through other people hinder, stop, block, distract, detour, delay, deny, successfully challenge, confront, change, alter, get you to resist, reject, refuse, seduce, trick, trap, and deceive, etc., you from believing, reaching, and being in a fairy-tale fantasy relationship. That is exactly what Satan desires. Don't let him take away your power of choice, your right to choose, and what you can and will accept, adopt, apply, etc. He is the master fairy-tale relationship deceiver and destroyer.

My Second Conclusion to This Matter

His strategy is to get you to yield, submit, and surrender to his demonically suggested and influenced corrupt, violent, aggravating, agitating, irritating, deceptive, delusional, etc., relationship methods, modes, mind-sets, and mentalities. If and when he has done so, he will then seduce, entice, draw, drive, push, persuade, pull, force and lead your thoughts, train of thought, thinking, and way of thinking when it comes to relationships captive and a slave.

The master fairy-tale and fantasy dreamer-vision relationship destroyer and deceiver wants to make sure he can overpower, overtake, overthrow any and everything God created your fairy-tale and fantasy relationships. And after he has done so, he will begin to take down, take over, and take out your natural function, natural relations, natural affections, natural passions, and distract your desire for a good, right, and pure relationship, distort your feelings, and detour your emotions.

My Final Conclusion to This Matter

Your relationship/marriage can and do still have the fairy-tale and fantasy potential in it. The only thing that you need to do is start making the right change within yourself, your heart, relationship thinking, and way of relationship thinking. Change your relationship mind, mind-set, mental state of mind, mental condition/conditioning, and change your relationship mental frame of mind and mentality when it comes to relationships.

When you do so, that will release the good, right, and pure fairy-tale and fantasy relationship power into your relationship and also open up the door for a godly relationship presence to fill you, your relationship/

marriage, and your relationship. In order to get God's relationship presence and power into your mind and into all of its components, capability, abilities, and capacity and into your relationship, you will have to (1) be consistent, (2) challenge, (3) confront, and (4) change. Being consistent is the most important of the three. You cannot be up and down, every now and then nor do all of numbers 2 to 4 when it is needed.

Transform—Changing Your Relationship

Exactly what are you to be consistent in challenging, confronting, and changing in order for you to begin getting and seeing a visible transformation change of your old relationship into a fairy-tale and fantasy relationship? You are to be consistent in challenging, confronting, changing, rejecting, resisting, refusing and refuting old relationship (a) arguments, (b) theories, (c) reasons, and (d) proud and lofty things that sets itself up against the true relationship knowledge that comes from God. You are to also be consistent in challenging, confronting, changing, and leading captive any, every, and all old tutored, trained, taught, learned, accepted, adopted, and applied old, hand-me-down, pass-around relationship thoughts and purposes.

It is important for you to know, that which you know of and you don't, won't, haven't or you are afraid to challenge and confront that is negative, bad, and wrong old irrelevant relationship legends, profane and impure relationship fictions, mere grandmother's relationship tales and remedies and silly relationship myths. Old relationship standards, practices, processes, procedures, principles, beliefs, behavior, behavior patterns, habits can and will eventually change you and the person you are in a relationship with change your relationship. They will change the nature, function, and flow of your relationship, and they will change the relationship direction, relationship path, and relationship patterns that you and your relationship will follow.

CHAPTER THREE

The Truth Be Told

We all want our relationship(s) to work. I don't believe that a person who is in their right mind will intentionally get into a relationship, expecting, believing, or wanting it to fail. We want to see our relationship(s) bring us all of that which we go into them expecting, and when they don't, we all—at some point, place, or time—find ourselves at the same dark place. That dark place is where there is hurt, pain, and brokenness. The other thing we all do when our relationship(s) don't work is we all eventually scramble around and try to find a reason or reasons why they didn't work. From that point, we move on over into what Satan really wanted us to do from the beginning, and that was and is to play the blame game.

He want us to do exactly what we know we shouldn't do and what the Bible tell us not to do and that is to "wrestle not against flesh and blood." We are to never get into contending with physical opponents, but we do. It is a lot easier to make someone we see our enemy rather than be mindful that there is a motivating corrupt force behind the scenes in a hidden secret place, making sure we do not end up in prosperous, productive, and successful relationships. This is especially true if those relationships are powered by the principles and presence of God. All of us are guilty of doing it, you know, looking at, treating, and making the other person the enemy.

And it is when we get into that mind-set and way of thinking that we end up being contributors to the divorce rate and contributors to abuse, neglect, someone being battered, abandoned, victimized, and so many heinous things happening. The people who end up in those kinds of circumstances, situations in most cases, only want to see the fulfillment of their fairy-tale relationship and their fairy-tale romantic relationship. There are always exceptions to what I just shared, but I'm not talking about those who have satanically and demonically twisted minds. I am not talking about a person who bully, badger, and provoke a person to a wrong act, action, or deed and then want to call the police for protection.

I am talking about people who have waited all of their lives and people who have endured through not-so-good other relationships who still believe in, endure through distracting relationships, and still wait for their fairy-tale relationship. There are three things you have to be aware of when you decide to get into a relationship of any kind, and the devil will masterfully and strategically put in motion a highly well-organized and well-balanced attempt to:

(1) assault, attack, and assassinate
(2) kill, steal, and destroy
(3) bring you hurt, pain, and brokenness

Satan knows your families' generational curses, and he knows how to get you over into opening yourself up to them and being vulnerable to them, and he knows how to get you over into compromising with yourself and with those family generational curses. He knows how to, when to, and where to begin getting us over into family generational curses, and he even knows whom to use for that wicked purpose. The devil knows how to get us over into and keep us trying to fight a spiritual relationship battle(s) with carnal or with fleshly means. The truth be told, we all have done it, and we do it.

He also know how to use and when to use whomever and whatever he can to get us over into fleshly fights that are part of one or both parties in that relationship and generational cursed genealogy. Why do we engage in such behavior? The reason(s) being is we feel like we have been betrayed. We feel hurt, pain, and brokenness. We feel like we have been taken advantage of, we feel like we have been used, misused, taken for granted, battered, beaten, broken, and bruised to some degree and in some way.

We feel like we have been tricked and deceived into believing the person we were in the relationship with would love us for who we are, what we are, and where we are. We felt like the person we were in a relationship with would be there for us and walk with us through the good times and the bad times in our lives. Our expectation is that person will walk with us and be there for us through the good and happy times and through the sad times in our lives. Deep down inside, you felt and really, really truly believed that person we were in a relationship with would love us unconditionally, do for us, stand by us, be faithful and truthful with us, and be really true to us and committed to us.

You went into that/those relationships believing and wanting that person to cherish you, provide for you, protect you and your dreams, hopes, and desires. You had high hopes and great expectations for the relationship and the person that you chose to get connected to. You believed that he/she would take care of you even when you would go through spiritual, physical, mental, emotional, and financial changes over the course of time when you were with that person. It doesn't matter whether we are male or female. We all want to feel safe, secure, and stable in our relationships.

On many occasions, we open ourselves up to relationship thoughts and feelings, and we do so and faith and with some degree of confidence. We believe and really want the person we are opening up to for relationship purposes to cause, create the atmosphere for, and contribute to the fairy-tale experience and encounter that we have dreamed of and have been waiting for.

The truth be told, we hold that person we end up getting into a covenant relationship with personally accountable and responsible to the vows they made and to the day by day, year by year promises they have made us. You should do that, but we have to be careful and make sure you are allowing that person to hold *you* accountable and responsible for keeping the same. Our heart hold that person we are in a relationship with personally responsible for loving us just the way we want and need to be loved, and we hold them personally responsible for spending quality time with us.

The Question Is

I'm sure you have a preprogrammed answer in your mind, but the questions I want to ask you are the following:

1. What will you do when, "life happens" and it happens in the form of the unseen, the unexpected, the unplanned, the

unknown, the unfair, the uncertain, the unaware, the unsure, the unforgettable, the unexplainable and the unthinkable and the unbelievable?

2. What will you do when your relationship began to collapse and breakdown?

3. What happens when you grow apart, become distant from each other, and don't feel the same way you felt about that person when you first met them?

4. What happens when what all you really do in a relationship is argue, fuss, cuss, and discuss?

5. What happens and what do we/you do when you meet someone and they look right and the relationship feels right, but as the relationship begins to unfold, things go wrong, and the relationship begins to unravel and what will you do?

6. What happens and what do you do when, as people say, "life happens," and when what happens in life is more than likely against us and not for us?

We all have seen it in the relationship(s) of others, and you and I may have experienced it in one way or another to some degree. As our relationship dreams and hopes collapse, we find ourselves in a place and at a point where we have to learn how to let go of what we hoped, prayed, thought, felt, needed, wanted, and believed would last until "death do us part" and let go of the very thing we want to hold on to.

7. When life happens and relationship death happens, and then the death of your feelings, emotions, and desires happens, and separation happens before actual, physical death happens, what do you do?

8. What happens and what do you do when you are still in a relationship, and you are just existing in that relationship/ marriage, and that something that kept your relationship alive and healthy has, for some reason unknown or even known to one or both of you, is no longer there?

9. What happens and what do you do when the thrill, happiness, laughing, doing all of the things that brought you both together and that made you, that person, and your relationship different

and worth being in, suddenly and without any warning start to decline, and then it dies?

10. What happens and what do you do when, for some reason(s), the closeness, communication, compatibility, oneness, unity, harmony, flowing, etc., you both once had is no longer there, and for the most part, the only thing you and that person do is sit in the room together barely talking to each other?

11. What happens and what do you do when the only thing you and that person you are in a relationship/marriage with do is talk about the basic relationship things or surface matters, the usual, such as family, the bills, the kids, work and occasional move, someone else's marriage, problems, etc.?

It seems you have more to talk about and to share with people you don't know, people you just met, and with someone who just got your attention, than you do with the person you have been in a relationship with for some period. Are you feeling me, and are you with me? If you are, e-mail me at write2reachplays@yahoo.com and let me know. Why do our relationships hit cold and dead places and hit points where we feel nonresponsive and in need of a relationship CPR, fix, a charge, or a boost?

There is no doubt that there is something wrong, but we choose to sit in our relationships and do nothing. A lot of things have happened, and you don't feel the same way you used to feel about that person like you did when you first met them. You don't say and do the things you used to say and do when you first met, which, in most cases, was what drew you to each other. It's true. It takes two people working together on the same page, working to keep their relationship alive, strong, and healthy.

But it will also take you having a (a) relationship reality, a (b) relationship revelation, and the (c) right relationship weapons that will ensure you can and will continue to have a strong, healthy, prosperous, productive, and successful relationship. It will take all three to help empower your relationship so that it will be alive, stay delivered, cleansed and purged, healed, made whole, have a heartbeat, function, and flow on its own and actually be living and not be in need of a relationship jump start or relationship overhaul.

The most we should have to do in our relationship is touch it up once, fine tune it up, and watch it work on its own. Every now and then, we may have to give our relationship an additional charge and change some things. The truth be told, there is nothing wrong with the institution of marriage itself. What then is wrong with our relationships and marriages, and why do they go wrong? The answer to this and the answer to the other questions I asked above can be attributed to what we, out of ignorance and out of selfishness, allow, give place to, and bring into our relationships.

We have to make sure we don't share our relationship matters to the wrong person or someone we say is a friend who has a hidden agenda and hidden motive. That hidden agenda and motive they have is something you will not ever be able to see because you will be/are too busy being emotionally driven and being so deep off into your feelings. Why do we one day wake up, look at the person lying next to us, or just stop and look at the person who is occupying space in your life, home, and in a relationship with you, and you feel like that person is a stranger in your bed and home. They are a stranger in your life and even a stranger in your relationship. Life, whatever that means, should never just happen to a relationship, our relationship. Our relationships should not end up in the key of day-to-day life.

The Answer Is

Tell me what happens and why do we end up being relationship thrill seekers. It is because there is an unseen, unexpected, unplanned, unknown, unfair, unaware, unsure, unforgettable, unexplainable, unthinkable, and unbelievable wicked force watching behind the scenes of our relationships, and this force is in a consistent flow, dominating, manipulating, and controlling the function and the flow of our relationships. What's really crazy is we have given him the okay to do so. Let me give you the three stages to the death of a relationship.

Stage 1: What Satan and the forces of/in darkness masterfully do is maneuver the real true God out of our relationships and trick us into replacing our relationship with gods, which, in the case of a relationships, is our selfish and hurt feelings, emotions, dreams, fantasies, selfish cravings, lusts, etc., to name just a few.

Stage 2: All of what I just named in stage 1 and many more selfish conceptions and births distract us, draw us onto relationship detours, cause our relationships to experience delays in moving forward, and deny our relationships the power to grow, develop, and mature as it should.

Stage 3: When all of stage 1 & 2 has happened, the next thing that happens is that which is wicked and makeup the works of darkness that is in the unseen, the unexpected, the unplanned, the unknown, the unfair, the uncertain, the unaware, the undetected and in the unsure will begin to make manifest in the visible and in our relationships. What we will end up having to deal with will be a lot of the unforgettable, the unexplainable, the unthinkable and the unbelievable that will end up being so negative that they are hard to overcome.

When stage 3 finally shows up in a relationship, Satan then will deliver the final blow that will bring death and destruction to our relationship. That delivered final blow will always be something that comes from one or both of your family's generational cursed bloodline that he can use as vicious cycle. He can and will use the both of you as weapons formed against each other. You will become a weapon that is formed against him, and he will become a weapon that is formed against you. Once you begin to allow yourself to be enticed into a generational cursed argument, fussing, cussing (using profanity), and enticed into a generational cursed discussion, he then makes sure you are entangled and entrapped in all three.

I'm going to say it again, "Satan knows all of both of your family's generational curses." He was back there when your first family member came into existence, and he made sure that first family member of yours was a recipient of your families' generational curses. Satan will keep both of the people that's in a relationship in a face-off and fighting a generational curse spirit. That generational curse spirit is something that you and I cannot humanly beat, kick, stomp, cut, batter, abuse, neglect, and abandon until it comes out and victimize the person Satan is using as a weapon formed against you, and he is using you as a weapon that is formed against them.

When Satan is able to bust and break up a relationship, it is always because of two reasons, and those two reasons are the following:

(1) One or both of the people in the relationship got caught slipping, or one or both got caught sleeping. There wasn't a watchman on the wall of the relationship, and there was no one praying and interceding on behalf of and for the relationship.

   Either you or the other person or people in the relationship got caught in the life-was-just-happening moments and matters. One or both of you were pulled, pushed, persuaded, drawn, driven, forced, tricked, deceived, and/or seduced into pursuing after the tangibles and not keeping the spirit of the spiritual in your relationship.

(2) One or both of you forgot that relationships, your relationship, was/is God-created (Genesis 2:18–25) and not for selfish nor for fleshly created fairy-tale fantasies. God created relationship, and he is the only one who knows why he created them and what they are supposed to do and what they can and will have the power and the authority to do if we keep him at the beginning of our, moments, in the middle of our matters, and at the end of our mess or mistakes.

Do you see it now? Everything that is bad, wrong, cursed, and negative acts, actions, deeds, choices, decisions, conduct, conversations, way or the lack of communicating, integrity, personality traits, etc., that has ever been in your family. What your family is known for, what your family has had problems with has tried to keep secret and think no one knows, Satan and all of his imps and cohort spirits know about them. They used them against your ancestors, and now you are the next recipient.

Why do we end up practicing bad relationship behavioral patterns when we don't plan, prepare, and position ourselves to do so? Why are there the unseen, unexpected, uncertain, unplanned, unknown, unfair, unaware, unsure, unforgettable, unexplainable, unthinkable, and unbelievable circumstances, situations, and confrontations that seemingly just happen or show up in our relationships, and we don't even know why?

Answer number 1: Satan know all of the wiles, trickeries, schemes, devices, deceptions, delusions, addictions, lusts, weaknesses, flaws, boundaries, limitations, strategies, deceits, seeds, traits, and spirit that he made sure was in your families' generational bloodline, and he made sure your first family member would easily be attracted to and attached to and would adopt and accept as part of your generational family makeup.

Answer number 2: He then made sure he cursed them, and he is always at work behind the scenes of your life and behind the scenes of your relationship(s), consistently at work trying to make sure what he has put in your families' generational cursed bloodline is what he can and will easily have the right, power, and authority to use to dominate, manipulate, and control your feelings, emotions, desires, acts, actions, attitude, choice, decision making, deeds, conduct, conversation, and communication.

Answer number 3: Once that was completed, he then assigned a despotism, a power, and a master spirit that is the world ruler of this present darkness and spirit forces of wickedness in the heavenly supernatural sphere to watch over and try to assault, attack, assassinate, invade, infect, and influence your mind, mind-set, thinking, way of thinking, thoughts, train of thought, mental state of mind, mental frame of mind, mental condition, and your mentality and then affect and effect it with the lust of the flesh or cravings for sensual gratification, lust of the eyes or greedy longings of the mind, and the pride of life or the assurance in one's own resources or in the stability of earthly things (1 John 2:16). This is why your mind and your relationships are a battleground.

Answer number 4: All of the wiles, trickeries, schemes, devices, deceptions, delusions, addictions, lusts, weaknesses, flaws, boundaries, limitations, strategies, and deceits are automatically brought to life within and manifest themselves in your integrity, intellect, character, and personality each time you yield, submit, or surrender to the lust of the flesh or cravings for sensual gratification, lust of the eyes, greedy longings of the mind, the pride of life, or the assurance in one's own resources or in the stability of earthly things.

Can You Now Really See It?

Maybe your relationship is not the way you planned it or thought it would be. Maybe you both know you are not the same or one of you have changed, and you or the other person is not the same person you got into the relationship with. When you look at your relationship, you can clearly see how you have gone from talking, sharing, caring, and pleasing each other, wanting to see each other, wanting to just be together, and wanting to do things together to barely wanting to do anything together.

The desire to have, to hold, to be intimate with, touch, etc., that person is no longer there, or just the thought of doing those things is boring or just something to do. Many of those who are at that point in their relationship have a better relationship with social media, sex toys, or stimulants of any kind, than they do with the person who, at one time, felt they just couldn't wait to get home to see.

You begin to think and feel the way I just described above and you want to know why the person you are with suddenly changed and they are not the same person you met. You are asking yourself what is or what was behind the drastic unexpected change for the worst that person made. You also really want to know "why is this happening to me, why is this happening to us, and why is this happening to our relationship?" You should never forget Satan is always behind the scenes, and he does not want you to have a fairy-tale relationship experience, encounter, dream, hope, and desire. He does not want you to know and see him working behind the scenes of your relationship.

CHAPTER FOUR

Fate Fairy-Tale and Faith Fairy-Tale Relationships

What you have to realize and fully understand is Satan will always have a counterfeit for whatever it is that God created. Satan will always try to make sure the spirit of fate, not faith, was/is the foundation for your fairy-tale relationship. Fate can look, feel, act, sound, make manifestations like faith and even have you thinking and believing it is faith in motion and in action, but it is not.

A fate fairy-tale relationship is a fairy-tale relationship that has a power of its own, and it is one that is supposed to or ultimately will and have determined the final outcome of events that will take place in that relationship. In other words, what will take place in that relationship and how it will end, its doomed destiny, has already been decided and determined long before the two people met. The unseen, unexpected, unplanned, unknown, unfair, unaware, uncertain, unnoticed, undetected, and unsure force(s) that is always powering fate-filled relationships, fate tale relationships, and fate fairy-tale relationships are always Satan, devils, and demons.

Faith and fate both have a destiny end results. Faith has, as its partner, a destiny of fulfillment; fate has, as its partner, a destiny of doom. Fate and faith are enemies of each other, and we should make sure fate get the faith fight it rightfully deserves. Fate is a faith counterfeit. Satan will lie, trick, and deceive anyone he can into thinking, believing, and feeling they are in a faith-filled fairy-tale relationship when in all actuality, it is a fate-filled fairy-tale relationship.

When satanic-sent and demonically influenced and suggested fate is the powering force that drew, drove, pulled, pushed, forced, persuaded, tricked, deceived, seduced, enticed, etc., and made sure two people who once had dreams, desires, expectations, anticipation, hopes, and aspirations would one day end up in a faith-filled fairy-tale relationship, Satan found a way to sneak in and poison that faith-filled, fairy-tale relationship with fate. When this happens, that relationship is doomed even before it can fully unfold, or the doomed end comes after it has fully unfolded.

The Two Relationship Paths

There is and always will be two kinds of relationship paths in this life, and they are the following: (1) fate relationship paths or fate fairy-tale relationship paths and (2) faith relationship paths or faith fairy-tale relationship paths. Now let me give you a visible illustration or image of what these two paths look like when they are an active power in that fairy-tale relationship. We will use Matthew 7:13–14 to help us paint the picture and get the facts I want you to see and know.

(1) *The wide-path, fate fairy-tale relationship*: The path that leads into a fate-filled, fate-faith fairy-tale relationship is a wide and spacious and broad path. It is the way that Satan has made for those who want to get into of their own free will or out of a deceived will a fate-filled, fate fairy-tale relationship that ultimately will end or lead away to destruction. And many are finding this path that lead into this kind of relationship, and they are entering into this kind of relationships.

(2) *The narrow-path, faith fairy-tale relationship*: the faith-filled, faith fairy-tale relationship is contracted by pressure, and the path is straightened and compressed that leads into/onto the path of a faith-filled, faith fairy-tale relationship and lead away to the satisfying and fulfilling life of a faith fairy-tale relationship finder. And few are those who find this path.

We should make sure we say and do all that we can humanly and spiritually say and do to reject, refuse, and resist the devil when he is trying to influence and suggest we get on to the wide, spacious, and broad fate fairy-tale relationship path that leads away to destruction. We must be consistent in fighting a good fight and warring a good warfare against any and all past brokenness and bad relationship mistakes, fears, doubts, worries, stress, unbelief's, patterns of behavior, conversations, communication, hurt, pain, vicious cycles of being abused, battered, abandoned, rejected, violated, etc., which are all fate fairy-tale relationship ingredients.

It is easier for us to get into fate-filled fairy-tale relationships because the way to get into them and the path that will lead and keep us onto them will ultimately have our mind, mind-set, thoughts, train of thought, thinking, way of thinking, mental state of mind, mental frame of mind, mental condition, our mentality, and even our heart drawn and locked into and held hostage to a carnal-minded, fleshly based wile from the devil that have the drawing power and the seducing, suggestive, and influencing satanic and demonic deceived images, instructions, information, and imaginations as the bait. If you get on to this path, fate will have you abandon looking and waiting for a faith-filled, faith-based faith fairy-tale relationship. He will have you lusting, pursuing, and craving for a fleshy fate-filled, fleshly fate fairy-tale relationship.

The path that can and will lead you into a faith-filled faith fairy-tale relationship and onto the path of a faith fairy-tale relationship is harder to get into and onto. "Why?" you ask. Well, let me give you the reasons why.

(A) The path is contracted by pressure or it is drawn together and made smaller, thus bringing about a challenge to change for every person who desires to be on the faith fairy-tale path. You can't get into and onto the path of a faith fairy-tale relationship with the wrong attitude, mental state of mind, mental frame of mind, mental condition, and mentality, and a right change have to take place first.

(B) The path is straightened or put into difficulties. When you attempt to get into and onto the path that leads to a faith fairy-tale relationship, you can expect to have the type of difficulties that are there for and is designed to restrict in range or restrict the range of your thinking, way of thinking, thoughts, and train of thought. You cannot get into a faith fairy-tale relationship nor will you be able to easily get on to the path that eventually will lead you into one as long as you demonstrate in acts, actions, deeds, in the way you say, do, and handle things, matters, circumstances, situations, and confrontations.

And you demonstrate in the choices and decisions you make that your thinking, way of thinking, thoughts, and train of thought is still yoked, in bondage, under the stronghold, bound, limited, still a hostage, captive, and captivated by your negative past experiences.

(C) The path is compressed, or it is pressed in less space, condensed, pressed together, and flattened. All of these definitions suggest that the path that lead into a faith fairy-tale relationship and lead onto the path that is going to require that your mental state of mind, your mental frame of mind, your mental condition to have been delivered, cleansed, purged, healed, and made whole so that is has not and is not swollen with memories of what has happened to you in the past.

There can't be no type of going down past hurt, past pain, past brokenness, past abuses, moments when you were being battered, violated, rejected, abandoned, etc., memory lane and bringing up, remembering and reliving former things and considering things and memories of old or that is old.

For those who can, will, and do get their faith fairy-tale relationship dream, hope, fire, desire, motivation, drive, passion, willingness to pursue after, made alive, restored, revived, renewed, and refreshed, they are going to have to be aware of the spirit of false care, false concern, false compassion, false feelings, false emotional attachment, false desire, false need and want, methods, madness, motives, motivation, memory, moments that is associated or connected to the person that Satan used to deceptively kill, steal, destroy, distract, detour, delay, hinder, stop, and seemingly deny you of the right God has given you to live in and out and see the visible manifested fulfillment of your faith fairy-tale destiny relationship.

All of what I just described above can and usually will speak to the hurt, pain, and brokenness that was/is on the inside of you in a prophetic way. And all of what I just described to you above will come into your consciousness, subconsciousness, and unconsciousness disguised as a sheep or disguised as being innocent and harmless ways to perceive, evaluate, analyze, sum up, come to conclusion, presume, and assume what you are led to believe are the right, good reason(s) why, and how you got into a fate-filled, fate fairy-tale relationship and onto the path of/with a person(s) who had a fate-filled, fate fairy-tale relationship spirit working in them and upon them against you. The spirit that is upon the person is not innocent and it brings with it devouring wolves reason and devouring wolves ways.

A Faith Fairy-Tale Relationship

A faith fairy-tale relationship is described as a relationship that has the assurance, confirmation, title deed of the things you hope for, that end up being the proof of things you do not see and the conviction of their reality; faith perceiving as real fact that is not revealed to the senses, that have magic deeds that have the power to ensure the unbelievable is turned into the believable and the untrue is turned into true because of the visible manifestations that prove otherwise.

In other words, when you are in a faith-filled fairy-tale relationship, you are in a *mental state of mind, mental frame of mind* where you have been strengthened, settled, and established in having complete trust, confidence, and unquestionable belief in the unbelievable being made believable and the untrue being true because of the visible manifestations that prove otherwise in the relationship.

You are in a *mind-set* where you have complete trust, confidence, and unquestionable belief that the unbelievable relationship that you have been dreaming of will end up being made believable, and the untrue magic-deed-filled events, moments, and memories that your believe will take place in that relationship and end up being true because of the visible manifestations that prove otherwise.

There is a deep personal conviction which in turn produce, prepare, and present a *mentality* that is yoked, in a stronghold and bondage, and a slave to having complete trust, confidence, and unquestionable belief in the unbelievable that you envision in relationship being made believable, and the what can seem like and feel like in the human and natural sense is untrue in a relationship being turned into truth because of the visible manifestations that prove otherwise.

What is made manifest are *thoughts, a train of thought, thinking, and a way of thinking* that is bound and limited totally to having complete trust, confidence, and unquestionable belief in the unbelievable in the relationship that bring about total satisfaction and total fulfillment being made believable, and the untrue way having total relationship satisfaction and fulfillment can and will make you feel free and end up being turned into truth because of the visible manifestations that prove otherwise.

There is a steadfast, unshakeable, undeniable, unmovable, having complete trust, confidence, and unquestionable belief in the unbelievable being made believable and the untrue being turned into truth because of the visible manifestations that prove otherwise.

Your *mind* is instantly and automatically drawn, driven, pulled, pushed, persuaded, and forced into having complete trust, confidence, and unquestionable belief in the assurance, confirmation, and title deed of the things you hope for in a relationship, being the proof of things you do not see and the conviction of their reality, faith perceiving as real fact, and a knowing that the unbelievable that you have high hopes for and a great expectation for, being made believable and that what others would say is "untrue" will produce facts that will take place as you with patience and perseverance wait for the relationship you know belong to, being turned into true because of the visible manifestations that prove otherwise.

To believe in a faith fairy-tale relationship is to have your mind, mind-set, thoughts, train of thought, thinking, way of thinking, mental state of mind, mental condition, mental conditioning, mentality, your mode, mood, and attitude locked, enticed, entrapped, and entangled into the assurance, confirmation, title deed of the things you hope for in your relationship, being the proof of things you do not see and the conviction of their reality, faith perceiving as real relationship fact(s) that bypass, overpower, overtake, take over, take down, and take out and remove any need for any unbelievable being turned into believable, untrue being turned into true relationship truths, images, information, instructions, ingenuity, ideas, and visible manifestations and proof having to be revealed to the senses.

A person who is in a fairy-tale relationship is someone whose *heart* is occupied, filled, and consumed with having the assurance, confirmation, title deed of the things in a relationship they hope for, being the proof of things they do not see and the conviction of their reality, faith perceiving as real fact what is not revealed to the senses.

Their heart function, flow, and follow any and all links, ties, leadings, and connections to the path that strongly suggest and totally influence having complete trust, confidence, and unquestionable belief in the unbelievable in their fairy-tale relationship being made believable and the untrue that is often thought of that exist in a fairy-tale relationship being turned into truth because of the visible and consistent magic-filled matters, moments, memories, and deeds manifestations that prove otherwise.

A Faith Fairy-Tale Relationship Mode

A person who is in a faith fairy-tale relationship mode is someone who is strong in supporting a way and a manner in which their faith fairy-tale relationship occurs or is experienced, expressed, or done. They will not allow anything or anyone to distract, detour, derail, delay, or deny them the right to see a visible manifestation of what they believe, feel, and know is real. They are very cautious, and they will make sure they do not share their faith fairy-tale relationship belief, dreams, hopes, and desires with those who are doubters, and they do not share their faith fairy-tale relationship facts with people who are dream stealers.

The mode that they are in will be one that can and will cause, create the atmosphere, and contribute to the right way and manner in which their faith fairy-tale relationship occurs or is experienced or how it is expressed or done. Because they know that everything they have ever wanted and needed in a relationship and in a person will be in the person they have dreamed, hoped, desired, and have even seen an image of in the spirit and in the natural. They can sense and feel that person's spirit and even their presence from time to time.

A faith fairy-tale mode is one that is filled with the right faith ingredients, which are hope, belief, confidence, and trust. It is important that you know it's not what others believe but what you believe in when it comes to your faith fairy-tale relationship that can, will, and shall bring forth the visible manifestation of it. I want you to look at two ways to view a faith fairy-tale relationship mode.

(1) A way and a manner in which your fairy-tale relationship will and shall occur or is experienced, expressed, or done that have the assurance, confirmation, title deed of the things you hope for, being the proof of things you do not see, and the conviction of their reality, faith perceiving as real fact what is not revealed to the senses in order for the belief in the unbelievable being made believable and the untrue being turned into truth because of the visible manifestations that prove otherwise.

(2) A way and a manner in which your fairy-tale relationship is destined to occur or is experienced, expressed, or done that have the power to produce, present, and prepare you having complete trust, confidence, and unquestionable belief in the unbelievable being made believable and the untrue being turned into truth because of the visible manifestations that prove otherwise.

I want to give you a tour of the words we have been using in their defined state so you can see for yourself how we have been connecting them. By doing so, you can feel and see how important the meaning of each is when it comes to how they function and flow, and what they have the power to produce, prepare and present; that can and will cause, create the atmosphere for that will lead to prosperous, productive and successful and more meaningful, rewarding and fulfilling faith fairy-tale relationship.

> *Faith*: the assurance, confirmation, title deed of the things you hope for, being the proof of things you do not see and the conviction of their reality, perceiving as real fact what is not revealed to the senses. To have complete trust, confidence, and unquestionable belief.

> *Fairy tale*: belief in the unbelievable being made believable and the untrue being turned into truth because of the visible manifestations that prove otherwise

> *Relationship*: the way in which two or more people or organizations are connected, regard, talk, deal, and behave toward each other

> *Mode*: a way and a manner in which something occurs or is experienced, expressed, or done.

Closing Questions

1. Are you in the right covenant faith fairy-tale relationship mode? () yes () no
2. How do you know you are in the right faith fairy-tale covenant relationship mode, signs, and signals?_____
   _____
   _____
   _____
   _____

3. How do you know you are *not* in the right faith fairy-tale covenant relationship mode, signs, and signals?_____
   _____
   _____
   _____

4. What are you going to do to challenge and change the faith fairy-tale relationship mode that you are and have been in if it have not been the right one or the wrong one? (a) right one _____
   _____
   _____

5. (b) wrong one _____
   _____
   _____

A Fate Fairy-Tale Relationship

I want to say it again—a fate fairy-tale relationship is Satan's counterfeit to a faith fairy-tale relationship. There are a lot of people who think and feel they are in a faith fairy-tale relationship when in all actuality they are in a fate fairy-tale relationship. The first reason they cannot tell the difference is because fate is always trying to hang out or hang real close to faith. Fate is your enemy, and that spirit is always roaming around, lurking around in fierce hunger, seeking a way to seize upon your relationship and devour it.

As a result, when the person is thinking they are in a faith fairy-tale relationship, they may be actually walking in a fate fairy-tale relationship. The most common thing that happens in this scenario is the person start out walking in a faith fairy-tale relationship, and one or both of the persons in that relationship open the door for the spirit of fate to come into their relationship, and they are not aware they have done so. They continue in that relationship patterns and behavior patterns, not knowing, recognizing, nor realizing fate had taken over the relationship and fate is in the driver's seat of their relationship. This fate occurrence is smooth, slick, and really shyster in how it manifest itself.

The other thing that happens is a person can start out in a fate fairy-tale relationship, and for some reason(s) that is either planned or not planned, knowingly or unknowingly, the persons in the relationship open the door for *faith* to come in and end up being in the driver's seat of their relationship. No matter which, the point is fate is always trying to disguise itself as faith. And so this is why there is always a fate-versus-faith fight. The person or persons in this type of relationship end up fighting hard to keep their relationship alive and active. In a fate-versus-faith fight, there will be as many fought rounds as the person(s) in that relationship can and will allow there to be.

Being a More than a Conqueror

The fate-versus-faith fight will come to an end, and you will end up being more than a conqueror over this spirit the moment when both people in that relationship

1. get on and stay on one accord
2. acknowledge and accept the truth about what is happening in their relationship, acknowledge there is something that is wrong, and it is something that is unseen manifesting itself through your relationship
3. get the information and gained knowledge concerning the spirit of fate and the strength and power of faith
4. go to God and ask him to give you the weapons of and for your warfare against the spirit of fate that is trying to kill, steal, and destroy your relationship. You can't use the weapons God has given someone else for their relationship fate-versus-faith fight.
5. you should take those God-given weapons, and you utilize them by being making them a daily part of your spiritual warfare weaponry, tactical artillery, and you should be strategic and

consistent in assaulting, attacking, and accurately assassinating that spirit. Do not let up because that demon spirit called fate won't let up on its warfare against you and your relationship

6. war a good, strong, steady, steadfast, unmovable, and unshakeable warfare along with some intimate and intense worship unto the God, who has already disarmed the principalities and powers that was ranged, attached, and assigned to your relationship. Fate is a principality. Jesus made a bold display and public example of them, the spirit of fate. Jesus triumphed over them, it, the spirit of fate, in him and in it—the cross (Colossians 2:15).

You are to war a warfare against an unseen spirit and not get into a war with a seen or recognizable person that the spirit of fate is using and actively influencing, suggesting in and through. Remember, God is not going to give you the victory over the spirit of relationship fate. He has already given it to you. That is exactly what Colossians 2:15 is telling you. Your relationship victory over this spirit is already a done deal. You already have won because of what Jesus did on the cross and after the cross.

Once again, I want you to be clear and fully understand you cannot and will not be able to use the relationship weapons God has given someone else for their warfare against the spirit of fate that is trying to dominate, manipulate, control, take down, take over, and take all the way out your relationship. Why? Because their weapons were catered to their fight and what act, action, deed, conversation, communication, handled matter, choice, decision, circumstance, situation, and confrontation that opened the door, caused, and created the atmosphere and contributed to them being enticed, entangled, and entrapped into their fate-versus-faith fight.

Just as no two relationships are the same and no two relationships have the same function, flow, and processes, principles, and procedures it follows, no two causes and reasons for the fight is the same. There may be some similarities, but they will be more differences. God gives specific fate-versus-faith fight information and instructions for each person's individual relationship fate-versus-faith fight.

The *second* reason why they cannot tell the difference between a faith fairy-tale relationship and a fate fairy-tale relationship is because they didn't know there were two types. Most people who did not know there was a difference in the types of fairy-tale relationships could and can basically take whatever negativities that happen in their relationships that end up, causing that relationship to end, and they charge it to the game. When a relationship is "charged to the game" it means the one doing the releasing basically assess or do an assessment as to what happen, the causes and reasons, and then they accept their assessment and then adopt a relationship cause and reason analogy and then move forward in applying an assumption.

How It Does What It Does?

The question you may be asking again is, "How does the spirit of fate get the power to do what it does?" That's a good question. The spirit of fate will need the cooperation from your feelings, emotions, and desires for any amount of time, and then it will need the assistance from your urges, tendencies, inclinations, intuitions, and instincts. The third assistance fate will need will be from your conduct, conversations, and communication. The last help it will need will be from your behavior and behavior patterns.

Once fate have access to these parts, pieces, or expressions of you, it will dominate and manipulate them all until it can control them, and then it will fill them all with its presence and power. All of this is strategically designed and carried out with accuracy and precision.

Fates Methods

Please understand and don't take this lightly or for granted. Don't play with this spirit, and don't discount its motive and motivation. There will be no hit and miss with the spirit of fate. It will consistently (1) hit, hurt, and hinder repeatedly until it can eventually kill, steal, and destroy. Sometimes that spirit will (2) hit, hurt, and hinder repeatedly and then it will change up and hit, hurt, hinder and then distract, detour, delay, deny, and then kill, steal, and destroy. Guard yourself against being a willing and even an unwilling active participant, full-time, part-time, or a seasonal participant.

Fate will be consistent with number 1 and 2 until it can break your human will, stopping it from building up any walls that resist, reject, refuse, rebut, and refute the weapons fate is using. Once your human will is violated and the trespasser called fate have trespassed, it will then begin with a wicked manner and in and with a power-packed power and presence, barrage and bombard your mind, mind-set, mental state of mind, mental condition, mental frame of mind, and your mentality until it is powerless against stopping fate from pulling, pushing, persuading, drawing, driving, and forcing you into self-willed, self-performance, and self-effort acts, actions, deeds, choices, decisions, leadings, suggestions, and influences.

Your thoughts, train of thought, thinking, and way of thinking will be so fatigued that it can't and won't be able to fight because of being bombarded with a barrage of fate-sent deceptive, delusional, and deceiving images, insights, ingenuity, ideas, instructions, and inspirations that explode like bombs when they hit. Every part of you will end up being halt between two opinions or double minded, and you will end up being heavily locked into procrastinating, hesitating, questioning, and second-guessing. This is followed by you being in a fate-sent, initiated, dangerous, destructive, deadly, damaging, depression-filled comfort zone, contentment, complacency, and compromises.

Looking at a Fate Fairy-Tale Relationship

When you are looking at a visible manifestation of a fate fairy-tale relationship or to be in a fate fairy-tale relationship is to function, flow, and follow in the development of events in your relationship that is beyond your human control, regarded and determined by a supernatural power that is destined to happen, turn out, or act in a particular way that cause, create the atmosphere, and contribute to belief in the believable being made unbelievable and the true being turned into untrue because of the visible manifestations that prove, dictate, decide, and determine the way in which the two or more people that is connected regard, talk, and deal and behave toward each other.

What's taking place in that relationship, the conduct, conversations, communication, type and kind of choices and decisions, the way a matter is handled, and the person's acts, actions, and deeds prove fate is the force that is behind working within, and it is the spirit that is powering their relationship. Fate basically makes sure the fairy-tale belief, thought, thinking, way of thinking, atmosphere, and surroundings is filled with so much negativities that will eventually stir up feelings of fear, doubt, worry, stress, and unbelief that come in and make that fairy-tale moment and memory seem and feel like it is/was a made-up story that is designed to mislead.

When we talk about a *fairy tale*, it can manifest itself in three different ways in a relationship, and those three manifestations are the following: (A) belief in the unbelievable being made believable and the untrue being turned into truth because of the visible manifestations that prove otherwise, (B) in a story in which improbable events lead to a happy ending, and (C) in a made-up story usually designed to mislead. Fate's main flow is through *c*. It will use *c* as its weapon of choice to change the final outcome of letter's A and B.

Fate have four ways in which it manifest itself in and through a relationship *defining it*, and those are the following: (1) the things that will happen to a person or thing, the future that something or someone will have; (2) an inevitable and often adverse outcome, condition, or end; (3) the will or principle or determining cause by which things in general are believed to come to be as they are or events to happen as they do, destiny, disaster, and death; (4) the development of events beyond a person's control, regarded and determined by a supernatural power, be destined to happen, turn out, or act in a particular way.

It's a 4D Relationship

A fate fairy-tale relationship will always have a *destiny* and a destination point and a place it is to arrive at that was assigned and attached to that relationship long before the two met and decided to get into a relationship. It will always be filled with so much *drama* that keep the persons in that relationship drawn and driven into being easily distracted, detoured, delayed, denied, and damaged.

It will always produce, prepare, and present *disaster* of some kind, and the end results will always be *death* of some kind to some degree. It can be a spiritual, physical, mental, emotional, financial, or relationship death or actual death to one or both person(s) that is in that relationship. I want to caution you once again: do not play with this spirit. You cannot and will not win.

A Fate Fairy-Tale Relationship Mode

If you ever encounter or have an experience with a person who is in a mode, you would be looking, listening, and talking to someone and seeing them manifest in and through their acts, actions, and deeds in and through their conversation(s) and through the way they communicate, a specific and often easily identifiable way or manner in which what they say things, in what they do, how matters are handled, how their choice and decision making is conducted, in how something occurs with them or is experienced, expressed, or done or there is a specific form or manner of expression they demonstrate.

To have an experience, encounter, or to be in a relationship of any kind to any degree and for any amount of time with someone who is in a fate fairy-tale relationship mode is to be with a person who is *caught* and *caught up* in the development of events that is beyond that person they are in a relationship with, beyond their human control regarded as events determined by a supernatural power that is destined to happen, turn out, or act in a particular way. That particular way of happening, turning out, or acting will then *dictate to*, *dominate*, and *control* the person that is in the relationship with a fate fairy tale person's ability to believe in the unbelievable being made believable and the untrue being turned into truth because of the visible manifestations that prove it is that person you are in relationship with *constant* and *consistent* form or manner of expression, their normal way or manner in which they allow dangerous, deadly, destructive, devastating, demanding and damaging events, circumstances, situations, confrontations, and matters to occur so that they are experienced, expressed, as the way it is always done.

The person who have compromised with fate will always be someone who is in a comfort zone, contented, or complacent with being in a fate mode that they are totally yielded, submitted, and surrendered and sold out to allowing themselves to fit, function, and flow in and out of a fate mode and follow the fate mode flow and fate mode path so that fate is what the person(s) that are in the relationship with, who have, or is in a fate fairy-tale relationship mode end up allowing fate occurrences, experiences, expressions, and fate doings to easily manifest themselves.

The persons mind cannot war a good warfare against the fate fairy-tale relationship mode, and their thoughts, train of thought, thinking, and way of thinking cannot reject, resist, refuse, rebuke, and refute a fate fair-tale relationship mode. Their mental state of mind, mental condition/conditioning, and mental frame of mind is hindered, held up, and held hostage.

Their mind-set have been tainted with and have been tutored, trained, and taught how, when, and where to have a reactionary, response, reactionary response, and how to receive fate relationship mode instructions, information, insights, images, ideas, inspirations, and ingenuity. Their mentality is or has been challenged, confronted, changed, and conformed to being in a fate mode.

A fate mode is dangerous, destructive, deadly, damaging, strong, and powerfully volatile and wicked when it is given place to and is fed fate food, which is fear, doubt, worry, stress, and unbelief to any degree. It can grow, develop, and mature into a dominating, manipulating, and controlling force that place yokes and strongholds, hold in bondage, and make a slave of the person's mind, mind-set, thoughts, train of thought, thinking, way of thinking, their mental state of mind, their mental condition, and their mental frame of mind.

If a fate mode is dangerous, then so is being in a fate fairy-tale relationship. There is nothing good that can and will ever come out of such a relationship. There are so much flesh, carnality, and natural methods, principles, processes, and procedures consistently being produced, prepared, and presented. The relationship is being based on, built by, and established in and through self-will and self-effort. Fate's dirty works and dealings are manifested in and through a person's self-will, self-performance, and manifested through a person's self-efforts.

The only thing that can and will come out of a fate fairy-tale relationship mode is depression, death, destruction, and self destruction. That is the destiny of a fate fairy-tale relationship mode. That was the destiny of it before anyone ever entered into such a relationship and into its mode. If you ever meet or find yourself in a relationship with someone who has a fate fairy-tale relationship mode or is playing around with one like it is a toy, my advice to you is to get away from that person. There are those who love to play fate games because of and due to them being in a fate fairy-tale relationship mode.

CHAPTER FIVE

Her Fairy Tale

Who is she? Who is this woman, girl, princess, someone's mother, someone's daughter, someone's friend, someone's relative, and someone's fairy tale? She was just like any girl growing up, typical in a lot of ways, different in most ways, the same as other girls on most days. She is someone who just wanted to live her life and be happy. Much like most girls growing up, her home life was, well, you already know because this is your story too, and her childhood was what it was. She is a person who loved her family, and she loved them with all of her life

The only thing she really dreamed of was to be loved, needed, wanted, accepted, and respected for who she was by her fairy-tale fella. She grew up in a world that was quite different from those she knew and from those who knew her. There were those days when her world was the same as yours—yes, you, the reader of this book. Like most of the girls growing up, she had dreams, hopes, desires, fairy tales, and fairy-tale fantasies. Of course, she would never tell anyone about them, even her closest friend(s) just know some of them, but no, never, not all of her fairy tales and fantasies. Some days she would easily be herself, and there were those days when it wouldn't be easy for her to be herself. And then there were those other days when she struggled within herself, and she wasn't or didn't know who she was.

There were those minutes, seconds, and hours when she really didn't know what she was, where she was, and where she was going. Sometimes, at times, most times, and in most cases, all of the time, she just felt like she was acting out her life on the stages in her life and on the stages of her life. You know how it is, just pretending. Pretending that you are planning, pretending you are preparing, pretending you are positioning yourself for what your life is to be, what you hope it will be, what you think and feel it will be, what you hope and pray you will be, become, and end up being. Is it real? Is she real? Is her life real?

When she is not pretending she is doing what all good little Christians that's her age, in her life, in her generation, in her family, at her school, and in her world do when they weren't pretending—they pray. Every day she exercises her parental-controlled faith, and she tries to find balance in her life. After all, it is her life, isn't it? No two days were ever the same for her. Yesterday it's a stage. Today it's a state—a state of mind and a state of being. Tomorrow it's a statement written by her acts, actions, deeds, choices, and decisions and written and authored by her change and changes. The next day it's her "yet to be" and she hopes it will be something so, "simple" that she can learn from it and make it a part of who she is. No, no two days are the same for her, and most of her days had some tests, trials, and temptations of their own. Yet she holds on and believes her life will be better, and there will be brighter days. No one really knows what's going on in the inside of her. That's because she is good at hiding it. Most just stand on the outside looking at her, and she intentionally keep them there. And they say, think, and feel they know her, or some even want what they think she has, but they don't know... They really don't know. They don't know how hard sometimes it is to be who she is—to be herself. They don't know how she is sometimes faced with and is filled with all kinds of a certain kind of fear(s). It's the fear that keeps her halt between two opinions. Come on, you know, being double minded, having two minds because that fear she knows all too well is fighting against her faith.

At times she appears to be constantly hesitating, dubious, and irresolute, and on other days she gives off the impression that she is unstable, unreliable, and uncertain about her life, love, living, and everything she think, feel, and decide. But that is just a pure pressure perspective. Sometime she can hear her future roaring inside of her, and she search within herself trying to find life's guarantees. And for just a moment, a moment in her month when she is all alone with what has happened in her last year and what is happening in her new year, she sits alone in her loneliness, in her quiet time, and she ask her future, and she ask her faith, "Is this all there is?"

She ponders the path she has chosen, the path that have chosen her. Some days she sees it, know it, accept it, adopt it, and understand it; and on other days she can't find it, don't want and need it, and resist, reject, and refuse it. Why? She's not sure if it's fate destiny or faith destiny. No matter what, she put on her "fact face" you know what I'm saying. That "you don't know the facts of my life but you think and feel you do", and she go out and put on a show that leaves her audience stunned, shocked and sensitive. See, they don't know. They really don't know… Nobody knows… The price she's had and is still having to pay to be a princess.

They don't know how much it cost to be in the home life she is living in. Speaking of her home life, well, it's a lot. No, a little different from yours, but on most days it is the same as yours. It's days that's filled with people, places, things, matters, moments, memories, circumstances, situations, occasional confrontations, and the pressures. Oh, the pressure that comes with just trying to be a person in a family that has a personality, image, intellect, identity, character, function, flow, and reputation of its own. The pressure of trying to find your way into fitting into a family that makes you feel like you fit in, but deep down inside, well, sometimes you don't want to feel you fit in the family, but you belong in the family.

She knows that in spite of the fit-and-belong issues, she has her family standing by her, and they are supporting and is very supportive of her. It's true. She had her family, she had her friends, and she had her inner fights. To some in her family, she was their favorite. To others, she was their foe. To a few, she was someone they feared. Every now and then, there were those who saw and perceived she was just some who was just a voice that had no face. Every day she still wakes up and says, "Power to the strong." But deep down, she often thinks and feels something's wrong. In the morning, she feels confident. In the afternoon, she feels confused; and at night, she finds her faith and feels cool, calm, and collected.

What about life, what about love, what about living, what about finding, and what about flowing? How about it? She went to school, she go to church, and she prayed. Some days she believes God know her life, knew what she would be going through, and he would hold her and help her. And then there are those days, decades gone by in her life when she wasn't sure if he cared about her or had time for her. She's being honest. Sometimes she felt like she wasn't important, and she really didn't matter. That's when it looked like her life was unfolding and unraveling right before her eyes, and her world was seemingly spinning and spiraling out of her control. Why? Because… just because!

At times—okay, majority of the time—she really and truly felt she was important, and she mattered. But what about those days when she could sense and even see life and love and how it would unfold for her and how, when it did, it made her feel minute and insignificant, but that was just out of sensing and not really seeing it. One day she looked into the mirror and hung her head in sorrow because she wondered what would happen when her usefulness is gone. And then she whispers, "Something is wrong in my heart right now," and she breaks down and cries. She somehow manage to lift her head and once again look at herself in the mirror, and this time, she sees all of the life she has lived running before her, and she asks her hurt, her heart, and her heaviness, "What about the love? What about my love? What about his love for me?"

She then bows and breaks down on her knees, and she speaks from her passionate plan and pursuit, saying, "Oh, faithless heart, you tempt me, test me, and try me to my core, but you can't and won't. I won't let you have a hold on me. I'm just telling you he's going to come… He's going to come for me, so don't you come around here anymore." This is just another day, another moment in her life when she have to remind herself of the fairy-tale love and the fairy-tale life and the fairy-tale relationship she has yet to have and live in and out. She's been waiting throughout the days and years of her life for that one moment when he will come and take away her hurt, aloneness, and loneliness.

God did not reveal to the mirror that she is looking at on the wall what her fairy tale would be. No, He never did, not a part, piece, not some, not a little, no part of it at all. She can, in a quiet whisper, hear a still small voice saying to her, "I am God, and I know the feelings you are feeling can wipe away your world. I'm going to hold you, and I want to remind you that the fighting inside you will pass." And once again she is able to pick her face up from off the floor, and she can pick her faith up from off that same floor because her Father won't let her fail, and faith in her Father won't let her fall.

Her friends and their families and their lives were different from hers, and then there were the friends and their families whose life was just like hers, some even worse. She struggled at times and didn't know who she was. Some days, most days, certain days, she felt safe, secure, and strong. That would be the days when nothing would go wrong, and she would get away from her life and her world and find her way to her fantasy island. There she would find her fairy-tale guy waiting for her, and she could hear her fairy-tale song playing so sweet in the background. It's just a moment… her moment… her secret place that she goes to just to get away from the quiet storm's that's raging in her heart. I'm talking about those quiet raging storm's that's in her heart she believes God can hear them and she believes only the guy who is her fairy tale can hear them.

Nobody Knows

Her teachers, mentors, friend(s), those who meet her for the first time, those who have direct interaction with her, and those who stand on the outside looking at her—they all say she is really smart, intelligent, bright, and quiet at times. Every now and then, she seemed distracted, but she always seemed to get her focus back and find her way back to reality. They said she had a lot of positive and good potential but at times didn't believe in herself. At times she was always trying to be what everyone wanted her to be—you know—live up to their expectations.

But nobody knows what she had to live with and through, you know, the acting out of hidden agendas and hidden motives of those she trusted, opened up to, those she let get close to her, get to know her, those who tested, tried, tempted, tricked her, trapped her, and took from her… you know. Yes, that… part of you that you can't get back… family… strangers… familiar foes with familiar spirits, lust, and desires. Nobody knows. Oh no, no. Nobody knows her secret, about her secret successes, triumphs, and victories. Nobody knows the truth about this, about that, and about the other… I know you say you have forgiven. She did too, but nobody know she is, you are, well, still having a hard time forgetting so you can release and not remember and not restore and not revive and not relive.

Nobody knows why she sometimes act the way she do. Maybe she cares, sometimes unconcerned and most times a little compassionate. Taken for granted, kindness taken for weakness, nobody knows. They just don't know how she can still be faithful, a little faithless, and then feeling like a failure. It's because… nobody knows. They really don't know that she have been running for her life, running with her life, running in her life, running into life while looking for love and looking for the light. Mmm, aah, nobody knows… Lord! please don't let them know how she can feel a cold wind and it's bound to come.

Another change nobody knows, and another end she cannot see. She's had her share of challenges and changes, just like most, some, a few, or all of the girls her age. Peer pressure, family pressure, faith pressure, parents pressure, survival pressure, performance pressure, pressure, pressure, pressure. Nobody knows the people pressure she feels, her stress that adds tension-filled times. Nobody knows… They should know because they see her when she sometimes falls down on her knees and ask them to tell her that it's all right. God will give her what she need. She's just growing, she's just developing, and she's just maturing.

Nobody knows she still believe, has faith, hope, confidence, and still trust that her fairy-tale prince will come and get her, and she will be saved by love. And she and he are going to be just fine. He will squeeze away her haunting fear and say the words she longs to hear. You see, nothing different, maybe a little different, every now and then a lot different, some days too different for girls her age, girls she grew up with, was close to, was friends with, connected with, knew of, associated herself with, and even hung out with. Nobody knows like girls her age, her weight, her height, her color, her race, her nationality, and her ethnicity, like girls she knew of and that knew her. It's clear. Just trust each word she says.

Nobody knows. No, no, they absolutely don't know the struggles with her identity and personality she has had. Nobody knows that there were moments when she was outgoing, assertive, felt good about herself and her life. Nobody knows that there was a time when she actually knew where her life was going. She had her direction clear, and she had got beyond the occasional clouds that came her way. Nobody knows, they, without a shadow of a doubt, don't know, didn't know she used to feel good about herself, and everyone knew it, felt it, saw it, was effected and affected by it in a positive way. But all of the things she's been going through, I'm telling you, if you only knew, nobody knows.

You see, they don't know about her heartache, your heartache, your heartbreak and how she, you struggled, strained and didn't, couldn't see and find her, your way through, the past, beyond those days when you felt hopeless.? You know, think about it, nobody knows, but you know. Nobody knows, can't, and won't let them know that at times there are two of her and two of you. One does the right thing, and one cannot see. And she sometimes doesn't know which one of the two of her was the strong one in the last act and scene in her/your life. It was a really good show she/you put on, but you and she still ask, "Who I am?" Some days she/you really don't know. Good home, good family, good life, going to college and getting a degree, planning your life, preparing for the future, and positioning yourself for your success and your happiness.

Nobody knows. How can they know that every path you take, every road you go down, every choice and decision you make can take you, me, and us right between the patches of the light that's in us and the darkness that's in us? Nobody knows. For the most part, she was your typical happy girl—complacent, contented with the way her girlhood was, oftentimes in a comfort zone, most of the time because of the way her life was/is unfolding. She had her share of moments when there was the good, the bad, the ugly, and the awkward, but nobody knows. Hey! They don't know. They really don't know. They just don't know. She won't let them know.

Just Living so I Can Love You

She was just seventeen when she had her first big fairy-tale dream, and like most girls, she wanted love, affection, and attention. Every now and then, the girl, woman, and princess that's deep down within her would wander far from home—her place of safety and refuge—and when she did, it was always because the fairy-tale faith deep down inside of her would lead her far from her reality. In her fairy-tale mind, she would live a life that chills her and those who knew some part or piece of fairy tale to the bone. She never really wanted to be some big star, but she did want to move away. She could see and feel herself living a fairy-tale love life. It's a life some people, most people, a few people, a lot of people, a select group of people that some days, most days, mmm, okay, every now and then, even her parents, certain people, peers, and even her pastor really didn't see nor want nor thought she could or would ever be living.

Why? It's because she was their good girl, their princess, someone they valued as priceless. They knew she had a sensitive and caring heart, and when she loved, she loved real hard. They were afraid that by her loving hard, it would bring her heartaches and heartbreaks that would take a long time to heal. To this she would respond, "What about love"? Her heart, well, it's just running into the arms of that fairy-tale stranger she have been longing ever since she could remember. She knew she was, would be, could be, should be, well, okay, she knew she was different. And her fairy-tale vision reflects just how different she is.

In her fairy-tale dream, she would want her fairy-tale man to always be true and to never have a faithless heart. To never be cold and blind and weak and to forgive her on those days when she's revealing she has a stubborn streak. Maybe write her some poetry and give her and unexpected kiss and show her you always want to be with her. She has walked away from her family, and she had found her strength to choose. It's him, her fairy-tale guy, the one she know who has been waiting for her, while she was trying to find her way. He's there waiting for her because he understands her, and his heart's desire is to protect her and provide for her.

Her Fairy-Tale Love Games

It's her fairy tale, and in her head, they play fairy-tale games that begin with small sweet surprises because he is her Boaz, and he is attracted only to her. In her eyes, he is the maximum fairy-tale man. Why? Because he is always making that extra effort to demonstrate that he cares, he's concerned, and he is compassionately connected to her, and he takes pride in being committed to chivalry at its best. He respect her for who she is, where she has been, what she has been through, what is important to her, etc., because he knows she is, at her best, a true woman, but he loves to play with the little girl that's inside of her. She knows he loves to draw and pull her out by using fun loving gestures and then entice and seduce her into an occasional fairy-tale love chase that end with him showing her he feels accountable and responsible for all that matters to her and for her personal well-being.

She loves how he does that because it's the little girl in her that time and life has hurt, bruised, beaten, battered, and took away her innocence. He is so attentive to the little girl inside of her and the journey she has been on that he has made himself vulnerable to her, and he has allowed himself to be emotionally involved with all that has to do with her. He doesn't have a faithless heart but a faithful heart that she knows belong to her. He knows how to tempt her to the core with his show of appreciation and his willing desire to spend time with her, the woman, and with her, the little girl.

When he touched the little girl in her, she comes to him in all of her regained and remembered attractive innocence with the style and grace of a shy yet vibrant and alive princess. She knows she is safe and secure in his hands and in his heart, and his machismo doesn't live strong with him anymore. For he is so much like her, a little boy that had to grow up fast and was forced to become a man that he had no intuitive instincts and knowledge. They meet, they play, and they have fun in the simplicity of a world that they have created for themselves. It's a world where they both can be who they are, say what they feel, do what they do, and live life the way they choose.

He knows he doesn't have to be her *daddy*, and she knows she doesn't have to be his *mama*, and that makes their childlike innocence blossom and bloom when they are together. He is a man, her fairy-tale man, and she knows she won't have to pamper his childish, manly ego because he has tutored, trained, and taught himself to demonstrate he is sensitive toward her. It's her fairy tale. He is her fairy tale, and they are their own fairy tale, one in which that has feelings, emotions, and desire. It's her fairy tale, and a faithless heart cannot prevail because she has a man who has the strength and the ability to love her and accept her for who she is.

It's the middle of her fairy-tale love game, and that is where the fairy-tale magic, fairy-tale moments, and it's where the fairy-tale love memories are made. It's where their love for each other is and it's where they will find a lifetime of love that they will share and have because it was there before they met and it made its own music. And when they finally meet, she knows both of them will begin to experience and encounter their made-in-heaven fairy-tale music melody. That alone is what strengthens her hope in the fairy-tale love she feels and believes in that her eyes have never seen. Before she allows herself to step into the middle of her fairy-tale love game, she prays hard to be worthy of that which she believes would one day, this day, in this fairy-tale moment, forever be hers. She wants to be found worthy of his blind loyalty to her and the fairy-tale relationship security he will bring into her life.

You see, she's wised up, and she doesn't think twice. She knows that when it comes to her fairy-tale love man, she can never leave room for compromise. She knows that her fairy-tale love game is not just about her only. It's also about him as well. She knows it won't be long until her faith in her fairy-tale love will be in sight, and the heavens will say, "It's all right."

And as her fairy-tale love game would go… they would meet in their innocence, far away from what her mama told her and far, far away from male mentors in his life has told him. Yes, they would meet in the middle where the magic of their fairy-tale music melody was setting the atmosphere, their atmosphere, for their fairy-tale moment, a place where nothing and no one else mattered. She knows they both are in the midst of a fairy-tale relationship revelation, and they are doing what a modern world, the world they both came from would say they wouldn't and couldn't do. That would be to share in the making of a fairy-tale memory that is consistently filled with fairy-tale truth and realities.

No, it's not a distant dream, and it's not a hopeless hope, nor is it a dry, desolate desire that she believes in. She can see him in her heart, and she can feel him in her faith and with her faith and their fairy-tale love relationship. Well, it's not just a fantasy. It's true, and it is filled with some fantasy, but it's a fact, and the evidence is not in found in what others can see. The evidence of the fulfillment of her fairy-tale love relationship is found in how it makes her feel and how it frees her faith so it can fly. It can fly far away from what was, what could be, what might be, what won't be, and what should be, and it will land in a place called fairy-tale love relationship will be!

He takes her hand and walks with her, and he walks her into the place called maturity, a place where both of them finally came to be, and it is there where the magic in a fairy-tale love begins. Can you see them? They both are mature, and because they are, they have set themselves up for the magic that's in a fairy-tale love. What she feels for him is calling out from a boundless love, for their fairy-tale love has lit a fire, and both of them are the flame. And everything that has brought them into their fairy-tale love is burning really bright into the darkness. What they will get out of their fairy-tale love relationship is shining out for inside of them both. It is the strength of their passion and compassion for each other.

When she was growing up, she used to meet him in her dream, and it would be there where they would proclaim love at all times. And in the places where she was really growing, she could hear herself say, "Let me say once more that I love you. Let me say one time, maybe two, that I love the way that you love me too." After which she would feel the strength of the person he is, and in a sweet sensitive way, he would be visiting her. And then she would take a deep breath and say to her fairy-tale visitor, "I wish I knew more of you."

When she was developing, she used to dream a lot about how he would love her and how he would listen to her heart. He would care about her feelings, and he would want to be with her. How he would take time to study her and get to know her, and out of what he would learn, he would have an even deeper and greater appreciation for the total summation of who she is. He would tell her he wouldn't let time erase the look of love that's in her face and how her life would always be richer because of all of the time she has spent in the magic of her fairy-tale love with him.

Oh, they are in the middle, and the magic has begun to flow like a river that runs deep. Time won't erase the way his heart see her face. He calls her name, and she hears his voice in the quiet whispers of everlasting, and she looks his way because it's clear. She trusts every word he says. Maybe this is not just magic. Maybe it's the melody that drew and pulled them into the middle of a fairy-tale love that has no real beginning, and it was created without an end. She's heard it said. When the rivers of a fairy-tale love is running high, you have to get to higher ground so the muddy waves of pain won't get a chance to wash over you.

When you are in the magic of your fairy-tale love, just stay in the flow and don't be afraid to let yourself go every now and then because it's going to be all right. Listen to her quiet heart singing loud. She's in the magic of her fairy-tale love, and she's been saved by his love. She knows she is a woman of promise, and she is an heir to her fairy-tale love and to her fairy-tale dream. While she is in the middle, in the magic of her fairy-tale love melody, she whispers to him, "I love you, I do. I need you more and more."

As her heart awakens and her fairy tale is still free, the magic has created a melody, and the melody has created a moment... just a moment. It was that magic-filled moment where her fairy-tale love met her fairy-tale life. And in the magic that's in the melody of her fairy-tale love, it creates a fairy-tale moment that will never end. Why? It's because time will never end in their fairy-tale relationship. You don't understand! You see, she found hope after she let go, so there's no need to question her and the feelings she have. Oh, you're wondering if she's really sure she found hope? Ask her again, and she will tell you the same over and over. She's sure enough to not want to be without him. She's sure enough to stay with him for good. She's sure enough in every little thing about him.

God, He knows the feelings she have for her fairy-tale man could wipe her world away. Ravaging the promises a strong heart one made. Her fairy-tale prayer is always the same. She prays that her fairy-tale man will stay with her and make their love ever new so time will not undo. She prays that as the years go by and their fairy-tale love is mellow and aging, oh, even when they are both old and wise, they will know then what they don't know now. Well, she prays he knows she will still be sure enough to never want to be without him.

She knows time will never end in their relationship. Why would she say this? Her fairy-tale guy is a man who loves to communicate, and she's a woman who loves understanding. So with that being said, she's laid it all on the table; and she's telling you, the reader of this book, what she's already told you before. And that is her love is not a soon-forgotten fable, and her heart is not a box with a lock in a five-and-dime store. Her fairy-tale love is a promise keeper, and he has promised that when life is long and problems come in their relationship, she will always be his only one. He's promised that they will always stand face-to-face, and with one look, his eyes will embrace her. He's her fairy-tale love, and she can hold fast, and rest assured he has promised to be a man, her fairy-tale man, her flame and her twin. He has promised he will hold her and never kiss her like they are married, but he will always kiss her like they are lovers.

He has promised to be a man that will tell her tomorrow will be brighter when things seem dim. He is her fairy tale, and she often wonders if he's out there somewhere looking for her. She just wants him to be there to hold her hand and dry her tears. Would he recognize her if he saw her? Yes, because they have met time and time again in their fairy-tale magic, in their fairy-tale melody when their fairy-tale love was in the moment. What a memory! I'm talking about her fairy-tale moments and her sweet fairy-tale memories that actually matter to her… Can you feel me?

CHAPTER SIX

Lord, Please Tell Me Why

Her journey hasn't been easy. In fact, it has been long and hard. She had tried to enter into every relationship with confidence, faith, and hope, but somewhere in the back of her mind, in a place where the unseen, unexpected, unplanned, unknown, uncertain, unfair, unaware, unsure, unforgettable, unexplainable, unthinkable, and unbelievable live, dwell, and hide, she still feel isolated and all alone. Every now and then, she will come face-to-face with facts, faith, fate, and finally her fears. Some days it's been a battle, some days it's been a war, and most days it's been a journey that she feels the need to get away or she just have to go on.

Some days it's been a struggle just to survive and get through all of the mental anguish, hurt, pain, stress, strain, frustrations, discouragements, disappointments, and let downs that she has suffered through and has, by the grace and mercy of God, endured through. When another relationship that she has put a lot into and had to fight past her past just to get into suddenly and without any advance warning take the path as the one that had put her in the unstable and unsecure mental state of mind, mental condition, mental frame of mind, and mentality, she is hurt and her pain is deeper.

She often feels like she is a hostage and a passenger in her own life, and the drivers are all of the pain-filled, hurt-filled, brokenness-filled feelings, emotions, past failures, past mistakes, and past wrong choices and decisions and past wrong judgments she made. When she has gotten into a what-seemed-right but end up in a wrong relationship. It's the same old story for her played out on a different stage, place, and point in her life. The person she met and got into the relationship with seemed different, and the people she met while in that relationship were different, but the end results of that relationship end up being the same.

She didn't see it, didn't expect it, hadn't planned for it, hadn't prepared for it, and she wasn't mentally, physically, emotionally, and financially positioned for an act and an action coming from a person she really loved and cared for. She never thought, felt, believed, nor had any inclination that what took place in their relationship would come from and through him.

You see, she had been through this before. It was years, and now here she is again dealing, facing, and even fighting with those same old hurt, pain, and brokenness that she thought she would never get past, get over, and get beyond just years ago. Is this history of her hurt repeating itself, or is this just an unfortunate, isolated situation? No matter, she is waking up once again to a lot of hurt and heartaches. God has kept him connected and in touch with her hurt and pain. He could feel her heart and her hurt. And when the time was right, he has brought to her the same regret-filled, remorseful, repentant heart he took to God. He brought it to her, and he laid it at her feet. He made sure she knows how sorry he is, and he would be there to walk with her through it all.

She knows the path she must take to get to inner deliverance. She knows so very well the point she had to reach to so she can receive inner cleansing and purging. She knows the exact place she had to get to so she can receive her inner healing. And she knows the presence she need in her life that will make her whole again. She's still a little afraid to be alone with him again because her last memory of the moment they shared was not a good one. She has forgiven him, not for his sake, but for her sake so she can move on past the moment and, one day soon, get past the memory of it all. But for now she is still in the back of her mind. She's having the thought it probably won't, might, might not, could, can, maybe or it will even happen again. In her heart, she knows that God has dealt with and is still dealing with the man. She can hear and feel his brokenness that surrounds his sincerity, and she knows he too is on the same journey she is on, different reason but yet the same need and want from God.

After a lot of years have gone by since she has been through something like this again, this one really hurt more. Why? It's because of the time, effort, and hard work she put into getting past the first time someone really hurt her. It's because it took a long time for her to finally be able to live again and open up and love again. It's because it was really a struggle and a fight for her to finally be able to trust and relax in a relationship again. It's because of this man, someone she never imagined, thought, felt, believed would be someone who would, through his action, remind her and force her to remember when... and now she's starting all over again.

You know, having to start at the beginning with the process she thought she had come to the end of years ago. He may be different. She may be grown up and more mature. But what has happened and the effect and the affect is still the same—emotional and mental anguish, pain, torturing and tormenting thoughts, feelings and emotions. It's this man and the mental and emotional hurt and pain that run deeper than deep. Not like the first time, there was just hurt and pain.

It's years later, and she's taking that old familiar journey all over again. And now—yes, right now—she clearly knows and understand what she has to do. She knows she has to once again try to find the mental strength and the willpower that will help her get up and get on to the path that will place her on the journey to mental and emotional releasing, recovery, and finally, mental and emotional restoration. But today, right now, at this moment, at this place and time, she's battered, broken, bruised, and once again, she feels like she has been beaten out of a relationship, out of something she had finally gained the confidence to believe would be hers.

Another vicious cycle is repeated in a different place, at a different point in her life, at a different growth, development, and maturity point in her life. It all happened at a different time in her life and at the hands of a different person. This person was someone she had opened herself up to, gave all she had to, and she had finally gained the mental strength and the mental ability to really open herself up to him and trust and love again.

Each time she find herself in that dark place, in this dark place, and at that dark point, it's like she is watching her own life on a big-screen TV. She never would have imagined in all of her wildest dreams he would do the same thing(s) that was done to her in her past. And yes, it's worth repeating, she once again is feeling those same old feelings she had felt before and had worked hard to free herself from. She feels betrayed, damaged, and destitute, and she has to find out just what she has to do with her life now that she has been hit with another round of unseen, unexpected, unplanned, unknown, unfair, unaware, unsure, uncertain, unforgettable, unexplainable, unthinkable, and unbelievable relationship abuse, neglect, being battered, being rejected, and being abandoned. She cries uncontrollably at times with no warning, and just like in the past, when she had been targeted and touched, tormented and tortured, she would once again find her way into a bathroom, and then she would crawl over into a tub of hot water. It's just a little something to help soothe the sore spots. She takes a look at herself and sees all of the bruises, and she can feel all of her body aches and pains. And then she cries, not really for herself, but for the parts of her that have really been hurt and is the real victim this time.

The part of her that she opened up and gave to him was a part of her she hadn't given to anyone else in years, maybe not at all. The hurt, pain, and brokenness she is feeling at the moment make it hard for her to remember. She cried for the part of her that once again didn't get what it thought, felt, was led to believe it would get but didn't. She would cry for the part of her that once again had been hurt and hit again and would need the time to heal. She would cry for her character, personality, integrity, and intellect because all of them once again would feel a present pain that was first a past pain.

After crawling out of that soothing hot tub, she would seek out a place that would be soothing to her soul and her spirit. She would seek out a place that would be soothing to her senses and her sensitivity. She would, with childlike faith, go to her father God again, and she would ask him, "Lord, please tell me why? I know you know. Please tell me why me, why us, and why this? And then just for a moment, she would listen, and she would finally cry uncontrollably for herself. She would pray and cry herself to sleep, wake up, and cry some more and then go back to sleep. She would cry because she doesn't know if he genuinely, out of a broken spirit and with a contrite heart, cares enough and is concerned enough about her to call. You see, in times past, when something like what happened between them happened, she would be left all alone with what he had done and abandoned.

Deep down within herself, a little past her hurt, down below the place of pain, and on the other side of where brokenness is, she would ask herself: Is this person who brought her to the same old familiar place, whom she felt was so different from the others, was he really just the same, or did he feel her hurt? Would he share her pain and bare her brokenness, or would he reject it all, make excuses, have an explanation as to why, and try to explain?

Or would he be the man she knows he was even though what he did wasn't right in no way whatsoever, not really him, not really of his character? She wondered, would he call her with a repentant heart and reach out to her? Her heart and her mind would be constantly bombarded with messages that she really didn't know which would be the truth. Her heart and her mind, thoughts, and thinking were halt between two opinions. She finds herself on an emotional roller coaster, and her feelings are numb sometimes. What she desires is what she had worked so hard to get before, and that is peace of mind, peace in her heart, peace in her spirit, and peace all around her.

At times she can't find peace, and most times she can't find her way into God's presence, but she tries and cries and prays. She knows she has to forgive so she can move on, but that, on some days, is hard especially when the parts of her hurt that she didn't know could or would hurt. She remembers the good times, the happy times, and the things that made him and their relationship so special and unique.

Her Maybes

Maybe he is gone on with his life. Maybe she never really mattered to him. Maybe he really didn't care like he said he did. Maybe he has someone else. Maybe he didn't really love me like she deeply loved him. Maybe, maybe, maybe—her mind is filled with maybes. Some days she remembers and finds herself reliving his touch, their kissing, their sharing, their caring, their pleasing each other, and even their lovemaking. She has those times when she is not really trying to think about it, but she finds herself remembering and reliving a moment and a memory that reminds her of the way they were, the way it used to be before it all started going wrong.

She tries to convince herself that it is time to move on without him, but some days that is a lot easier said than done. She had finally thought and felt she had found someone who would fit into the role and image of her fairy-tale man, and after what has happened to her, them, their relationship, she can only wonder if all along he was really just a stranger in her heart. And maybe she was just a stranger in his house. He was her fairy-tale guy, and this was supposed to be her fairy-tale life. She remembered what her mama said about fairy tales. She told her she'd one day understand relationships and their story, and what she learned would be good for her.

She replayed the times they were sharing the same space at his place and intimately in each other's face. Was he still a stranger in her house. You know the one she was trying to build for him, for her, and for them. She remembered the day when he changed, she changed, they changed, and their relationship changed. That was the day she couldn't figure out whom he was. In the quiet whispers of her, I remember when she kept saying to herself there's no way he could have been whom he said he was that day. He had to be someone else.

With tears in her eyes and her heart filled with brokenness, she kept saying to herself, "My fairy-tale guy, he wouldn't touch me like a stranger would, and he wouldn't treat me like I was once treated in my past. He would truly adore me, and he would listen to me, and he would hear me. He wouldn't walk by and ignore me. He would come to save me even if it meant he had to swim through raging stormy seas. He would never let me stand alone and leave me, abandon me and let me stay out in the wilderness and standing alone in the cold." That day there was a stranger in her house, their house, and in their relationship. And she would break down and cry.

"Lord, please tell me why! Please tell me. Why me, why us, and why this?" she cries out in a whisper, under her breath, in her pondering and wondering mind, and with a silent scream. She is hurting, and her soul and her heart is filled with and is singing those heartfelt blues. Part of her still want him to put some music to her hurt, put some passion to her pain, and put some loving to her brokenness. She knows what's in her heart when it comes to him, and she knows what she feel is real, but she doesn't know how, when, and where to begin letting him in after hearing him share how he feels out of his brokenness and out of a humbled heart that is filled with godly sorrow, regret, remorse, and finally, repentance.

She can feel his words, and she can feel his heart, and she can feel his spirit, and she knows that what he is saying is real, sincere, and what he is saying and showing is coming from a place where God has dealt with him. She knows she really miss him, and in their conversations, she discovers he feels the same. He has felt and said what she has felt and said about him when it comes to her. Yet her heart is still filled with so much hurt and Harlem blues even though she knows he is physically there but gone because the mental and emotional hurt she has suffered makes her feel isolated and all alone. The part of him she thought she really loved, knew, once knew has left, and she can't find him in the midst of her hurt, pain, and brokenness. He doesn't know that her heart cannot hear him at times, and she sometimes cannot feel him. Yet she still listens and make sure she do her best to hear him because this time she knows it's different and he's not the same as the one before who abandoned her after he hurt her.

He is different, and he is reaching out to her, and he wants to reconcile. Even though he's the one who brought her to where she is, she still knows he's the man who can and will put some music to her heartache, pain, and troubles and bring an end to her mental and emotional blues. Where should she begin? Where would you begin, and what would you do? Where do they start? That's the question that needs an answer. I'm talking about fairy tales in relationships, and believe it or not I'm talking about fairy-tale romance! Holler if you hear me!

CHAPTER SEVEN

Starting Again

It is said that honesty is the most important ingredient in love, and I will agree. After seventeen years of being married to the same person and learning how to love her, I one day found myself right in the midst of something I never thought would happen to me again. You see, it takes a lot to love a person that has loved others before they started loving you. Most of what you experience and encounter on the road to learning how to love that person is all of the things they had been taught by the person(s) before you on how to love them. Over the course of your relationship with the person you are in a relationship with, all of the things that someone else had taught them about love and relationships will finally begin to surface.

Some of what will surface will shock you, a little of what surfaces will stun you, and most of what surfaces will downright steal you and bring you to a place and point where you feel like you have been living in someone else's relationship and not the one you wanted or expected. That is exactly what happens when you got into the relationship with someone's ex. Why? It's because you have spent most of your time in that relationship trying to get the person to fit into your image of your fairy-tale or fantasy person, and at times they get it and begin to walk in it and live in and out of what you are trying to get them to see and do. But a majority of the time, there are a lot of rejecting, resisting, and refusing by that person to conform to the image and end up being what you would like them to fulfill in your life.

Most of the time in a new relationship is spent trying to deprogram that new person you are in a new relationship with of their bad-tutored, trained, and taught love and relationship habits. The truth being we get into relationships for the purpose of fulfillment or so that we can feel like we are not someone who is still running on empty. Our desire is to think and feel we have what we need in that person we have a covenant with, and we don't have to look no further. In all actuality, we don't know what we are going to get out of most and many of the relationships we get involved in. Most of the people we get into relationships with only tell us what they want us to know about themselves, their life, their bad and wrong choices and decisions, where they have been, and what they have been through. So we get into a relationship with that person and things are good for a while, and then one day you run into something that has come out of or from that person that you never seen before and you never expected.

That's the moment when everything in your relationship suddenly will begin to change either for the better or for the worse. The persons that came before you who were in a relationship with the person you are now in a relationship with had taught that person how to love them, need them, want them, satisfy them, and how to do for them. That same person(s) had taught the person you are now in a relationship with their interpretation of what love and a relationship is. They had been tutored, trained, and taught how to fit into the fairy-tale image of the first or last person(s) they were in a relationship with, be that a twisted or a right interpretation. The person you are now with was tutored, trained, and taught how to be a/the covenant relationship companion that they are by someone else who does not know you and have never met you.

As your relationship with that person begins to unfold, you begin to notice they are saying and doing things, handling you and matters, making choices and decisions, demonstrating acts, actions, deeds, and expressing feelings, emotions, and desires that you have not expressed to them that you need or want. They will also begin to act out that part of themselves that the person(s) before you would not let them express. They will do so in a manner that you don't know really how to understand, and you don't know if you should demonstrate a negative reaction or respond in a positive manner. It all comes down to you, the person, what you also have been through, what has happened to you while you were on the relationship road as to how you interpret the display the other person is showing you.

The bottom line is somebody who was in a relationship before you tutored, trained, and taught the person you are now in a relationship with their view, meaning, and interpretation of love, loving a person, and how and what they felt was and is the art of sustaining a healthy, prosperous, productive, and successful relationship. They didn't learn it from you. They learned what they know from the person they are saying is their first fairy-tale man/woman. Some of what they learned may be good, a little of it may be okay, but most of it is bad and ugly.

He or she may have held your relationship person a certain way. He or she may have kissed that person a certain way. They may have been intimate in a certain way. And now that other man and the other woman are gone, there will only be you and that new man or woman. You will find yourself standing all alone with the covenant relationship principles, procedures, standards, boundaries, limitations, restrictions of someone else, and the new relationship person. Not only so, but you will also find yourself having to challenge, confront, and deal with the type of relationship mind, mind-set, thinking, way of thinking, thoughts, train of thought that you have been tutored, trained, and taught by someone else and that you have, in turn, were in a relationship(s) with.

Once you have tasted and been touched by their concept of what love and relationship is and mean, and based on what you learned, you will then began tutoring, training and teaching the ones you were in a relationship with, what you learned. As I said before, be that what you have learned and now have become a teacher of is all yours, some of yours, part of yours, one-third, one-half, two-thirds the less or the more of yours. Every love and relationship standard, principle, process, procedure that you practice and believe in is and can be a mixture of some or all and a portion and piece(s) from yours and someone else's relationship definition.

The truth is we pass our relationship values, principles, standards, conditions, process, procedures, and teachings around in a haphazard manner just like a cold is being passed around. Someone breathes their relationship interpretation breath on you, and you catch it. If and when the relationship ends, you are still infected, affected, and you are still effected. Instead of getting treated by the master relationship doctor and the creator of relationships, who is Jesus, for any and all learned bad and wrong relationship belief illnesses, belief diseases, and belief infections that show up in our relationship behavior and behavior patterns, we/you pass it on to the next person you meet and get into a relationship with.

The other thing you are left with is a relationship mental state of mind, relationship mental condition, and relationship mental frame of mind that your mental capabilities and abilities have been tutored, trained, and taught by others you were in a relationship with, to accept and adopt and keep. As twisted as it may sound, you have come to develop a liking or love for what you were taught. It feels good to you. It makes you feel good about yourself. It makes you feel alive and important, like you count, and you hold on to that, and you are now trying to incorporate what she or he tutored, trained, and taught your mental capacity, capabilities, and abilities to respond and react to in a new relationship.

Every time we do try to incorporate what we learned and liked in previous relationships that was taught by the person(s) you were in a relationship with, your new relationship and the person you are sharing it with will end up in a conflict. Why? The new person you are with may not like what you have been tutored, trained, and taught to like, love, or it may not fit in your new relationship, or it may not fit in that new person's idea and image of a fairy-tale relationship. Maybe the new person you are with do not have a want, need, or desire for what someone else has tutored, trained, and taught you.

What do you do when what you have been taught in a previous relationship do not fit in the new relationship you are in? The answer and solution is simple. If it doesn't fit, don't force it. Just relax and let your relationship find its own flow. As you relax and let the new relationship find its own function and flow, the process will lead you into being tutored, trained, and taught something else from the new person you are in a relationship with that you will love, like, need, and want. It will always be something you have never had in a relationship, or it may be something you have had, but it will be interpreted in, through, and by the new relationship person in a different way.

Or you can just get out of the relationship and keep running in and out of other relationships until you do or might find someone who can and will give you that one something you loved and liked that someone in a previous relationship of yours tutored, trained, and taught you to desire, need, and want. But what about the other things you need and want in a relationship that you don't know you have a need or want for?

What I'm Saying Is

What I'm hoping you will see is how we take good and bad, right and wrong, positive or negative, happy or sad relationship seeds from one relationship into another and from one person to another. We, without our knowing it, will end up placing unrealistic expectations upon a new relationship and placing unrealistic expectations upon a new relationship person and those unrealistic expectations don't fit. So why do you, I, and we continue to try and force them to fit? There may good and healthy things in a past relationship that you liked or loved, but those things still cannot and do not and will not fit in a new relationship. Why? It is due to the fact that it doesn't fit into the new person's fairy-tale relationship image. What you are trying to fit, that which you have been taught to like and love and learned to like and love, is, in all actuality, part of the person who tutored, trained, and taught you fairy-tale portrait.

In the course of my seventeen-year-marriage, I discovered that there were relationship things my ex-wife liked and loved that she was tutored, trained, and taught and learned to like and love by someone in her past relationship(s) that she kept hid or was lying dormant in her for years. And one day, when I didn't expect it nor saw it coming, the love and relationship thing(s) that she learned from the one(s) from her past that she loved or liked, manifested itself; and when it did, it was expected of me to accept, adopt, recognize, and receive it. Then implement it in our personal relationship and into our marriage. It didn't fit, but she tried to force it. I too was doing the same thing, and I didn't see or realize it. Satan had the both of us so distracted with our own selfishly learned relationship desires that we allow ourselves to get consumed and busy trying to force things we learned, liked, and loved that was taught to us by our friends, family members, associates, and more so from a person(s) that was in our past relationships that did not fit into our seventeen-year relationship.

My *first point* is this: someone from a past relationship(s) you were in tutored, trained, and taught you their version and interpretation of what a relationship value, meaning, purpose, plan, process, procedures, etc., are, and you either accepted, adopted them, initiated, and applied them and made them your own, or you resisted, rejected, and refused to accept them even if they felt good and looked good to you. My question to you is who tutored, trained, and taught you what you know about a relationship?" My second question to you would be who was the person that tutored, trained, and taught the person who tutored, trained, and taught you about relationships? And who taught them, etc.?

She showed me something that I had never seen before nor knew was in or a part of her. She brought something into our relationship that I didn't know she had an attraction to and an appetite for. She said and done something that just surprised me in a negative way. I'm sure I did the same to her. My *second point* is this: we have to stop hurting each other, and we have to stop trying to force something from our past to fit into our present. It won't happen. We sit in our relationships and try to smoothen, suffocate, hide, and protect something that someone from a previous relationship has taught us, so it doesn't show up in our new or present relationship.

We try to prevent what he or she tutored, trained, and taught us, be that good or bad, right or wrong, happy or sad, from showing up when all along we have tasted and tested that relationship something and we like it, love it, but we would rather sneak and partake of it and then lock it up. What happens is eventually what's inside of us will come out. I one day found myself starting again after a seventeen-year marriage relationship. It was really hard for me ending it and then having to regroup and start all over again. I wasn't in another relationship, while I was ending my seventeen-year marriage relationship.

The thing that hurt me the most with starting all over again was I knew I couldn't and wouldn't get back those seventeen years I invested in a person and in a relationship that I thought would end up being my fairy-tale relationship. I thought and even felt that I had found the one person that I could and would share my life with, and she and I would conquer the world, our world and the part of this world that belonged to us. I believed we would do great things for the kingdom of God, and we would help sighing, dying, crying, and hurting the homeless humanity. From the first day she and I met, I sat down and shared my heart, what my dreams, hopes, and desires were.

My life has always been an open book, and I opened up and pulled out the dirtiest pages of my life that I'm not at all proud of and shared them with her. I let her ask me any question she had. No matter how embarrassed or how shameful I felt, I would answer her question about my past. I really wanted her to know the real me and to know what kind of man, person, husband, father, provider, minister of the gospel, and human being she was getting into a covenant relationship with.

I expected her to do the same for me, but she didn't. She gave me a really quick look at the pages of her past and then quickly shut them up. She shared the things from her past she wanted me to know about, and the others she kept locked from my view. I didn't press the issue, and I felt in time she would open up and talk to me about her relationship experiences and tell me about her relationship teachers. She never did, and years later, her past relationship secrets, hurt, pain, brokenness, abuse, neglect, etc., begin to seep out and the sputter out and finally flow out of her. But what came out of her came out in a bullying manner.

It all started when I began to challenge her relationship behavior patterns and challenge her to change with me for the sake of ourselves, each other, and our marriage relationship. I really wanted her to share my life with me. I really wanted us to be together, "until death do us part." But that didn't happen, and I found myself starting all over again. I found myself starting again with no one to share my life with me. I am a man whom God has given a sensitive, caring, concerned, and compassionate heart. And I do feel hurt, pain, and brokenness.

I am the type of man who pushes for the excellence in all that I do because I do not want to live below or just live equal with my Christian privileges. Everything Jesus died so that I can have that is what I want and even need. I had a vision for our marriage relationship, I had a vision for our personal relationship, and I had a vision for our home and life. It was a vision that God gave me. The day I walked out of that courtroom, I did not feel good about myself and about what happened. I walked out of that courtroom and out of a seventeen-year marriage and out of her life feeling nothing but hurt, pain, and brokenness.

I had to begin preparing myself for starting again. The last time I was single seventeen years ago, and I knew times and people and relationships are not the same as they were. I did a lot of crying and praying, and I kept asking God, "Why me? Why this? Why us"? I had to accept that I had not found and married the woman who would share my life with me. I want to tell you there is a big difference between someone who *fit* in your life and someone who *belong* in your life. What's the difference? People who fit in your life do just that. They fit. They give very little, the bare minimum. They take a lot off the table, bring out the worst in you, just take up space and time in your life, exist, and make selfish demands, and they just don't say and do the right things that help you.

People who *fit* into your life are always inconsistent with the good and right they say and do. They want control. They do not help you build but always have a way of tearing down. Their love is conditional. They are selfish, self-centered, self-righteous, self-justified, driven, motivated, etc., and no matter what you try to tell them or try to point out that you don't like when it comes to themselves, they will never see it, and they will stay in a place of denial. In their eyes, you are the problem, and they didn't say or do anything wrong.

The people who *belong* in your life are those who are consistent with the good and right they say and do. They know how to bring out the best in you. They push you to your lifelong dreams, and desires. They stand by you and with you, and they show their support for you. They are givers, and they give and love unconditionally. They will use everything and every resource they know of and have to help you build and be all that God created you to be. They pray for you always, and they listen to God when it comes to you. You and that person are twin flames and not soul mates, meaning you and her are driven by like passions and pursuits, and you have the same twin fire burning inside of you. There's so much more, but I believe you get the picture.

I'm starting again, and I still believe God will send me my fairy-tale twin flame. I'm starting again, but this time I'm armed with Rhema Relationship Revelation wisdom, knowledge, and understanding, which is where what I'm sharing with you in this book is coming from. I'm starting again, and I never would have believed, thought, or felt I would be doing so. I'm starting again, and I still believe God will send me my fantasy woman, and we will live a fairy-tale relationship life. She will be the one who will share my life with me until death do us part.

CHAPTER EIGHT

Fighting with Myself

One of the things I have discovered through all of the things I have been through is the worst kind of hurt is the mental and the emotional hurt. The physical part eventually will heal, and the scars are gone, but the mental and emotional hurt, pain, and wounds is much deeper and take longer to heal. Being that I am a man who has a sensitive and caring heart, I can feel the hurt of others, and that usually keeps me emotionally broken. For some, it is easy for them to hurt someone and walk away and leave the person they hurt wounded, broken, in pain and in brokenness. I happen to not be one of those kinds of men, and I thank God I'm not.

The hardest part about fighting your feelings is at times you don't know which feelings you are fighting and where those feelings came from. The other fact is you can be fighting feelings, and you don't know who those feelings you are fighting is for. Whenever you hurt someone that you really do love and care about and you feel godly sorrow, regret, remorse, and you have a repentant heart, your feelings are connected to the person you have hurt, and you are feeling that person's feelings. The most important thing to avoid is being emotionally entangled and being emotionally entrapped.

Fighting your own feelings is not an easy thing to do, especially when you are not really sure why you feel the way you feel. To have feelings involves the sense of touch and the ability to experience physical sensation. Satan want to keep you tied to a conscious awareness to something that God has forgiven you of and the person you have hurt has forgiven you for. So what Satan do is bring about a sensation within you or the receiving of sense impressions through seeing, touching, smelling, and through hearing that he has tainted, twisted, dominated, manipulated, and controlled.

When a person is having or receiving satanic- and demonic-influenced and suggested conscious sense impression, they are receiving an inaccurate conscious sense effect that is produced in their mind. The physical sensation or sense impression that a person may be feeling is prepared, produced, and presented through that person's expressed emotions. When I found myself in that place where I was asking God why me, why us, why this, I was experiencing a physical sense impression; and when I started to experience that, I became emotional or became easily aroused to a strong feeling, such as regret, remorse, repentance, love, hate, fear, doubt, worry, stress, unbelief, hate, etc.

Satan wanted to use the mistake I made as a weapon he could form and use it against me. He wanted me to beat myself up and live in total self-condemnation. Every day he was trying to pressure me into opening myself up to accepting and adopting feelings of guilt and being worthless. He would use my conscience or my knowledge of right and wrong with my urge to do right as the instant replay player that he would use to replay every moment of what I had done. He wanted my conscious to be flooded with condemnation. My conscious is the place where I have an awareness of myself as a feeling and thinking being.

Let me paint the picture for you: Satan wanted to contaminate my conscience—my knowledge of right and wrong with my urge to do right with condemnation, and he wanted to contaminate my conscious awareness of myself, feelings, and thinking being with condemnation. In order to do so, he had to find a way to get me over into my conscience; and from that point, he would bombard my consciousness with self-condemnation messages and images. His way of doing that was to involve my feelings in what he wanted to do. He wanted to get my conscience to bother me so much because of what I had done, so that I would be, become, and end up being really consistently conscious of what I had done. Thus, I would be opening the door for self-condemnation and a lot of others degrading, demoralizing, damaging, dangerous, and self-destructive feelings.

I came out of that seventeen-year marriage relationship with a lot of feelings, and I knew I had to fight against them if I was to move forward. I felt a lot of things, and I knew that most were good, and some were not good because they would lead me down the path to self-condemnation and self-destruction. It was not easy for me, and I did a lot of crying and lying at the mercy seat of God. I really needed him to help me make it through the day and help me bring order to the feelings that I was having that was out of order. Through what I had been through, Satan had got me over into negative reactionary responses, and I needed to get delivered from that.

What was happening to me was I had stopped yielding to he who has the right of way. What this means is if you were driving a car and you came to a yield sign, what would you do? What you should do is (1) slow down as you are coming up to the sign, (2) come to a complete stop if you have to and look both ways for oncoming traffic, (3) take caution before proceeding by giving way to the oncoming traffic, and (4) slowly merge into traffic. When it came to what I was going through, I wasn't doing that. I would hear the voice of God giving me instructions, and I would heed. But for some reason, I would later indulge in the conversation that I had received a caution prompting on.

Let me make it plain for you: In my mind, I was thinking I was under control, and what I had to say was important. So I would, at a later time in that day, proceed to engage in sharing what I had to say, and that is when Satan was able to draw me into the wrong place. I rationalized with what I wanted to say, and I even started out the conversation using a cool, calm, and collected tone of voice. I was watching to make sure I was not distracted and detoured onto a stray or bait conversation that the person I was talking to might have in their selfish way of thinking, just waiting for me. Sounds good so far, right? Well, that's when things would go wrong. Before I knew it, I had fallen right into the trickery and trap of the enemy.

The conversation started out in the right flow, but as I would go on sharing, the person I would be talking to would rudely interrupt me with a lot of dangerous, destructive, damaging, and disrespectful accusations and assumptions that may or may not have contained some or no truth to them. And then Satan would use that person to say what they were saying out of pure emotion. So I was being hit with a strategic well-organized, masterfully designed arsenal of assaulting, attacking, and assassinating accusations and assumptions that Satan knew would get me out on his grounds and away from my spiritual safety zone.

Once he had this happening, he would then fill the person that I was trying to talk to with so much anger-filled, bitter-filled, resentment-filled, judgmental-filled, spiteful-and-get-even-filled, prove-my-point-filled, self-justify-what-I-said-and-done-filled, and selfish-filled emotions that everything they would be saying or doing would be emotionally driven and charged. And the next thing he would do was to make sure once he had the person I was talking to heavily into this mental state of mind and mental frame of mind, he would then lock that person into it, and then he would draw, drive, push, persuade, force, suggest, and influence that person over into using a tone of voice that he knew would get to me, hurt me, hinder my right way of thinking, push my buttons, and finally push me beyond my breaking point and my rational reasoning boundary and limitation.

The attitude of our heart would change, and the atmosphere in the room would drastically change. Neither one of us was able to recognize it and realize it. I was quickly drawn away from trying to share my concern(s) out of the right spirit into trying to prove my point or trying to defend myself. I wasn't consciously aware I was doing so because the room and the atmosphere were so emotionally charged, and the spirit in which I came into the room with had changed. The things Satan had the person I was trying to reason with saying to me was spoken in a violent, judgmental, hurtful, and spiteful-intended motive and tone of voice. He had the person I was talking to locked into trying to tear me down and take me down.

No matter what I said or tried to say, he had that person's head and that person's heart locked and loaded with more selfish, self-centered, self-righteous, and self-justified reasons, accusations, and assumptions. After which Satan had the person I was trying to talk to locked into a highly emotional state, and that person would be firing at me everything Satan would be seducing and suggesting. Whatever he had that person to say and do, they said and done it. And the person spoke words that Satan had them speaking, and those words would hit me in the sensitive, caring, concerned, and compassionate part of me that I had opened up and given to them.

They would hit me in the vulnerable part of me that I had shown to the person, and I had opened up to the person because I trusted that person with my vulnerability, and I was confident that they would not betray my sensitivity and vulnerability. With every hit I would hurt, and Satan knew he had me. He would get the person to close down their sensitivity, feelings, emotions, heart, and hearing to me and what I was sharing. He would get the person to focus their mentality or their mental capacity, power, attitude, and outlook on all of the wrong I had done and on all of the relationship mistakes I had ever made.

After getting the person to lock in on the mistakes, I had made he would get the person to bring them up in a way that they would be used as a weapon formed against me. As all of this was unfolding right before my eyes, I was fighting the feeling to fight back. I kept trying to walk away, but every word the person spoke was mean-spirited and personal, and they hit me in the private places within my heart, which in turn really opened me up to a mental and emotional breakdown.

The person was constantly being used by Satan to say and do things that had a badgering and bullying spirit behind it. With each thing the person said and done, all of it was intended to try to bait me into whatever I was that Satan and all of his imps and cohorts spirits had schematically designed for my failure. The person wouldn't stop, and it felt like they really wanted to hurt me and make me look like someone I wasn't. I knew we had some tough times, and we didn't always agree on everything, and we said and done some things to hurt each other. But what was it that was so bad that it could have and did change this person seeing me as their husband to seeing me as someone they felt the need to tear down, hurt, and humiliate? What had I said or done over the course of our relationship that would constitute their malicious-intent-filled desire to condemn and convict me?

I didn't go to the person to fight with them. I went to the person for the reason of talking to them and to hopefully find a place or point where we could start a new beginning in our relationship and not an end to it. I had no idea they felt the way they was telling me. They were bringing up negative feelings they had and dislikes they had when it came to me, and how I went about being the head of my household that they kept hidden from me. I had no idea I was walking into a *problem waiting to happen*. And on this particular day, that problem no longer had to wait. It was about to happen. Everything I shared with them was being processed through their selfishness, selfish sensitivity, selfish emotions, and selfish feelings and not through the heart I was used to reaching and touching.

My truth: Satan knew if he kept using the person who is closest to me as his weapon formed against me, at some point in the moment, my human survival urges, tendencies, desires, inclination, intuition, and instincts would kick in, and I would come out fighting for myself. So on that day and in that moment, Satan made sure they violated every part of me that he knew and they would know was my weakness. He knew just what to have them say and do that would get to me and would get me to put down my spiritual guard, and to my shame, it worked.

Meet My Best Friend, Self-Effort

After a period of time had went by, I was so caught up in the moment I had lost my conscious awareness; and to this day, I still have no conscious awareness of where my mind and the mental part of me was. And with my feelings being so distracted, detoured, and delayed, and our conversation and communication connection was disconnected and broken, from somewhere on the inside of me, I can't tell you where I just sensed and felt the urge and had the instinct to end it all.

My reality: Self-effort had taken over, and I was no longer yielding to him who had the right of way. The person who knew the right thing to do and who had always had the strength to walk away from previous moments like this one was no longer in control. Self-effort had taken over and that self-effort spirit functioned on and flowed through wrong reactions, wrong responses, and on wrong reactionary responses.

What was self-effort saying? What part of me was my self-effort speaking to? Self-effort was saying to me, "You have heard enough. Bring an end this." My human self-effort was speaking to my urges, tendencies, inclinations, intuitions, and instincts. Whatever my self-effort spoke to my human urges, tendencies, inclinations, intuitions, and instincts, they all obeyed. Self-effort tells us to help that circumstance, situation, and confrontation out. Satan is the power behind and is the one who is powering your self-effort. Self-effort and self-will cannot and will not work with the spirit of God, and they reject, resist, and refuse faith principles. Self-effort cannot, will not, and don't know how to work with the spirit of God, and it cannot and will not follow the leading of the Holy Spirit. Self-effort and self-will cannot because they are powered by another force that thrives on staying in the unseen and thrives on doing the unexpected, uncertain, unplanned, unknown, unfair, unaware, unsure, unforgettable, unexplainable, unpredictable, unthinkable, and unbelievable, and it needs the help of carnal means.

Faith principles do not function and flow with and through human effort or through human self-effort. When our self-effort and self-will get out of the way, the faith of God and the God kind of faith can and will work. We always feel like we have to help God help us and have been led and taught to think, feel, and believe we have to do something to get something from God, and that is not true. God does not need our help with matters of the heart, circumstances, situations, and confrontations that are warring against us. God just want us to yield, submit, and surrender to his power, presence, and authority. He will work it out, and we just walk it out. He will work things out through us without our help because it is for us and without our help. And we just walk out whatever it is that he has worked out for us.

That day, in, through, with, and out of self-effort, I was trying to fight my wrong feelings. That day I was so caught up, entangled, and entrapped in self-effort that I was trying to fight the feeling to fight back by using self-effort means and methods. Satan had got me to yield, submit, and finally surrender my self-will and my self-control over to self-effort. And self-effort took control of my urges, tendencies, inclinations, intuitions, and instincts and then took over the whole conversation, moment, atmosphere, and the both of us.

Neither one of us could or did see this coming, nor did we plan and prepare for it happening. We both walked into a well-orchestrated, masterfully strategic, well-organized, unseen, unexpected, unplanned, unknown, unfair, uncertain, unaware, unforgettable, unexplainable, unthinkable, undeniable, eventually unavoidable, and unbelievable satanic and demonic relationship setup. We both fell for it. Once all of what I just described happened, he had me and us and our relationship just where he wanted it.

My power point: Just maybe to the person I was involved with in that moment I was a, "*stranger in her house/our home*", but on that day, at that moment and in that atmosphere they, she was, a "*stranger in my* *heart"*. I had to walk away from that relationship, and I spent a lot of time fighting my feelings when it came to the person I was in that moment with. Walking away and fighting with myself and fighting my feelings for that person weren't easy. It was really hard because I loved her. I had to accept the fact, the truth, and the reality that I had failed, and the only thing I would have left would be the memories of her, the memories of our moments together, and the memories of the things we both believed mattered.

Her Memories Matter

There were those things we did and those memories we made that nothing and no one can repeat because it all took place while we were in the moment. In the moment, memories are very different from plain old memories in that they themselves come out of a moment that happens when two very different people who share the same feelings, share the same desires, share the same dreams, and they are yet the same in what they want out of a relationship. When they are the same, they have allowed themselves and their relationship to be positioned to enter into a moment that will eventually come out of a moment that is made whenever there is a divine connection. Yes, we once had a divine connection, and we shared a common cause. We were compatible, but we failed at communicating. She was one who, most of the time, just went along with whatever I said or done and wouldn't say nothing. I was her opposite. I would be the one who would take the time to share and communicate my concerns with her. She was more passive, and she often said she wasn't confrontational and didn't like to be, so she went along with whatever choices and decisions I made and went along with the way I would say, do, and handle things.

She would be the one who would sweep things under the carpet as they say, and I was the one who kept removing the carpet, so everything hidden was exposed, so we could deal with them. We had more good times than bad, and the good we both did in our marriage relationship outweighed the bad. Why did it end? Well, now you know why I spent a lot of time fighting with myself and fighting my feelings for her. Memories... our time... our place. Moments... in our space and in our face. Intimate things we shared and even at our end, not God's end. We both knew we still cared.

But what do you do when you just don't know what to do? How do you disconnect yourself from an atmosphere that you know is dangerous and destructive? How do you hold on and let go at the same time? I could find an answer to those questions, but the answers I could come up with would only be answers and not the truth that would make and set her, me, and us free. We are both are free from the fighting, but I was not free from my memories of her. The funny thing about moments and memories is once they are made, they are just like monuments. They are always larger than life, and they always take you back to the person that helped you make them.

CHAPTER NINE

His Fantasy

From the first time he saw her face deep down within, he knew, without a shadow of a doubt, she was the one and he needed, wanted, and had to have in his life. From the first time she shared her heart, her hurt, she shared her past and her pain. In his heart, he felt she was someone that deserved to be happy. He absolutely was sure she was someone that was purposed, prepared, and presented right out of his faith-filled imagination. And the first time she opened up and let him come into her world, her life, her dreams, her hopes, her desires, and come close to her it caused, created the atmosphere, and contributed to him clearly seeing and knowing she would always and forever be the reason he would consistently have an idea or ideas about saying and doing something for her and with her.

Okay, even because of her, what he would find himself thinking, feeling, and wanting to do for her would be far removed for his normal reality and far removed from her normal reality. You see, she was, is, and will forever be the woman of his dreams. And he will never forget that first time when she looked into his eyes, and knew his heart, had an understanding of his vision, and out of care, concern and out of the compassion she felt in her heart for him, she said to him, yes. She then said to him, "I love you".

That was a moment that enticed, entangled, and entrapped him into a memorable moment when there was a free play of his creative imagination that, once she fulfilled, he would find himself really into her like he had not ever been into any woman, and they would have a life and a lifestyle that would consist of them loving each other as their way of living. They both would be living for the love of each other. Some of his friends said their love wouldn't last, but he knew the God he served said their love wouldn't end. The faith he had inside of him said their love would survive, go through just so it could and would get to the place and point where it would grow, develop and mature, function and flow out of a love unlimited. That place where love never end, you know, always and forever until the twelfth of never.

What you don't know, what you don't understand, and what you don't see is their fantasy had a secret. They were secret lovers, and from the first time he was close to her, he felt her spirit and yearned for her touch. He was drawn, driven, pulled, pushed, persuaded, led, and forced into meeting her in a secret place that only the two of them would know of. There would be no directions, and there would be no instructions, directing them to their secret place. There would be no path that could and would tell, show, and lead them to that place they would meet at. Oh, that place. It had a secret.

Secret lovers, secret place, passionate people meeting in their place called there. Free to come and go, free to experience and encounter. Free to follow the plan and their purpose and their pursuit of their destiny. No boundaries, no limitations, and no expectations. What you really, really don't know is their plan had a secret, their purpose had a secret, and their pursuits had a secret. That could only be revealed and heard in the quiet whispers of their "I remember when." He would meet her there in their eternity and would wait for her in time. He couldn't wait to see her, touch her, hold her, and cherish her in time, every second, every minute, every hour, in a day, in a week, in a month, in a year every decade. No one would ever know their moments had a secret, and their memories had some secrets. Listen, I'm trying to get you to understand when and where the first time he met her, and they had their first time flowing into the creation of his imaginative faculty that was expressed or merely conceived. It was in their place called there, where they would meet and share some sweet fairy tales and fantasies. It was also the first time he sensed her presence. He felt her heart. He knew her spirit. He experienced her feelings, he encountered her emotions, and they shared the same desires. Oh, what a first time for him to find out her fairy tale and his fantasy had a secret too.

Heart Secrets

He would never forget the first time when they finally got the opportunity to meet. He echoed the words that he had heard deep down in the quiet whispers of his heart. That he would make sure he would be to her what no man had ever been to her, and he would make sure he proved to himself and to her that he would not be, and he wasn't like any man that she had ever been with. That was the only secret he has ever kept from her.

Down through the years of their relationship, he had done his very best to stay true to the secret vow he made when they first met. And as they would spend time together, talking, listening, and getting to know each other, he knew, without a shadow of a doubt, his secret vow was the right one to make because she was the right one that really needed and deserved such a vow. Some secret vows are verbalized and vocalized, and some vows are declared and decreed with words unspoken. Such was the case of this man, her fairy-tale love.

Unlike most men, he remembered their first kiss. He remembered the genuineness of her touch. He reminisced back over the first time he held her hand. He relived the time when he looked into her eyes, and he saw his best friend, his number 1 supporter, and his number 1 fan. He saw his life traveler, his lover, his twin flame, twin fire, his soul mate. Yes, he saw everything he would need in a helpmate and wife. His heart had a secret, and now his soul would have one as well.

Soul Secret

In a quiet whisper that is shouting inside of his soul with a deeply committed conviction, his soul would secretly vow to love her always and forever at least until the twelfth of never. He never just said it, but the way he cared for her, provided for her, and protected her and the way he went about loving her just the way she never knew she needed or wanted to be loved would prove his feelings, emotions, and desires was connected and committed to her. They would meet in a place called there, and they would, over the course of their relationship, make wonderful memorable moments and memories that would be forever etched in eternity.

He would walk her down the aisles of what made her happy and meet her time after time at the altar of her heart, where he would confess and repeat how much he loved her so, and he would lay prostrate in her love until the twelfth of never. Oh, and did I say always and forever? Because of the way she loved him, because of the way she needed him, because of the way she wanted him, and because of the secrets he had, he became a man on a mission. His mission wasn't impossible, and he knew he was a man who was not perfect, but he had something that most men have but chose to hide.

He had a tender and sensitive heart toward her, and she could feel him, flow with him, and follow him to the place where time will never end in their relationship. His soul had a secret, and his mind knew it. His soul had a sweet secret, and his will was willed into watching over his secret. His soul had a secret, and his emotions powered the secret until it became a promise. Until the twelfth of never mind. Until the twelfth of never will. Until the twelfth of never emotions.

Spirit Secret

He vowed within himself to walk with her through the days of her life. He promised to hold her through the times in her life. He was committed to walking with her when it was time for her to walk into another world, the world that he knew she never had but always wanted to live in. You see, his spirit, his human spirit would dedicate itself to walking in harmony with her and staying in the rhythm of her heartbeat.

His spirit had an unspoken secret. His spirit would connect and communicate with her spirit, and together both of their spirits would soar from beyond her human expectations and find a safe haven place within him that she have not ever found in any other man. He would make sure she would always be at peace with him, with herself, with her journey, and with their life and love. For the first time he saw her face, he felt her hurting human spirit. She didn't say it. She didn't even tell him, and she surely wouldn't and didn't show it, but his spirit knew it. His spirit knew her spirit needed the breath of everlasting life and love breathed into it. His spirit, her spirit, and their spirits.

Love Secret

His love had a secret that her love for him didn't even know. That love secret that his love kept secret came to life and came alive the first time he saw her face and heard her voice. From that moment, that first love he felt for her would forever be a song being composed whenever they would be together. Gentle is the melody… sweet is the sound. He would love her in the unlimited, need her in the unspoken, want her in the unforgettable, desire her in the unexplainable, hold her in the unthinkable, and cherish her in the unbelievable. In his world, in her world, it's just in their world.

His love had a sensuous sensitive secret. If only she knew how much loving her really made him want to love her even more. He wanted to love her like she have never been loved, hold her like she have never been held, love, need, and want her with a fire, desire, and a passion that will take away her pain. You see, he is so into her, and his love sometimes find it hard to keep its secret because she brings out the best in his love for her. Sometimes he knows she senses something when he is sharing, caring, and pleasing her heart. Sometimes he knows she can sense him saying something when they drift off into the secret side of their soul, you know, the secret side of their mind, will, and emotions.

He knows she has never really been in love so much that it's so right, and it removes everything in her life and everything in her love that has been or gone wrong. You don't understand what they have and what they share. It's much more than they, those who didn't know how to love her, could see. The secret that his love had gives her something he knows she never felt and dreamed of. His love had a secret, and it is kept in a heart that's true.

They were meant to be, and he knows she is one of a kind, and he's honored to have her by his side. His love had a secret that it's trying so hard to hide… They both deserve each other's love. His love has a secret… She doesn't know he's a man that is falling so fast. His love is trying to keep its secret, you know, the fighting inside will pass because his love is no longer a boy's, but his love is a man's love. She inspired his love to make a secret… He can't and won't walk away. God has given him the strength to choose… to be the man who will always wait for her. And walk her heart home to the secret his love have. It's a secret that's held in the heart of a woman's-man, her heart, her man, their love secret.

Into you secret

They met, they shared, they cared, they loved, they touched, and they both felt. It's theirs, it's real, it's sensual, and it's sincere. He's into her heart, and she is so into his love. Which is something neither one of them have ever experienced before in their previous relationships. His "into you", have a secret, and sometimes when he is into her and they are into a moment where secrets are shared and memories are made, he remains true to the one he is into.

Remaining true to never share his secret but show it when he is so into her and giving her all of the love she has been missing long before they met. His "into" have its own secret too. You feel me? Into loving her to the limit while listening to her share her heart. While hearing what she had his love into. It's hers, and she can always get into and come out with that which will give her what she didn't verbally ask for. He is her fairy tale, and she is his fantasy, and they both share a dream that keep them into the reality of what they share. He asked, and she said I love you; and she asked, and he would say, "Because I love you."

For each into moment they share, something great and wonderful always happens. They both get out of their "into moment" everything that matters. God knew what they had need of. God has given them the opportunity to meet and find their way into what would make them both feel complete. Have you ever been into a moment, a memory, and a matter and you got out of it everything that you went "into" it looking for?

Lord, you know what the destiny is for their relationship. You know how important it is for both of them to be into what you have joined them together for. Everything they are into is because of you. She is into him, and he is into her. They both are into each other. That's the way they both thought their life and love would forever be. Do you know how it feels to really be into loving someone, and the only reason you could give for loving them the way you do is just because of the I-love-you reason?

CHAPTER TEN

Lord, You Know Why

Men, yes, we are different; and no, we don't and usually won't say it, but we are the same. Just like every woman is not the same, not every man is the same. Men, well, we feel the same way women feel, and in a lot of ways, we think the same as women do. Some men are not good at expressing themselves and sharing what's really in their heart. When it comes to what we are looking for in a woman, well, we are not looking for a woman who will be our fairy tale, but men look for a woman who will be their fantasy.

Yes, it's true, we want to be her fairy-tale guy, fairy-tale dude, fairy-tale fella, fairy-tale man, and the only thing we want is for her to be our fantasy, the center of our affection. From the very first time, a man sees a woman he really desires to be with. She instantly becomes his idea about doing something for her that is far removed from normal reality. He want to say and do something that is so real and so right that she would never forget him. He wants her to know he is so into her, and there is nothing he wouldn't do to satisfy and fulfill her every expectation. When a man is really into a woman, she becomes his dream and his reality.

And there are men who are really loving, caring, giving, concerned, and compassionate. There are men who are not afraid to open up and show their sensitivity and who really want to be in a serious relationship. Most men spend their time looking and trying for the way, and in most cases, they get lost on the way to wherever it is they are trying to get to. What you have to understand is when a man really, really loves a woman, his woman he will find himself constantly thinking about her. She is always in his heart.

He is so into her and the only thing he desire is to protect her and love her more than words can ever show. You see, that is his case, this man's case. His heart was filled with all of the right things when it came to her, but it just kept coming out the wrong way. Every time he would close his eyes, he could see the tears rolling down her face. He could see the sadness that was in her heart, and he could feel what she was feeling. He just didn't know what to say, what to do, and how to undo that which he never intended to do. He knows he was blessed to find someone like her, and to have her love him the way she did was so much more than his fantasy revealed. He cherished every moment that they shared.

As he stood there watching her crying from the depths of her brokenness, guilt is what he felt when she would look up at him. The same things that made him a hard man would be the same things that made him a soft man on that day. A man that was so tenderhearted because he knew he really loved her, and he wished and wanted to take away the hurt, pain and brokenness that she was feeling. The reality had already hit him, and that reality had let her down, and he had done what he vowed he would never do because he knew what she had been through in her last and other relationships. How could he? Why would he? He didn't have any answers, and he couldn't explain.

He just knew he would not see her smile again. He just knew she would not let him into her heart again. He knew he would not have that same open heart she kept available for him that he had absolutely came to love, value, and appreciate. As he stood there feeling helpless, he could hear her heart asking him, "Why me? Why us?" His heart would finish by asking himself, "Why this? Lord!" Why this circumstance, this situation, this confrontation and why, why, why this kind of matter?" Every tear she shed would tear his heart up and shatter it into thousands of pieces. On this day, when they would meet to talk, he found himself standing at the edge, looking at the end. How he got there, he's not really sure. He somehow feels like their love was so vicious that it had its own way, and it tore their lives apart. And now she's standing there, looking at him through her hurt, pain, brokenness, and through her feelings of disappointment.

He can feel her anger, and he can see she is upset and hurting. He can hear her heart, her hurt, and her pain. He can hear her heart, but he knows deep down inside she can't hear his heart whispering, "Baby, I still love you." Her hurt, pain, and brokenness won't let her heart hear his feelings, saying, "I miss you so bad, and I realize you were the best I ever had in my life." Her disappointment in him won't let her soul hear his emotions cry out, "I'm so sorry for all the wrong I've done." Her feelings being so numb just can't let her hear him say, "You were the only one". As he stand there looking at her and feeling her, feeling the moment, his desires cry out with a silent scream, "I need you to hold me, baby, baby, like you used to." Yeah, those words and that kind of song!

He can't find the words that will make his wrong right. It was just a day, just a moment, a circumstance, a quick choice, and a wrong decision. All of his life he knew he had so much to give, and knew if he would meet the right woman, he would spend all of his life being found guilty of loving her in the first degree. He knew that they were opposites, and they were attracted to each other. He knew they were different in a lot of ways and the same in most cases. How and why their relationship ended up where it was that day as they are at the place they are meeting is still a mystery that's still unsolved. You see, he's not your typical guy, and he doesn't say typical guy things.

When he got into the relationship with her, he did what most men do. He applied all of the relationship principles, processes, and procedures he was taught by the men who mentored him. They never told him which were right and which would be wrong to accept, adopt, and apply. They never told him when and how to apply what they taught them. His story is one that I'm sure you have heard before, but on this day and at this time, I'm asking you to just step back for just a moment and look at his story from a different perspective.

That different perspective would be from that of a man and a human being whose life has been everything but a normal one. His story doesn't require you to show him pity or sympathy. What it will require is something I hope you have. He's been through more childhood, teen hood, and adulthood challenges and changes that forced him to go from being a boy to a man. It's not sympathy that he is looking for. It is an understanding heart and an open mind. That's what he hoped you will have. They never told him it was okay for a man to cry, be sensitive, caring, concerned, and compassionate. No one ever took the time to sit down with him and explain how important it is to listen and then hear and how important it is to communicate.

He wasn't told or taught that communication equals understanding. The men who he learned what a man is, from, well, they never told him how important it was, is and would be for him to listen to her and hear her. They should have told him he needed to make sure he said and done everything he could to let her know how important she was and that she mattered. He never meant to dominate, manipulate, and control. He wasn't trying to reject, resist, and refuse. Why didn't they tell him that whatever it was he did wrong to quickly repent or he would eventually have to repeat. And now here they are in the same space, at the same place, but not for the right reasons.

As she looks across the room at him, he can see the sadness that's in her soul. He can feel her heavy heart and her wounded spirit. And he just can't take it anymore. He loves her so much that he doesn't want to hurt her anymore, and he doesn't want her to hurt him anymore. He had decided that he would rather not be with her than hurt her again. Long before they agreed to talk, he had ran over and over in his mind what he wanted to say; but the moment he saw her, his once fantasy, he opened his mouth, and what came out was these words, "Sweetheart, I'm trying so hard to get over you, but I'm really having a hard time doing it."

"Because the love we shared through the years had really meant so much to me. My heart is yearning for her love. Please tell me, what I have to do to just get through to you. I'm so sorry for the wrong I have done." And then he heard these words deep, deep, weigh deep down within him, saying, "Nobody warned me that love would own my heart." He has learned that you don't hurt the one you love.

He knows that he is to blame, and nothing with him have been the same because he loves her and he misses her. He remembered how they used to talk all night. He finally got the courage to lift up his head again and look into her eyes and say, "I miss you." He told her he missed the way she used to hold him, and he missed her laugh. He wanted her to really know the promises and secrets he made. He deeply regrets that he broke them, and he shared them. All he can do is think of her.

In utter frustration and in disappointment in himself, he turned to walk away because he felt he had lost the heart he loved listening to and that he knew belonged to him. Before he could take his second step, he fell down on his knees and cried out to God, "Please help me. Please tell me what I have to do, what I can do to get things back the way they once was between us." He asked God to please show him what he had to do to get through to her.

You see, somehow they both got into something that they couldn't shake loose. Every night he prays more for her than he does for himself. Some say they would pass by his door and hear him say, "Lord, you know why things happen in a relationship the way they do. Is it just one of things that all of us in relationships are going to have to get used to happening?" Their hearts would break as they heard him tearfully cry out, "Lord, you know what all of us can and will eventually get into when we don't get out of our relationships that which we got into and went into them looking for. Lord, will you please tell me how a perfect love like ours went wrong?"

They could hear him crying out, saying, "Lord, you know we at times get into the wrong mind-set, have the wrong thoughts, wrong thinking, way of thinking, and how we get into the wrong mental state of mind and into the wrong mental frame of mind when we are in relationship. And because we at times open ourselves and relationships up to the wrong type of feelings, emotions, and desires, we end up getting ourselves into the wrong mentality, attitude, and into the wrong people." Lord, when will I see her smile again and hear her laugh again? He knows she was supposed to be his forever fantasy, and he was to be her forever fairy tale. She's gone far away from him. You see, he can physically see her, but his words can't, won't, and don't reach and touch her now because he forgot about the unspoken secrets that was made, and how he shared them with the wrong person. He still loves her, but he's going to have to get used to her not being with him. They will never be able to go back to the days when they both knew and felt their love was so strong.

He let her down, and he did what you should never do, and that is you should never hurt the one that you love. And he knows he will have to accept and get used to seeing her with someone else. Just the thought of that is really hurting him deep down inside. As he drifts into a place within himself where he knows there is total and complete silence, it's a place that he knows all too well because he have been there before with her and with what has happened on more than one occasion. He knows he now have to open up his eyes now and face his reality. His reality is and would be, every moment of his day and maybe every day of his life he will have to spend them without her, his fantasy. He remembers the days when they would drift off into that place where their love and life would never end it felt like they had loved and lived an eternity.

CHAPTER ELEVEN

This Unbelievable Story

What do you do when you see and meet someone you really would like to get to know for all of the right reasons, and from the first day you and that person spend time getting to know each other, you began to see that there is no real (1) connection, but everything becomes about, (2) competing, and about (3) comparing. As you begin to try and establish a good, strong, solid foundation for your relationship that other person is saying and doing things that is a distraction to the relationship, and they are opening up detours away from the type of relationship you are trying to establish and build.

As you begin to open up and share what you have been through as a way to help build a bridge of communication and understanding between you and that person, they in turn, instead of having the right communication and understanding, response to what you are sharing. They have a wrong reactionary response and begin to say, "What about me, and what I have been through?"

From the first day you met that person, you in the course of your relationship discover exactly what is the central theme for that person's life, and that is they are trying to replace and remove any attempts you are making in trying to build a sound and solid foundation to build your relationship with them on. You are trying to build a foundation that is based on communication and understanding, and they are wanting and trying to build and base your relationship with them on what has been and still is the central theme for their life, which is "What about me and what I have been through?" The more you talk to that person, you end up being thoroughly convinced that those words are the ones they spend so much time in passionate pursuit of establishing.

As you share a piece from your past that you feel is important at that time that will ultimately help that person gain a greater and deeper understanding of who you are, where you have been, what you have been through and share that which will help them know what it is they can and should do to help you have a good, right, prosperous, productive, and successful relationship with you. Instead, that person began to block out what you are sharing and begin to tell you how they feel. And what they are saying is driven out of their selfishness, self-centeredness, self-justification, and self-righteousness. They are talking out of their past hurt, past pain, past experiences, past brokenness, past not delivered, not being cleansed and purged, not healed and not made whole places within them. And they get locked into forcefully sharing a what-about-me-and-what-I-have-been-through story.

Throughout the course of your time in the relationship with that person you are demonstrating, you have a loving, caring, concerned, and compassionate heart, and you are attentively listening to that person share their past hurt, pain, brokenness, abuse, neglect, challenges, changes, etc., with you. Out of an understanding heart, you listen, hear, and you have tried to make sure you did not say or do anything, handle a matter, cause, create the atmosphere for, nor contribute to you bringing about any type of flash back, déjà vu, etc., moments, memories, occurrences, circumstances, situations, and confrontations that will bring about a setup and a setback for them. You have been attentive, a good listener, and have tried to help in the rebuilding of that person's drive, will to win, self-confidence, self-esteem and helping in the rebuilding of any and other part and piece of that person's life, world, heart, being, etc., that has been broken, hurt, shattered, damaged, taken advantage of, etc.

You have listened to God and have obeyed to the best of your ability what he was saying and leading you to say and do to make sure you are helping and being an instrument and a vessel. He can, will, and did use in the building up of that person in all of the places they have been battered, abused, and torn down in. When you feel the need to and want to share something that is out of your past that is still a sore spot, a deep wound that God is still at work delivering, cleansing, purging, healing, and making you whole.

You are trying to share something that is out of a place where you are not where you want to be with what has happened to you. It's a place where you know you are still in recovery from what you have been through, and you know you are still under the master physician's (Jesus) hands and care. As you continue trying to share with that person how they are saying or doing something that reminds you or bring back negative flashbacks from what you have been through in your past, they totally ignore what you are saying and go back to that what-about-me-and-what-about-what-I-have-been-through mentality and mind-set.

They do not want to hear what you are saying. They are not concerned about that which they knowing or unknowingly are saying and doing that is causing, creating the atmosphere for and contributing to what you had been through and what you have fought hard to get past that you don't want to see happening again to you. Every attempt that you are trying to make in getting them to be aware of a sore spot, a tender place, a place where you are still in the process of being healed that place where you haven't been delivered, cleansed and purged and made whole in that place yet; instead of that person listening and hearing what you are saying that person in that "sharing moment" they cut you off and say, "what about me and what I have been through"? And from that point on, they take over the conversation and say things that have no reference to what you were sharing or talking about.

The things you are sharing from your past, out of where you have been and what you have been through, are moments, memories, matters, circumstances, situations, and confrontations that you feel will give that person a deeper and greater understanding as to who you are, and it will help them build a communication-and-understanding bridge over into how they can help you and what will help keep them in your life. You are trying so very hard to keep that person in your life and make them a part of your life and future, but they are in that what-about-me-and-what-I-have-been-through mode, mind-set, thinking, way of thinking, thoughts, and train of thought. They are trapped, locked, entangled, and entrapped into that type of mental state of being, mental frame of mind, mentality, and their mental condition has been satanically and demonically tutored, trained, taught, and conditioned to reject, resist, refuse, refute, and deny hearing anything that have to do with what anyone else have been through. Over and over again, they end up being moments when you know you are in the right place, at the right time, and you are in the right atmosphere to share something that you have been through that have an in-the-moment significant meaning that in turn can and will help in the building of the type of communication and understanding relationship you both will have, can have, and should have. Yet instead of them having an open heart to that which you are sharing in that right place, time, and moment being received in a good and positive way, that person's mind, mind-set, thoughts, thinking, way of thinking, mental state of mind, mental state of being, mental condition, and mentality is and have been so demonically and satanically influenced, suggested, infected, effected, affected because of past hurt, pain, abuse, neglect, being battered, brokenness, etc., they instantly, automatically, and without thinking clearly or yielding take over the moment and go into a defensive mode.

All kinds of bad, negative, and wrong things end up being said and even done that leave you, the sharer, at a loss for words and feeling a little lost because you did not expect that person to, as we say, go off on you. No matter when, where, and what that person have shared with you, you have listened attentively and heard them, and you have tried to help them. Those kinds of moments can and will often leave you with memories that keep you at loss for words when you are talking to that person and leave you with a feeling of extreme caution. And that in turn produces boundaries and limitations on what you share with that person, and it also produce and place boundaries and limitations on the relationship.

Those kinds of moments often can lead a person into putting up or building up what-I-can-and-will-share-with-this-person walls. Why? It's because you never really know when you should or should not, if you can or can't share anything from your past that will help in building a strong, safe, sound, solid communication- and understanding-filled relationship foundation with that person.

You never know what will trigger a negative, wrong, combative, and rejection-spirited moment, conversation, and type of communication that can, could, and often do lead into a wrong, bad, or negative conduct being displayed. It is hard to talk to, communicate with, share with, build a relationship with, reach out to, try to help and be there for a person who is dominated, manipulated, controlled, possessed with/by, tainted with highly satanically disguised, blinded to their human or consciousness; unseen, unexpected, unplanned, unknown, unfair, unaware, and undetected traits and traces of "what about me and what I have be through" feelings and emotions. It is also hard to connect with that same someone who is up under the heavy influence of a satanic and demonic suggestive, led, mentality infected, "what about me and what I have been through" power filled messages, images, instructions, information.

When those infected and affected areas of that person's heart, personality, character, intellect, integrity is being bombarded, assaulted, attacked, and assassinated with what seemingly seem like to that person's distorted and detained mind, someone is trying to ignore, downplay, overlook, mistake for weakness, take advantage, show total disrespect and total disregard what they have been through and what has happened to them, that person's mind-set, thoughts, train of thought, thinking, way of thinking, mental frame of mind, mental state of mind, and mentality instantly, automatically, and without any type of procrastination, hesitation, questioning, and second-guessing draw, drive, force, push, pull, lead, seduce, trick, etc., that person into urges, tendencies, inclinations, intuitions, instincts, and into intuitive instincts of being in a survival mode.

It's as though the person has lost any type of control over their being in control consciousness and will began to block out what the person they are talking to is sharing from their heart. No matter how much love, care, concern, compassion, feelings, and emotions the sharer have for them and no matter how hard the sharer have been trying to establish and build a healthy, profitable, productive, successful, strong, safe, solid, secure relationship with them, etc., they will, out of that satanically and demonically deceived mind, see, feel, think, and perceive and begin to treat the person who is sharing like they are an enemy to them and an enemy to their what-about-me-and-what-has-happened-to-me mind-set and way of thinking.

That "what about me and what has happened to me" way of thinking will be, become, and end up being the belief system, motto, passion-driven focus of the distracted, deceived, and distorted persons attention. When a person who is in that what-about-me-and-what-has-happened-to-me mode, mind-set, and mentality, what basically happens is that person has made themselves or consistently allow themselves to be, become, and end up being vulnerable to compromises in areas they normally wouldn't when it comes to a relationship.

For you to open up and try to share and show that person a wound that you have or show them a place that is still wounded through you sharing a piece from your past, that person, without yielding, thinking, listening, and hearing you and your heart, will often fire back at you quickly out of a vengeful, mean-spirited, angry, aggressive attack mode with a what-about-me-and-what-about-what-I-have-been-through bullet that pierce the very core of vulnerability and compromise. The very core of your open feelings, emotional trust, attachment to that person and confidence in that person and your open sensitivity is also pierced.

That person basically feel the urge, have the tendency, inclination, deceived desire, intuition, and instinct to protect and defend their "what about me and what about I have been through in my past" that has and is still hurting me, hindering me from moving forward and getting past my past, keeping me in and feeling pain from my past even though my past is not happening right now in my present. I'm still in a state of brokenness because of my past abuse, neglect, being battered, betrayed, etc., and because of my past hurt, past pain, and past brokenness.

What has happened to that person in their past has been carried and found a way into the persons present and is forcing that person's past to become their future. When that happens, it will ruin, kill, steal, destroy, hinder, hurt, handicap, delay, and deny any and all present Holy Spirit anointed deliverance, cleansing, purging, healing, being made whole, happiness, good, freedom, victories, overcoming, winning, etc., from manifesting itself and thus blocking, keeping in chains, yokes, bondage, and in a stronghold that person's God-given, ordained, destined destiny.

When a person is reacting and negatively responding out of a what-about-me-and-what-have-been-through thought, thinking, feelings, emotions, mind, mind-set, mental frame of mind, and mental state of being, their mentality have also been deceived, tricked, trapped, enticed, entangled, and entrapped to the point where nothing else positive or good can nor will flow in and through their heart. The person and all of their human mental capabilities, capacity, and abilities in turn will end up being a slave, bound, and limited, and in and under a what-about-me-and-what-has-happened-to-me yoke and bondage. All of that person's mental capabilities and abilities will become a hostage to that person's past hurt, a prisoner to their past pain, and bruised so badly by their past brokenness that they are bound.

No matter what good a person tries to bring out in a person who has, is living in and out of, is seduced into saying, doing, handling, making choices and decisions that is out of feelings and out of an emotional-driven   what-about-me-and-what-I-have-been-through, what-has-happened-to-me, what-I'm-afraid-will-happen-to-me-again attitude, that person will struggle, have a hard time, most often cannot and will not believe, nor will they be able to conceive, and they will have a hard time conceiving something good, what they prayed for, hoped for, wanted and wished for is happening and can happen again and again.

What is the driving force behind their what-about-me-and-what-I-have-been-through, what-has-happened-to me, what-I'm afraid-will-happen-to-me-again thought, thinking, feelings, emotions, mind, mind-set, mental frame of mind, mental state of being, wrong drive, motivation, ambition, motive, agenda, character, conduct, conversation, communication, lack of understanding, etc.? We know the driver is Satan and all of his demonic spirits. But what he is using to drive it all is fear.

The Fear Factor

Fears of all kinds bombard, assault, attack, and work to assassinate their faith in a new relationship. They live in fear of the unseen, unexpected, unplanned, unknown, unfair, uncertain, unaware, and unsure showing up or could show up. Even though what is showing up at that present moment in that relationship and in their life is good, right, and happy, fear won't let them plan, prepare, and position themselves for it.

They have been consistently tutored, trained, taught, inundated into/with, practiced, know how and when, is so in tune with, used to seeing, feeling, thinking, expecting, believing, being a victim of, a product of, a recipient of, had to learn how to live with, learned how to adopt, and accept as their only truth and reality the unseen, unexpected, unplanned, unknown, uncertain, unfair, unaware, and unsure showing up in their life and in their relationship(s). Each time the unseen, unexpected, unplanned, unknown, uncertain, unfair, unaware, and unsure have shown up, it is always in a negative, dangerous, destructive way.

And when those fear-driven unseen, unexpected, unplanned, unknown, uncertain, unfair, unaware, and unsure negatives show up, they always will have connections, links, roots, and ties to the person's past abuse, neglect, being battered, abandoned, being rejected, and they will always derive from the person's past hurt, pain, and brokenness. Those fear-driven unseen, unexpected, unplanned, unknown, uncertain, unfair, unaware, and unsure negatives can and will always have connections, links, roots, and ties to that persons what-I-have-or-I-am-working-so-hard-to-forget-and-get-past thoughts and thinking.

Fear of the unseen, unexpected, unplanned, unknown, unfair, unaware, and unsure in a new relationship tortures and torment that person no matter what positives they may see being made manifest. Satanically and demonically influenced, suggested, and acted upon fear will always deceive, trick, trap, and lock that person's human will into fighting against having and demonstrating the God kind of based faith in a new relationship, and fear will keep that person fighting against the good and right that they can visibly see showing up.

Fear has them locked into and have all of what they have dreamed, prayed, wished, wanted, needed, expected, believed, thought, felt, worked hard to get and accomplish, achieve, acquire, accumulate, change about themselves when it comes to their way of thinking, how they flow and function, changing their choice and decision-making process and procedures, etc., that would help them have confidence in a new relationship, and in the person that they are in a relationship will really work. Fear is behind the scenes drawing, driving, dominating, manipulating, and controlling every I-really-want-this-to-work effort, feeling, emotion, and desire.

There are so many who can't fight the feelings of fear, and as a result, they have made an unseen, unexpected, unplanned, unknown, uncertain, unfair to themselves and to others, especially the person they are in a current relationship with, unaware and unsure pact, agreement, compromise, bargain, deal, etc., with fear-filled, driven, and motivated what-about-me-and-what-about-what-I-have-been-through thoughts, train of thought, thinking, way of thinking, mind, mind-set, mental frame of mind, mental state of being, mental condition, mentality, and a fear-driven and motivated heart.

Fear Factor Pact

That pact, agreement, compromise, bargain, deal, etc., was made and is made and continually strengthened each time that person demonstrate acts, actions, deeds, make choices and decisions, handle matters, moments, and memories, and say and do things that is usually without them knowing it, and it is without them knowing what they are demonstrating, is born, and conceived out of fear-driven and motivated what-about-me-and-what-has-happened-to-me reactions and response.

All of this activity is showing up or taking place in their unseen, unexpected, unplanned, unknown, unfair, unaware, and in the unsure part of their consciousness and subconsciousness to the point and place where the person gets to the place and point or into the mind-set, mental state of mind, mental frame of mind, and into the mentality where they begin to become complacent, contented, and in a comfort zone as a result of the unknown to them or known to them pact, agreement, compromise, bargain, and deal. The truth be told, Satan knows how and when to assault, attack, assassinate, dominate, manipulate, and control your what-about-me-and-what-I-have-been-through, what-could-happen-to-me-again feelings and fears.

Fear of the unseen, unexpected, unplanned, unknown, uncertain, unfair, the unaware, and unsure keeps the person you want to build a relationship with fighting against the good that is happening in the relationship. That fight against the good that is happening to them in the relationship will keep that person working in agreement with, working in cahoots, with and working in harmony with what the spirit, thought and feeling of fear and how fear is easily influencing, tricking, trapping, and deceiving the person's sense of perception. And as fear is continually assaulting and attacking their consciousness and subconsciousness with suggestive pictures, images, imaginations, giving instructions, and providing deceived and distorted information to what the person will use to believe with, their level of comprehension when it comes to that "what about me and what about what has can and might happen to me again" will become that person's only friend and not a foe. In the end, that relationship more than likely will end up being another failure, disappointment, and not a friendly or faith-filled relationship.

Fear is telling, driving, drawing, forcing, etc., that unbelieving person's consciousness and subconsciousness out of instinct and to compete and compare with the person who is sharing their heart and has opened themselves up to being vulnerable. The sharer have also made some compromises they wouldn't normally make just to include the rejecting person into their life only to hear the rejecting person continually talk about what-has-happened-to-me-and-what-I-have-been-through, what-could-happen-to-me-again stories and do not listen to the person who is sharing.

The rejecting person do not hear the sharing persons heart and do not step away from their own what Satan and fear has turned into a now selfishly, self-centered, self-righteous, self-justified what-has-happened-to-me-and-what-I-have-been-through, what-could-happen-to-me-again, victim-spirited, woe-is-me, why-is-this-always-happening-to-me, you-need-to-listen-to-me, I-have-been-through-the-same-or-similar-experiences personal stories.

Every time you try to share something that is important and share something that can help build the right relationship with that rejecting person and help them really get to know you, they feel the need and the urge to share a similar story. They are locked into a fear-driven and motivated mind-set to where they feel the need to compare a similar story just like the one you shared that can compete with the one you have shared.

CHAPTER TWELVE

Compare and Compete

To have someone that you are in a relationship with having a fear-driven and motivated what-has-happened-to-me-and-what-I-have-been-through, what-could-happen-to-me-again spirit dominating, manipulating, and controlling their thoughts, thinking, way of thinking, mind-set, and mentality is to have that person coming up with a personal story of their own that can compare and compete with the story that you are sharing that is from your past experience(s). A compare-and-compete spirit will be the force that will be suggesting and influencing and leading the person you are in a relationship with into finding a story that is similar to yours.

That same compare-and-compete spirit will have the person you have been trying to talk to and reason with locked into trying to compare one of their past experience stories that is equal to the one you have been trying to share with them. They will find a personal story of their own that can demonstrate the same magnitude of what has happened to you, what you experienced, what you went through, the effect and affect what you went through or experienced had on you, your life, others, and the affect and effect that experience had when it came to your choices, decisions, etc. Satan's hidden plan is to get you and that person into comparing, competing, debating, arguing, fussing, cussing, getting into a heated discussion, and getting mad because listening and hearing is not something that is happening in the conversations that you are holding.

And before you know it, Satan will have the both of you heavily locked into a mind-set and mentality where the both of you are basically trying to get the other person to listen, hear, and help. As this type of thinking and way of thinking is being demonstrated, before you know it, Satan have sneakily got you to compromise your character, conduct, conversations, and communication, compromise your human will, strength, and ability to do what you know and have always done before when that compare-and-compete spirit showed up, and that was to just walk away.

Without you realizing, recognizing, and knowing it, he has gotten you over into compromising your Christian character and strength. When there are two people who are competing to talk and be heard, neither one of them is nor have the ability to hear each other's heartfelt relationship desire or need. That is exactly what Satan wants both people to do, and that is to compete in being heard. The moment he can get either one of them in that place, mental state of mind, mental frame of mind, mind-set, and mentality, he knows he has the opportunity and power to tear that relationship up, and he can get the people in that relationship into a halt between opinion disagreement that can and will divide and conquer their personal relationship and tear it up.

Standing on the Outside Looking In

If you were to stand on the outside looking into your relationship that is just like this kind of relationship, here's what you will see. I truly hope you will clearly understand what I'm sharing. Here's the story.

The only thing he wanted was to talk to her, the person he had spent time in a relationship with. He just wanted to talk to her about something she was saying, doing, had made a choice and decision concerning, a way in which she handled a matter, circumstance, situation, or confrontation that he didn't like nor care for because it reminded him of or was the same exact thing that he had gone through and experienced in the relationship he was in before he got into a relationship with her.

Yes, she was a different person, and this was a new relationship, but she was saying, doing, had made a choice and decision. She handled a matter, circumstance, situation, or confrontation in a way that he didn't like nor care for. When she did so, he was reminded of something he had gone through before and had prayed and fought hard to get delivered from and get past, but in some or a lot of ways, it was still a very sensitive matter and still a sensitive place with him. He wasn't having a flashback of any kind. He was just seeing and hearing her say and do something that reminded him of what he had gone through.

When he saw what he had went through before happening again, he could not help but to remember how things turned out the first time. He remembered how the wrong end results had come out of it and the state of mind, frame of mind, mind-set, and mentality he and the person he was with during that time had ended up in. He remembered what condition his heart ended up in and what kind of direct or indirect effect and affect those wrong end results had on those who was close to one or the both of them. He remembered how he ended up in a place of brokenness and in a dark place. It was a place that he thought he would never heal from and be able to get over and get past.

It was only by and through the grace and strength of God that he made it through that dry, desolate, empty place. When he came into the conversation that he and the person he thought would understand how he felt, he came into that moment as he always had, and that is with an open heart, open mind, being transparent, and allowing himself to be in a vulnerable state with her. As he was cautiously and carefully picking and choosing his words, as he was engaging in communicative conversation with her and expecting a positive and good end results, he was not prepared for what would and eventually did take place next.

He wouldn't had imagined in all of his wildest dreams she would, with a vicious and vengeful tone, began to assault, attack, and try to assassinate him and what he was sharing. The words she was using were words that were a weapon she would constantly and continually use in the course of their conversation and discussion to form against him and to form against what he was trying to share with her. When she, with a mean-spirited voice, would say, "What about me and what I have been through?" and continue talking by saying, "You act like you are the only one who has been through something. I am not her." She would not stop with those words. She would continue beating him down when he was at his most vulnerable state and place with her. She would continue with the word weapons that Satan had suggested and influenced her into using to help break him down, while he had allowed himself to be caught with his protective walls, guards, and spiritual weapons laid down.

Neither one of them had realized Satan was at work behind the scenes abiding and dwelling in the unexpected, unplanned, unknown, unfair, unaware, and unsure, and he was masterfully and meticulously planning and plotting the whole scene and moment. Satan was strategically planning and plotting how he would kill, steal, destroy, take down, and take them out of their relationship. On the day they had got into a compare-and-compete moment, those spiritual weapons he had been using consistently in times past to keep those what-about-me-and-what-has-happened-to-me-and-what-I-have-been-through, what-could-happen-to-me-again word weapons that had been formed against him from prospering and penetrating, he, for some reason(s), would let and lay them down.

The moment he did that, he had put himself in a compromising way and place. And like a lion that had been watching and waiting for the moment when it could and had the right to attack, the person he had been in a relationship with that said she loved, cared for, had demonstrated concern and compassion for, cooked for, laid next to, prayed for and with, had stood with him through the good times, the bad times, the hard times, and the through the ugly times, she was not launching at him with and through the mean, hurtful, spiteful, damaging, and destructive things she would say and do him and to their relationship.

Those hurtful, mean, spiteful, damaging, and destructive things she would say and/or do came out her with a malicious intent with the goal of taking him down and taking him out. He could hear what he was saying, and he could feel his lips moving, but his heartfelt, sincere words were falling on deaf ears. In that moment, he felt like he was no longer the man she said she loved, cared for, wanted to be with, and wanted to marry. On that day, he was made and led to believe and feel like he was her enemy, a sheep led and ready to be slaughtered, a prey that she had watched, waited, baited, and had set up for failure, for the takedown and takeout.

He had heard it said, and he had said it himself, "Sticks and stones may break my bones but words will or can never hurt me." He quickly discovered on that particular day and with that particular situation, that is not true. The wrong-right words coming out of her mouth were also words that was being spoken out of the heart and mouth of the right person whom Satan know can and will hurt you deeply. Words that are used as a weapon formed against you coming out of the mouth of someone you thought really felt, knew, and who said they loved, needed, and wanted to share their life with you and would be there for you when you needed and wanted them to would and did hurt deeper.

Words that are used as a weapon formed against you coming out of the mouth of someone you trusted, had confidence in, relied on, allowed yourself to be vulnerable with, showed your vulnerability to, had opened up your heart, mind, and soul to, can and would hurt you deeply. And when you hear words that are used as a weapon formed against you coming from someone you felt like you didn't have to defend yourself with nor had you ever felt like you were a target. To have that person suddenly speaking words out of their mouth and what seem like and feel like words that was coming from their heart, in an aggressive nature and spirit, that person's words can, will, and did hurt him that day because her words would aggressively assault, attack, and assassinate what she knew made him who and what he was.

There he was, still committed to trying to talk to her. He was still trying to share and still trying to reach out to her, still trying to reason with her, still trying to get her to open up her heart and hear him. He was still trying to get her to open up the eyes of her understanding and be sensitive to what he was sharing, demonstrate she was listening to him, hear him, and demonstrate she had some love, care, concern, and compassion for him because of what he was sharing. He was waiting and hoping she would reach out and draw him closer to her.

But that's not what she did, and in that moment, he felt like she wasn't the same person he had been in a relationship with. He realized the person he was talking to suddenly had a different personality and perspective. She became someone that had a predator's spirit, and he was her prey. Based on what was happening in that moment and based on what she was saying and the spirit in which she was speaking out of, he knew he would be the one who had to pay the price for all of the people, especially men and that last man from her past who had caused, contributed to her pain, hurt, problems, sufferings, abuse, neglect, being battered, and being rejected, etc. He was in that moment, the one who had to pay the price and pay the penalty.

The what-about-me-and-what-has-happened-to-me-and-what-I-have-been-through, what-could-happen-to-me-again word weapons she used to form against him were sharp and had precision piercing pain especially when those word weapons are spoken in a moment when they were not connecting and communicating and when she was competing and comparing. He could feel himself running into and hitting her walls of resistance and rejection. She was defiant, and she would refute and refuse to receive what he was saying. She made it clear through her resistance and through her rejecting what he was trying to get her to understand. She refused to change.

If you were in this situation, I'm sure, in the back of your mind, you would want that person to stop talking and to stop trying to make their self-justified point. You would also want that person to do the one thing they were not demonstrating they were good at and that would be to listen, to hear and to help you. Compare and compete used what that person had been through as a weapon used to challenge and change the conversation. What started out as you trying to build a covenant and establish communication and understanding compare and compete had challenged and changed and beat up your feelings, emotions, and desires. Compare and compete had stolen the conversation, challenged and changed the nature, flow, and spirit of the conversation, and the end result you desired was broke down and disconnected.

Any and all lines of communication and understanding that had been built between you and that person was no longer there, and compare and compete had you caught up in the moment and in a compromising state of mind and frame of mind. Everyone is shouting and screaming at each other, talking at each other and not talking to each other. Both people are trying to prove their point, trying to get the other to listen, hear, help, support, build up, and not tear down. The atmosphere in the room has suddenly changed, and without you and that person knowing it, the both of you have been set up by the spirit of compare and compete.

And at the point, your character, conduct, conversation, and communication is being set up to be compromised. You may be thinking and asking yourself, "How does Satan use the spirit of compare and compete?" Satan uses the spirit of compare and compete as if they are two kids that are and have been playing together, and both of them are trying to say or do things that outdo the other person. For instance, one kid may say something like, "My dad has a blue hat," and the other kid being in the compare-and-compete mode and mind-set may say something like, "My dad has a blue hat that is taller than your dad's hat." Back and forth they would go comparing and competing.

In all actuality, no one person's painful past is greater than the other. When you are seduced into that compromising place, you get caught and then caught up. The more you try to communicate that which you don't like, need, want, what you need to be changed so that it would help your relationship, the more compare and compete is telling the other person to challenge what you are saying, resist, refuse, and reject your humble plea, and, forcefully out of a "what I have been through," make and prove their point. The compare-and-compete spirit also wants you to get into trying to make and prove your point as well.

When that point can't be made and proven, you will find yourself driven into functioning and flowing out of a sensual mode. Everything that comes out of you is derived from your carnal mind and everything that you are processing in that moment is being processed through your carnal understanding. All of this is happening at a rate of speed that keeps you from really thinking things out. The compare-and-compete spirit will then draw, drive, pull, push, persuade, and force your thought, train of thought, way of thinking, and thinking process into conducting itself as if it is a video camera.

Your mind, your mental state of mind, and your mental frame of mind will act as the instant replay screen, and the spirit of compare and compete will have all three driven and locked into reviving, restoring, and reliving any and all old past feelings, thoughts, and emotional connections and ties to what had been said and done in the past that was not liked. Anything positive and good about the person you were talking to in that moment would not stop them from pulling up negative references from their past. They would ignore what you were saying and would continue to tear down anything that you would say that would be a source of motivation for them.

Whatever it was they had ran into in their past that was similar to what you were trying to talk to them about, they were reliving it in their present, while you were at the moment talking to them. Their past had become their present, and whatever it was that brought them the hurt, pain, and brokenness, the spirit of compare and compete was making sure they were not only reliving the moment, but the person was also beginning to repeat what they had said and done during that actual moment. What will you do when you find yourself caught up in a corrupt conversation? What started out as a clean conversation, you know, you just wanted that person to listen, hear, help, understand, and make an adjustment to help make sure you don't go through the same things again. Compare and compete used the what-I-have-been-through past experiences to challenge and change the flow of the conversation, and now there is a breakdown in the conversation, and no type of understanding is taking place.

That person's not delivered, not cleansed and purged, not healed, and not free feelings, emotions, and desires that is linked, tied, connected, chained, yoked, in bondage, in a stronghold, bound, and limited by "what I have been through" has taken control of the conversation. You are vulnerable, and you are open; and at that moment, compare and compete is using that person to assault, attack, and assassinate your vulnerability. The conversation start to get more heated, and with every negative word spoken, they hit you hard, and it hurt.

You want it all to stop. You don't realize what's really happening in that moment, and without you knowing it, you are being pushed into your survival mode, and you weren't trying to do it. The more you try to share, the more the other person out of their selfish-driven and motivated urge, tendencies, intuitions, inclinations, and instincts and without being cautious and careful, begin to challenge what you are saying and charge back at you with a comparison conversation that in the end gives the person you have been trying to reason with what they feel is the right to do what you did. It is true, and we must not be deceived and misled. Evil companionships, communions, and associations, corrupt and deprave good manners and morals and character (I Corinthians 15:33).

The only thing it took was one corrupt and depraved conversation while you are in the heat of the moment that would eventually overtake, overpower, and overthrow you and then corrupt and deprave your good conversation intentions. It's all right to compare and compete if both are for all of the right reasons, and there is a prize worth having, but to compare and compete for all of the wrong reasons and for the prize of being and looking just as childish and immature as the other person is not a prize worth having or winning.

Another Compare-and-Compete Perspective

Let's just step back for a moment, away from what Satan have you locked, seduced, deceived, tricked, trapped, enticed, etc., into comparing and competing for and look at it from another perspective. Just think about it, you are essentially comparing your childish and immature behavior to that of another person or to that of other people. And you are absolutely competing for the prize entitled "the most childish and immature person." Both of you are traveling down the wrong conversation path, and the question then becomes, who is more childish and immature than the other conversation competitors?

Are you sure you want to be recognized for being weaker than the person who is also weak and do not have the strength to resist, reject, and refuse childish and immature temptations and compromises? We all say and do things for various reasons, and when we do so, we at that moment may think and feel we are saying and doing what we are into for all of the right reasons only to later discover the end results are not what we expected them to be, or we discovered that we were really deceived in our acts, actions, deeds, and in the choices and decisions that we made and in how we handled a matter. The following are some facts that I want you to look at and consider: (a) Sometimes you can be saying and doing all of the right things for all of the right reasons, (b) you can be saying and doing all of the wrong things for what you think is the right reasons, (c) you can be saying and doing all of the wrong things for all of the wrong reasons, and (d) you can be saying and doing all of the right things for all of the wrong reasons.

Final Compare-and-Compete Q&A

Why do our relationships lose their rhythm and their rhyme? Why do we feel the need to compare and compete, challenge and confront, but never change? Why do we assume, accuse, assault, attack, and assassinate? Why do we struggle when it comes to attracting, accepting, adopting, and applying the right conversation and communication principles, processes, and procedures? Why do we keep hurting each other?

Reason number 1: It's because we keep allowing demons, deceptions and delusions, our close friends and family, our past hurt, pain, brokenness, our past negative relationship experiences, the words, acts, actions, deeds, etc., of those who were/are the abusers, batterers, those who rejected us, etc., to define us and our relationships.

Reason number 2: We have not been disconnected from the thoughts, feelings, and emotions of hurt, pain, and brokenness. Neither have we not been delivered, cleansed, purged, healed, and made whole. Now let me break these down for you.

1. To be delivered is to be set free so that someone or something is aimed or guided to an intended target or destination.
2. To be cleansed and purged is to be rid of impurities and infections as if by washing (cleansed). To be purged is to be made free of something unwanted, clear of guilt, to cause evacuation from any type of defilement.
3. To be healed is to be restored, to make sound or whole, to patch up a breach or division. To restore to original purity or integrity.
4. To be made whole is to put together the various ingredients that will complete or fill, not lacking or leaving out any part. Mentally and emotionally sound and healthy. Constituting the total sum or undiminished entirety.

Reason number 3: We keep hurting each other because we forget the serpent still want to and is at work deceiving people in relationships just as he did in Genesis 3:13. The devil, your enemy, is still roaming around like a lion roaring, seeking someone who is a relationship that he can seize upon and then devour the relationship (1 Peter 5:8).

Reason number 4: We keep hurting each other because we forget that the weapons needed for our relationship warfare are not physical weapons of flesh and blood, but they are mighty relationship weapons that God gives for the overthrow and destruction of relationship strongholds (2 Corinthians 10:3–4).

Reason number 5: We forget we are not contending or wrestling with flesh and blood but a highly organized army of satanic and demonic spirits (Ephesians 6:12).

Reason number 6: We forget to apply the leave-and-cleave principles, processes, and procedures (Matthew 19:15). The moment comes when you will have to leave some people, places, things, previous relationship moments, memories, methods, motives, motivations, principles, processes, procedures, learned behavior and behavior patterns, etc., behind you cleave to making and meeting new ones.

Revelation relationship insight: We have forgot to leave past and old bad, negative, wrong, right that is wrong, wrong that look and feel right, hand-me-down, etc., relationship habits, and we forget to cleave to new relationship habits that God can and will send someone to tutor, train, and teach you and the person you are in a relationship with.

CHAPTER THIRTEEN

Caught Up in the Moment

It seemed like the more you share, the more hard-hearted the other person would get. Things are really getting intense and heated up. And before you know it, everything is happening really fast, and everything that you were trying to establish is going the wrong way, and you realize you are caught and you are caught up in the moment. You are caught, and you are caught up in a moment and in a conversation that you unknowingly have been baited, enticed, seduced, and tricked into getting into. You're trying to reason with the person, and that has turned into you trying to and having to defend yourself. Because you feel that you are led to believe you are not talking to the person that you have been trying to reason with but a person who is under the influence of a predator's spirit. And that predator's spirit has made you the object that it wants to prey upon.

The person you have been trying to reason with and share with keeps talking and talking without listening to you, and they keep making assumptions and accusations that assault, attack, and assassinate the part that you had been trying to share and your reasons for trying to share just like a predator that is after its prey. You are still trying to establish communication and understanding, and the person keeps on making accusations and assumptions. Some may be the truth that really hurt, but most are lies.

After a while and without you really knowing it, you begin to defend yourself from the barrage of allegations, assumptions, accusations, assaults, attacks, and assassinations, and you then become so defensive minded that you begin to look at the person who is provoking you just like a mean, vicious, hitting defensive lineman on a football team would look at a quarterback that have no protectors and have left himself vulnerable and open to a ferocious hit, which no defender could resist no matter how hard he tries. In that moment, when things are happening so fast and the person keeps talking and talking and getting louder, more boisterous, even bragging but mostly blaming you there is no one to protect your blind side. You know, the side or part of you that is left vulnerable to a hit, hurt and pain

And the person's speech and body movements and tone of voice comes across as that of a badgering bully. Satan has, without the provoking person knowing it, tricked and deceived them into being so cocky and confident that they feel they can say and do anything and compare and compete in the way they feel they want to and in the manner in which they want to and you won't do anything. It's a very intense situation and conversation, and you are caught and you are caught up in the moment, and you do not have the time to think about what you are saying and what you are doing. You do not have the time to think about what you just might do. You have, without you knowing it, once again have entered into that defensive-minded reaction, reactionary response mode.

Drawn and Dragged into the Moment

The provoking person is still talking and trying to make *what* they are saying or doing, right, and as they do so, they are really arrogant, and they enter into a mode of thinking where they will begin to dare you to do something, and they keep pushing your buttons. You see, Satan and that person know just what to say or do to you. The provoking person know exactly what are the wrong-right acts, actions, deeds, and words that will get to you. Their spirit, words, character, conduct, conversations, communication, heart, mind, thinking, way of thinking, thoughts, train of thought, mental state of mind, mental frame of mind, and mentality have been transformed from that of being that loving, caring, concerned, compassionate, affectionate, giving, and understanding person you once knew or thought you knew into being someone who is totally the opposite.

Their attitude, words, and spirit have, in that moment, conformed into that of a rude, disrespectful, non-caring, cold, heartless person who pushes you to and into urges, tendencies, inclinations, intuitions, and into instincts that boldly say, "Stop her from trying to compare and compete with you." The only thing you can feel and hear deep down inside of you in that moment are the words "Stop her from talking. You have heard enough." Your mind is telling your urges, tendencies, inclinations, intuitions, and instincts to quickly react and deliver a quick reactionary response that will stop the provoking person from saying, "What about me, and what has happened to me, and what I have been through, what could happen to me again" at all cost, by any means necessary.

You can hear something inside of you telling you the provoking person is and will continue to be selfish, self-centered, self-righteous, and they will continue to try to self-justify and make right the wrong that they are saying and doing. It's not so much as what they are literally saying that's really bothering you, and it's not what you are thinking about that is the problem. But somewhere in the midst of them consistently provoking, badgering, and bullying you with their annoying, agitating, aggravating, assumption, and accusation-filled words, without you knowing it or planning and preparing for it, you enter into a dark place that you did not know was there.

Caught in the Moment

While you are there caught and caught up in that dark place with the unseen, unexpected, unplanned, unknown, unfair, uncertain, unaware, unbelievable, undeniable, undetected, unforgettable, and unsure, you are not consciously aware you have stepped out of your rational reasoning mind, mind-set, thoughts, train of thought, thinking, way of thinking, mental state of mind, mental frame of mind, mental condition, and mentality, and you have entered into a dark place with a strong deceived feeling and emotional desire, urge, tendency, inclination, intuition, and instinct that is linked, tied, chained, or is somehow connected to your physical reaction and reactionary response mode.

Which in turn has access to the power, authority, and freedom to speak to and control your bodily functions, and because your rational reasoning mode is held hostage, in a yoke, in bondage, and in a stronghold in that moment, your selfish, self-centered, self-righteous, self-justified, self-effort, and self-willed-filled and motivated carnal mind, feelings, emotions, and desires are under satanic domination, manipulation, and control will begin to draw, suggest influence, tell, push, persuade, and force all of the parts of you and your past that you have not been delivered, cleansed, purged, healed, and made whole from that is still filled with hurt, pain, brokenness and is still a sore spot or wound shouts out to your bodily functions, "Do something," and it does.

My point with all of this is, if you do not go to God and let him deliver, cleanse, purge, heal, and make you whole from being dominated, manipulated, controlled by/with what-about-me-and-what-has-happened-to-me-and-what-I-have-been-through, what-could-happen-to-me-again feelings, emotions, thoughts, train of thought, thinking, way of thinking, urges, tendencies, inclinations, intuitions, and instincts, you will always be lead into and kept in a dark place where there is hurt, pain, and brokenness.

And you will be, become, and end up being consistently at a point of no return when it comes to your reactions and reactionary responses. Let me tell you exactly what will get you into a place or at a point of no return. It will be the human part of you being so weak that it cannot consistently fight against, beat, and defeat your self-effort, selfish, self-centered, self-righteous, self-justified-filled past hurt, past pain, past-brokenness-filled self-will.

You are caught up in the moment, trapped, yoked, in bondage, in a stronghold, and a slave to trying to defend yourself, and your mind has finally comprehended that there is something strange in the tone of the provoking person's voice. The love, care, concern, and compassion are no longer in the atmosphere, and you can't feel it coming from the person you had been trying to share your heart with. In that moment, it feels like there is a stranger in the room with you, and there is a strange heart that is hearing your words and hearing your heart. The heart that you are or was used to talking to and sharing with has, in the course of your conversation, left the room.

And now there is a strange heart in the room, and it is not trying to receive anything that you are saying. There is a strange mind in the room, and it's not the one that you are used to sharing your thoughts with. And the mind of the person that is now provoking you have shut itself down, and it is refuting your words. The provoking person know very well they could and usually would comprehend what you are saying, and they would communicate they understand. There is a strange feeling in the room, and it's not the feeling the person you are used to sharing your feelings with that's in the room with you. The room is filled with feelings of resistance, rejection, and a refusing to feel you.

Nothing you have to say is important. Why? The selfish point that the provoking person you are talking to is what is important. There is a disconnection in the room, and nothing you can say connects with the person you are talking to. While you are feeling the disconnection, the provoking person tells you the disconnection you are feeling has been there for a long time and not just at that moment. You hear those words, but as you are into this now-corrupt, caught-up moment, you are still trying to visualize the moment when you and the person was disconnected or did get disconnected, all while you are still trying to guard your heart.

Split Decision

You are caught up in an atmosphere that drastically changed. You could feel it change, but you couldn't stop it from changing. Why? It's because you are a vital part of the change. You are involved in the change, and what you are saying is the object of the change. It's a split decision, and you better make up your mind. You are caught up in the moment. You better wise up. I caution you to think twice, never leave room for compromise… and when room was left, before you knew it, you were caught up in a confrontation. I have a question that I want to ask you, and that question is, "Are you a conversation coward, or are you a brave conversationalist?" Can you keep your composure when your conversation is challenged, and your courage is being confronted?

That soft answer that turns away wrath is gone, and you are caught by and caught up in the moment with grievous words that stir up anger. The conversation is headed for a head-on collision, and you are about to get caught up in that collision. You can hear everything inside of you telling you to walk away, leave it alone, but when you try you can't. It's like something keeps pushing, pulling, persuading, drawing, driving, and forcing you into that you-will-get-caught-up conversation. With every word the provoking person speaks, your mental frame of mind and mental state of mind is being challenged and changed.

You try to caution the provoking person, but they won't comply. You try changing the subject, but that person changes is back. No matter what you try to do to get yourself out of the conversation so you can leave the room, like a bullheaded bully, Satan keeps the provoking person pushing you and keeping you struggling, trying to get released from the corrupt conversation so you can leave. You are caught in a conversation that is challenging and trying to corrupt and change your character and conduct. You are caught up in a moment that your mind and heart tell you it really matters. And before you know it, the tolerance boundaries you have set have been crossed and broken, and the limitations you have made for listening have been violated.

Before you know it, your mentality is caught up in the moment, and now you are now ready to be pushed to a point of no return. Why won't the provoking person stop badgering and bullying you with their words? Why won't they stop trying to push and pull you into putting up with them trying to prove her point? Satan had the provoking person emotionally charged, and he had that person believing they are right, and they don't have to change. They are caught, and you are caught up in their emotional moment. There are no holds barred when it comes to what the provoking person will out of being totally emotional, say and do.

The provoking person is caught up in their emotional state of mind and in their emotional frame of mind. And because they are there in that condition, everything that is absolutely wrong feels right to them, and whatever they feel, they say it and do it. The provoking person heeds none of your warnings. They keep talking and talking and accusing and assuming and badgering and bullying and pushing and talking until your mentality finally says, "I heard enough," and your urges, tendencies, intuition, inclinations, and your instincts are all being caught in the moment and say, "React—end it. Stop them." With your rational reasoning being caught and caught up in the moment, your reaction is free to respond to the provoking persons resisting, rejecting, refusing, and refuting. Beware of caught-up-in-the-moment conversations.

CHAPTER FOURTEEN

The Compete-and-Compare Curse

You see, you are to close upon it. That whole circumstance, situation, and confrontation. You can't see it, and you are not able to see yourself the right way. You can't see what really happened, how it really went down because you want to feel and believe you were right when you were really wrong. You want to think and believe the other person was wrong when they are really right. Your selfishness, self-centeredness, self-righteousness, and your self-justification won't let you see the truth, the reality. Selfishness won't let you see yourself as you really are and was in that matter. Self-righteousness and self-justification is making sure you see yourself as you want to see yourself and not see your trusted truth and your raggedy reality.

The question I have for you is, is it as it really is? Is what took place, happened that day in that moment is as it really happened? Is the way you are looking at it really the way it went down, or did you say and do more than you should have to make it worse? Is that whole matter is as it really is, or are you so close upon it, so emotionally entangled and entrapped in emotionalism, and you were so deep into it that you couldn't, can't, and you still don't really see how it really is? Self-deception and self-delusion is not allowing you to see what really took place. You still can't see it! You are still in self-denial.

What really happened on that day and with that circumstance, situation, and confrontation didn't go down the way you want to believe it did. You can't and won't see the mistake you made that really made things worse than what it already was/is. But what! There is no but!

Don't be like that little kid who throws a rock and then hides his hands behind his back and say, "I didn't do it." Yes, you did. You know it, and God knows you did. You did what you did, and you said what you said. You compared and competed, and a curse came. A family-inherited generational curse came into that conversation, eased its way into the relationship, and sneaked itself into that matter. And *you* opened the door for it to come in. The only thing you had to do and should have done was to not do what you did, say what you said, and just be quiet and not let your hostile prove-my-point, say-what-I-have-to-say words be the bait, the bully, and the badgering words that provoked, agitated, and aggravated the whole already-tension-filled relationship, matter, environment, and atmosphere. You just had to keep on comparing and competing. The devil spoke to your selfish feelings, emotions, and desires and told you and them to stand up for yourself and don't be a doormat anymore, and you followed Satan's plan.

He didn't want you to see, what you wanted to say and do, and your reasons may have been right, but you said and done what you ended up, saying and doing (a) the wrong way, (b) at the wrong time/moment/place, (c) in the wrong spirit, (d) with a hidden agenda and motive, and (e) out of the wrong attitude. To make an already-negative and tense situation even worse, you then demonstrate the wrong behavior and behavior patterns when you were expressing yourself, standing up for yourself, and trying to establish your own selfish identity.

Instead of being more concerned about making sure you and the person you had been in a relationship with were on the same page and the both of you were communicating and had an understanding, you selfishly deemed what you had to selfishly say, how you selfishly felt and thought, and your own selfish agenda and motives to be more important than the relationship matter itself, etc., that brought the both of you together for the conversation.

Maybe, just maybe your (1) timing is bad and off, (2) Satan turned your right into a wrong, (3) Satan turned your wrong into Satan's concept of right, not yours nor the other person's, (4) Satan played you and used you. He preyed upon your selfish feelings, selfish emotions, and selfish desires, and you let him do it. You listened to Satan suggest to you what seemed and sounded right to you. Stop it! Stop making excuses and stop trying to explain and trying to justify the fact that you opened the door for all of the wrong reactions, responses, acts, actions and deeds to happen. Satan caught you slipping, and he caught you sleeping, and he slapped you and the other person(s), and the people who opened that door real hard and now, right now, there is hurt, pain, and brokenness. You just wouldn't let it go!

You just had to keep pressing your issue. You just couldn't control yourself, and you just had to say and do what you felt you had to say and do and you really showed no willingness to wait until there was a better day and time. You just had to push and press your issue and hidden agenda until it provoked the wrong negative reactions, responses, and reactionary responses. But what! We cannot and will not engage in talking about the other person and what they said and done wrong. They are not reading this book with you. God is holding you accountable and responsible for what you said and what you did that pushed, pressed, and provoked.

Compare-and-Compete Power Thoughts

Power thought/point number 1: I want to share the following power thoughts with you that is important, and they are ones you need to clearly understand: (a) God *does not* and will not hold you accountable and responsible for what others say and do to you, (b) God *can, will, and do* hold you accountable and responsible for the things you say and do to others. You provoked, pressed, and pushed, and now you are in pain. You started a fight, and now you want God to finish it for you. That is not what God can and will do. You provoked, and in doing so, you pushed yourself out of the place of protection and placed and positioned yourself in harm's way. You showed no absence of restraint, and you became your own worst enemy.

Power thought/point number 2: Just like God came into the garden to deal with everyone that was responsible for what Adam had done by eating the forbidden fruit, God is coming after you, and he is going to do just what he did with Adam, Eve, and the serpent in Genesis 3:8–19. He is going to deal with you, and the wrong you committed. You cannot and will not escape the loving, caring, and corrective hand of God. He loves you. You are accountable and responsible for any and all provoking, pressing, and pushing you allowed yourself to engage in and get entangled and entrapped in that brought about whatever took place on the day when you ended up in hurt, pain, and brokenness.

The blame game cannot and will not work with God, and He won't accept your buts. Everything that you said and done out of (a) selfishness, (b) pride, (c) stubbornness and out of the wrong attitude, spirit, mind-set, and mentality led and brought about whatever consequences and repercussions that *Satan* set you up for. The truth be told, what really led you into and brought about what ended up happening could have been avoided if you would have just yielded, submitted, and surrendered to the leading of the Holy Spirit and not yielded, submitted, and surrendered to your selfishness, pride, and stubbornness.

Power thought/point number 3: The truth and reality is that Satan used you. Yes, the devil used you to bring hurt, pain, and brokenness to the both of you, and he used your not wanting to control your attitude, mind-set, and mentality to bring into your relationship a compare-and-compete thinking, way of thinking, thoughts, train of thought, mental state of mind, and mental frame of mind. Satan used you, and he treated you just like you were nothing and nobody. He used you, and he treated you just like someone that is insignificant and unimportant. There's the truth! Can you handle the truth? No, you can't handle the truth! The truth is too real, and it is too right.

Power thought/point number 4: Satan set you up for failure, and he used those who said things like, "If I were you, I wouldn't" and "don't let him/her treat you that way and talk to you that way." You see, what they didn't and don't know is you never told them the whole truth and story. You never told the person and people you confide in or talked to about what happened to you and what really led up to that wrong occurrence taking place. You didn't tell them what led up to that wrong happening was a product of minutes, hours, days, weeks, months, and even years of you being

❖ constant and consistent with the wrong things you said and done over the course of your relationship with that person;
❖ you demonstrating a selfish, self-centered, self-righteous, and self-justified arrogance when it came to the compare-and-compete retaliatory, get-even acts, actions, deeds, and things you

were saying and doing on that day and prior to that day when you ended up being battered, violated, hit, hurt, abandoned, rejected, etc.

❖ you would never admit you were wrong when you were
❖ you wanted everyone else to change for you, but you refused to change
❖ you didn't demonstrate you had a repentant heart
❖ You continued ignoring the person who ended up hurting you and you also ignored their request for you to stop pushing your selfish pursuits and endeavors at them. You knew by doing so what kind of negative feedback and negative reactions, responses, and reactionary responses that would end up being the final end results.

Power thought/point number 5: You have to stop allowing yourself to get caught up in causing, creating the atmosphere, and contributing to compare-and-compete circumstances, challenges, changes, and confrontations that provoke, push, press, and bring out the wrong responses in those we love and care about. Your feelings, emotions, and desires are not your best friends especially when you are involved in relationship circumstances, situations, and confrontations. The provoking, pushing, and pressing happens whenever you allow or give place to your feelings, emotions, and desires. Every time there is a breakdown in a relationship, it is always due to one or both persons giving place and functioning in harmony, flowing in and out, and following the leading of their feelings, emotions, and desires. Truthful facts can and always deliver, cleanse, purge, heal, and make whole any and all relationship matters and issues and not a person's feelings.

Don't Get It Twisted

I'm not, in any way whatsoever, *cosigning* and advocating any wrong acts, actions, or deeds of another, nor am I trying to make any excuses and provisions for wrong happening. What I am hoping, believing, and trusting is you will look at what happened to you in that relationship and in all of your relationships from another perspective, God's perspective. In doing so, I really believe you will find the reality and the truth that can and will make and set you and your relationship free so that you, the person you are in a relationship with, and your relationship can move forward into its fair-tale-fantasy fulfillment. I do *not* and will *not* ever support anyone being hurt or harmed in any way whatsoever. I do not support domestic batteries, assaults, and attacks of any kind.

What I want you to see and clearly understand is we, you, and I are accountable and responsible for the things we say and do, the choices and decisions we made/make, the way we handle a matter, circumstance, situation, and confrontation that can, will, and might lead and that led up to what happened to you. God gave you the right and the freedom to exercise your power of choice, and he provided you with every way to escape Satan's corrupt conversation temptation. In fact, while you were being drawn, driven, pushed, pulled, forced, enticed, seduced, tricked, bamboozled, and sucked into that wrong outcome moment, something told you… "Isn't that what we say and you say? Didn't you get that feeling something wrong was going to happen?"

Power thought/point number 6: Be honest. You knew that subject matter that brought about the wrong things happening to you on that day was a subject matter you and that person had already (a) discussed before and you couldn't come to a mutual agreement and agreed to let it go (b) discussed before and the wrong end results came about, (c) discussed before and you were cautioned, asked, or told to not bring it up again, (d) discussed before and you still didn't get the end results you needed, wanted, or expected. For a moment I want to ask you to put aside all of the dramatic emotion that you are trying to keep alive and stop accepting, adopting, and applying Satan's victim spirit principles, processes, procedures, attitude, mind-set, and mentality. Let's look at some truths and realities when it came to what happened to you. No one made or forced you to stay in that negative and explosive atmosphere and environment. You had every opportunity to walk away, end the heated conversation, or just be quiet, and you chose to do none of them. Protecting your relationship wasn't that important on that day and protecting yourself and the other person wasn't that important on that day when you were in harm's way. Everything that took place that day wasn't the devil. It was all *you*! You were not *completely* ignorant, blind, deceived, or naïve when you went into that negative atmosphere and environment.

And when you found yourself in that negative conversation and environment, you *still* had every opportunity to get out of it, but you didn't, and you chose to continue trying to defend yourself and justify your choices, decisions, acts, actions, deeds, accusations, assumptions, etc. You had every opportunity to not go into that conversation, meet that person, or leave that person, but you didn't choose any of those options. Now if what happened to you was just you really and truly being a victim of an unknown circumstance and situation you really and truly had nothing to do with directly or indirectly is one thing. But in most cases, what happens to us take place because we allow ourselves to get involved and/or we put ourselves into a place and a position where we set our own selves up for failures.

Here It Is

We have to stop allowing ourselves to be put in a negative or in a selfish circumstance, situation, and confrontations where we compare and compete for the prize of hurt, pain, and brokenness. We have to wise up and never leave room for (1) compromising circumstances, (2) compromising situations, and (3) compromising confrontations. Satan is always working behind the scenes of our relationships in trying to entice, entangle, and entrap us in all three. You should never leave room for anything that can and will compromise your character, conduct, conversations, and your communication, and you should never allow yourself to get caught and then caught up in compare-and-compete corrupt conversations and communication.

Compare-and-Compete Conversations

Satan has seduced, tricked, lied, and deceived and led so many men and women into comparing and competing with each other. In fact, that way of thinking and mode of thinking have become the norm in our society today. Men and women are easily enticed, entangled, and entrapped in satanic- and demonic-influenced and suggested competitive comparing and competing. We engage in such activity without even questioning, challenging, and confronting what we see. As we continue to competitively compare and compete, the effect and affect of such activity is visibly seen and recognized in our relationship, in our mood, and in our attitude if we are paying attention.

Competitive compare-and-compete conversations always bear the fruits of consistent and continuous arguing, fussing, cussing, attitudes, and disagreeing discussions that are damaging, dangerous, destructive, and deadly in that they open the door for the wrong acts, actions, and deeds being committed. Satan is behind the scenes dominating, manipulating, and controlling our competitive nature and spirit, and he is tearing down and tearing up marriages and relationships that God have brought together. We are the ones, out of our own free will, who are letting him do so. We compare our selfish causes, and we compete with our selfish causes. We do so without ever thinking about what we are saying and doing and we get into the mind-set and mentality easily. We are more inclined to challenge and confront the person we are in a relationship with rather than challenge and confront our compare-and-compete mind-set, thinking, way of thinking, thoughts, train of thought, mental state of mind, mental condition, and our mental frame of mind.

I'm Waiting on You

The spirit of compare and compete with all of its causes and curses was already there in that room, in that place, in that space at that time where you and the person who was used to hurt you, waiting for you. The moment when you entered into the room, the spirit of compare and compete had completed your conversation script. That spirit had placed them on loud, fluorescent, illuminated mental memory flash moments that you could not miss seeing. They were placed on your mind, and they were placed in your memory. The spirit of compare and compete was there waiting on you. All of your wrong feelings, emotions, desires, urges, tendencies, inclinations, intuitions, and instincts was also working in cahoots with compare and compete. Both had already determined it was in your best interest that they overthrow your right to a rational mind.

They also had decided it was in your best interest that they take over and take control of whatever conversations and communication that would be spoken in your meeting with the person you were in a relationship with. The spirit of compare and compete had decided you were not smart or intelligent enough to converse and communicate. Are you getting this? The moment when you entered into the room to meet with the person that you had shared so many good and happy times with, Satan and the spirit of compare and compete had already decided and determined they didn't want you to be with that person and in that relationship. They had decided and determined they would try to find ways to take away your relationship power of choice

So you entered into that room to meet with the person that ended up being used to hurt you. The silent unseen assassins known as Satan and the spirit of compare and compete loaded up their weapons they would use to form against you. Their weapon of choice would be accurate and precision striking, generational cursed, relationship corrupt conversation artillery. And they would put their devious, dangerous, deadly, destructive, and damaging relationship plan and strategy into effect. When it was your time to talk, the spirit of compare told you to compete with whatever the other person you are/were talking to had to say and compete with whatever they would be trying to share with you.

Satan had you thinking you are and were proving a point when you said, "You see, you don't like it when the shoe is on the other foot." And then you said something like, "If you say and do it, I can too. You won't like it." Every person that is locked into a compare-and-compete mind-set will end up being dominated, manipulated, and controlled with what-has-happened-to-me-and-what-I-have-been-through-what-could-happen-to-me-again words, thoughts, train of thought, thinking, and way of thinking. When used as a weapon, "what has happened to me and what I have been through, what could happen to me again" can and will open up a past wound, an act, action, and deed and bring that into a present-day war. It's just human nature for us to try to protect ourselves and try to prevent ourselves from reliving our past. But it's not how we do those things that we do. It's when, where, and why we go into a protective mode and take our selfish stands, selfish hidden motives, and selfish hidden agendas into our own protective custody.

Compare will have the other person believing they have the right match, that which you had been saying and doing, and they have the right to make the same kind of choices and decisions you made. Compare will also have the person believing they have the right to handle matters the way they want to because of what you have been saying, doing, etc., that's wrong. The conversation of compare says,

"I did it, said it, handled it that way, made that choice and decision, etc., because you did the same." Compete will have the other person thinking, feeling, and believing they have a right to protect themselves by saying and doing whatever has been said and done to them. To do so is what we call retaliation, trying to get even, or trying to initiate payback. No one wins, and everyone ends up hurt and hindered.

Compare says, "You know what I have been through." Compete says, "You know what has happened to me too. I've been through some things too." When both of these are used as a weapon formed against a relationship, the people that are in that relationship, the person, and the relationship is challenged, and both is then changed. The person and the relationship will end up being filled with so much conflict that both will begin to conform to the compare-and-compete curse.

When a person is in a compare mind-set, they are in mental state of mind and mental frame of mind and the mentality where they deem the wrong act, actions, deeds, matters of another to be worthy of comparison, can be held equal to their retaliatory get-even acts, actions, deeds, and matters. They want to make the other person's wrong acts, actions, deeds, conversations, etc., to appear in a similar standing. The conversation that the person's mind-set is articulating is, "If they said or did it, I can and will too, and we will be equal or even."

Compare-and-Compete Mode

When a person is in a compare-and-compete mode, their mind, mind-set, thoughts, train of thought, thinking, way of thinking, mental state of mind, mental condition, mental frame of mind, and their mentality have accepted, adopted, and applied a specific or particular way or manner in which the spirit of compare and compete occurs or is experienced, expressed, or done. Not only so, but the person's mind and all of its components, capabilities, and abilities are locked into a specific and particular way or manner in which it releases compare-and-compete standards, principles, processes, and procedures to be made manifest because it has been tutored, trained, and taught to do so.

That tutored, trained, taught, accepted, adopted, and applied specific or particular way or manner in which the spirit of compare and compete occurs or is experienced, expressed, or done has locked that person's mind, mind-set, mentality, and their thoughts, train of thought, thinking, and way of thinking into a compare-and-compete yoke and stronghold. Their mental state of mind, mental condition, and mental frame of mind is held hostage, becomes a slave, and is held in bondage. The demonic term for this is called a "mind-binding spirit."

If your mind and all of its components, capabilities, and abilities are locked in a compare mode and what happens is all are locked in an order that can be considered or described as similar because of the way or manner in which everything is processed in and through the person's mind with the help of all of its components, capabilities, and abilities occurs or is experienced, expressed, or done is always the same way. A person whose mind is always in the compare mode can be described as someone that is always trying to strive to outdo another in, with, and though their thinking, way of thinking, thoughts, and train of thought for acknowledgment, prize, supremacy, profit, etc.

Their reactions, responses, and reactionary responses have engaged in a contest with that of another person's. The conversation that the person's thinking, way of thinking, thoughts, and train of thought has transmitted to their reactions, responses, and reactionary responses is, "Say and do whatever they say and do for the same reasons and/or to the same degree or to a greater degree than theirs and show them how it feels."

To do so is just a way of inviting in the compare-and-compete curse. The compare-and-compete curse will always have a what-goes-around-comes-around boomerang attachment assigned and attached to it. The compare-and-compete curse is caused, a created atmosphere and it is contributed to each time one person or both persons in that relationship tries to prove a selfish point that can and will make the other person look bigger or smaller or equal. The compare-and-compete curse becomes active or made alive whenever the person(s) let their self-will and self-effort get involved and take control in trying to teach a person or persons a lesson as a way to self-justify what they did.

Are you caught up in the mode of trying to outdo the person who has done you wrong? Are you tricked and trapped into mental frame of mind where you are trying to prove a point? Have you been seduced and deceived into the mind-set where you want to show a person how it feels to be wronged in the way they hurt and wronged you? Do you feel the urge, have the tendency, feel the inclination, sense the intuition, and have the instinct to show a person what if feels like to have someone you love and trust and in a relationship to wrong you?

Do you have that state of mind and frame of mind where you say, "I'm going to say and do what you say and do," and/or do you have that I-just-said-and-did-what-you-did mentality? If you answered yes to any of these questions, you have and you are constantly and consistently opening the door for the compare-and-compete curse. When Satan is the force that is powering and leading you into comparing and competing, your conversation and communication will be corrupted, and each word spoken will bring nothing but chaos and confusion. That's the curse that comes with trying to compare and compete.

A Different Perspective

I dare you to do it! Do what? I dare you to step back and look at what really happened in your life and in your relationship from another and different perspective. Not from mine, not yours, not another or the other persons, but from God's perspective. It's time to stop running. Stop blaming the other person and others for what happened or is still happening in your life. It is time to stop blaming them for the failing of your relationship. It is time you stop acting like you are a victim. God is calling you to consider your ways, consider your previous and present conduct, and how you have fared. Look at the end results. Was it the ones you wanted, needed, or expected?

You have some ways—the method and system that you use to do something, your usual habits, actions, qualities, how you do something, how you behave, appear, feel, etc., that consistently cause, create the atmosphere, and contribute to the collapse of your relationship. Your ways have brought about some unbelievable, unforgettable, and unreal costs you have had to pay for the life and way of living you have chosen, or you have allowed your ways to connect itself to you. Consider your ways because they very well may be family generational-cursed ways.

Compare-and-Compete Perspectives

I want to commend you for accepting the challenge of stepping back and looking at what happened to you and looking at your relationship from another perspective. It takes a big person to take on such a journey. I can assure you God is and will open the eyes of your heart to the truths and realities of what has happened to you and what is happening in your relationship. He will also enlighten the eyes of your understanding because you have dared to do so. Now let's look at some perspectives concerning what happened to you and why your relationship ended up where it did.

The first perspective: You basically have sown, given, and put a lot into your life, relationships, and to the person(s)/people that is in those relationship(s) with you, but you have reaped little from your past relationships and is reaping little from those you share a relationship with now. And you have reaped little out of your life.

The moment when you need something from your relationships, need something from the person(s)/people you are sharing a relationship with and you need something out of your life that will help sustain and satisfy you, the truth is, you do not have enough in your life and in your relationship, and you don't have enough coming from the person/people you have been or you are in your relationship with that will do so. You have poured so much into your life and in your relationships and into the person(s)/people you share a relationship with, but you do not have and cannot get enough out of your life, your relationship(s), and the person(s)/people that you are in a relationship(s) with. You can't seem to get that one something that that can and will fulfill you.

You do your best to show and give a lot love and care for your life, your relationship, and the person(s)/people that you invite and involve yourself into a relationship with, but in the end, it seems like and it feels like your life, relationships, and the person(s)/people that you really love and care for and share a relationship with, well, that love and care you have given seems to be not enough and/or just enough but never more than enough.

And when you do your very best to try and earn a better life, better relationships, and the right to be in a relationship with a better person(s)/people, that which you have said, done, matters handled, and the choices and decisions you have made that you knew, thought, or felt would bring the better, in reality, has felt, seemed, and looked like your better has been put into some part of your life, relationship(s) and the person(s)/people you share a relationship(s) with where there are holes of some kind and to some degree. I want to challenge you to consider the method and system that you use when you go about your usual habits, actions, qualities, how you do something, how you behave, appear, feel, etc. Take a moment and consider your reasons and your reasonings.

The second perspective: The other thing that you have been doing that keep bringing the compare-and-compete curse into your life and into your relationship(s) is you have been talking so very proudly about your life, relationship(s), and the person(s)/people that was in those relationships with you. In doing so, you have let arrogance go forth from your mouth and you have become overbearing in being boisterous and really proud and pride filled when it comes to you talking about your life, relationship(s), and the person(s)/people that you share a relationship with.

To do so is just like you making or putting your life, relationship(s), and the person(s) and people that share in those relationships on pedestal, and you are worshipping them as if they are a god. You have to remember God is a jealous god, and you should not idolize anything or anyone. But more important than that, when you are arrogant and you are talking proudly about your life, relationship(s), and the person(s) and the people, you are basically allowing Satan to set you and that person(s), people, and relationship up for failure.

As you continue to do what I just described, what happens is Satan will let you continue to do so; and when you least expect it, Satan will bring out the unseen, unexpected, unplanned, unknown, unfair, unaware, uncertain, unsure, unforgettable, unexplainable, unthinkable, and the unbelievable, something that you nor that person knew was in their family's generational curse that the person(s)/people inherited. Satan knows all of your family generational relationship curses, and he knew which ones the person and people that you have been and is in a relationship with inherited. He knew that if the curses were used at the right time, it would kill, steal, and destroy all or some parts of your life, that relationship and the person(s)/people who did not know they had inherited a relationship curse or curses.

The reason(s) many do not know is because some of the family generational curses and compare-compete generational curses they inherited did not show up immediately. They may have skipped other family members and was lying dormant in that person. Nothing in that person's life, relationships, and in the person(s)/people they had/have/ is in a relationship with have ever pushed them to their boundaries, limitations, or had pushed them too far. And one day someone did, and that person reacted and had a reactionary response that was right out of and right in line with what type of generational curses that is in their bloodline.

It was something that was said or done, a matter that was handled in a certain way, a choice and decision you made, or it was an innocent and unsuspecting person who wasn't intentionally trying to say or do so, but they did. What you said, done, the way you handled something, and the choices and decisions you made may have been one(s) that you have done on different occasions, and nothing remotely went wrong nor was there any type of reactions taking place. But on that one particular day and in that one particular circumstance, situation, confrontation, conversation, and communication that which was lying dormant in their bloodline or your bloodline was triggered.

The point I want to make is when Satan sets you up for failure and he set you up to fall, he will do it in a big way. He will do it in a way that he knows will ultimately kill, steal, and destroy you, your life, reputation, image, hard work, dedication, drive, motivation, ambition, will to win, and will to live. He will deliver your inherited relationship generational cursed and compare-and-compete curse at a time when it seems like, feels like, and looks like everything is going good and right for you, and then he will open up his arsenal of family-inherited relationship generational curses and compare-and-compete generational curses. When he do so, he will start bombing your dreams, hopes, desires, vision, ministry, marriage, money, and even bomb your with that which he know can and will break your spirit. He is always behind the scene. Be aware of this!

Let's Get Real

Whatever it is that have you into a compare-compete mode, spirit, and attitude, Satan has set you up to be a recipient of it. Satan has set your life, relationship(s), and the person(s) and people you are in a relationship with up for failure. You see, Satan not only set you up, but he also used you. The truth be told, you were his pawn, patsy, and he punked you. On that day when your life, relationship(s), and relationship with the person(s)/people you were/is in a relationship was attacked, assaulted, assassinated, killed, destroyed, stolen, taken down, Satan had you thinking and feeling like you were going to go into that conversation and make your statement and stand your ground and all would be well.

He had you thinking and feeling like you were going to stand up for yourself, speak your mind, say what you have to say the way you wanted to say what you had selfishly wanted to say what you felt you had the urge, tendency, inclination, intuition, and the instinct to speak your mind. *But* he didn't tell you, let you see, make you aware, send you a memo, etc., to inform you that it would be the wrong place, wrong time, and wrong moment for you to take your selfish stand. He didn't give you a hint that would let you know the person you were meeting with wasn't in the mood nor was that person in the frame of mind for that kind of selfish act, action, deed, or to hear your kind of selfish conversation.

Satan did not whisper in your ear, "It's not the right conversation for that which you wanted to begin establishing your hidden agendas and hidden motives. He set you up for failure, and you fell for it. He sent his, your, failure-filled and fate-filled friends to help you out. You know them real well. They are your feelings, emotions, and your desires. All three of them have been getting you in trouble for a long time. Let's cut to the chase. To be honest with you, your feelings, emotions, and desires are not your best friends. In fact, they are your worst enemies. You have been a fool for Satan.

Let's get real. Satan pimped your feelings, emotions, and desires. He played you! How does that make you feel? Everything that happened that day, in your life, in your relationship(s), and in your relationship with that person(s) and people wasn't about you. It was about Satan trying and finally finding a way to sneak into that meeting and steal the conversation that you and that person were going to have. He would distract, detour, delay, damage, and deny you and that person any kind of communication and understanding. And the both of you and everyone that was there fell for it.

Please do not misunderstand me. That's not to say the wrong reaction and reactionary responses of the other person was and is right. There is no justifying any such wrong acts, actions, and deeds. What I'm talking about is you owning up totally and completely to your part in what has caused, created the atmosphere, and has/is contributing to the collapse in/of your character, conduct, conversation, communication, choices, decision making in your life, relationship(s), and relationship(s) with the person(s)/people that is in those relationships with you.

Accountability and Responsibility

Yes, you are accountable and responsible for whatever it is that has caused your relationship to be in the condition it is in and what have/is causing it to fail and not work. Please stop making excuses, and please stop trying to give an explanation as to what happened. I'm asking you to please stop trying to give your version of what happened and to please stop trying to explain and justify you coming into the conversation with a compare-and-compete spirit. You did not go into that place meeting and gathering relationship with a pure heart. You did not go to see, meet, or talk to that person to communicate and gain an understanding because your heart and mind wasn't clear. Be honest. You went into that meeting and into that conversation already ready to compare and compete.

Satan had already prepped and prepared your heart, mind, mind-set, thoughts, train of thought, your thinking, your way of thinking, mental state of mind, mental frame of mind, your mood, mentality, and attitude with the compare-and-compete weapons. He tutored, trained, and taught your urges, tendencies, inclinations, intuitions, instincts, reactions, responses, and your reactionary responses how to rebuke, resist, reject, refuse, and refute any attempts by the persons and people whom you will be holding a discussion or conversations with.

Satan made sure you would be deceived into thinking and feeling they would be trying to stop, hinder, delay, deny, reject, resist, tear you down, talk at you, belittle you, or say and do something that would eventually stand in the way of you standing up for yourself, stand in the way of you speaking your mind, being heard, and, yes, even stand in the way of you comparing and competing no matter what your reason(s) are and what they think your reasons or motives would be. Satan had you deceived into thinking and believing you would be right in comparing and competing.

He did so by highlighting, placing the wrong people in your life and in your pathway, keeping you thinking, mad, angry, upset, replaying, pulling out what he wanted you to hear in conversations being held by others, on television, etc., that he could get you to feel like you had a right to speak your mind and stand up for yourself. He twisted the truth. Yes, you do have the right to stand up for yourself; and yes, you do have the right to stand your ground. Your rights are right, but it would be your reasons that would be wrong. Your reasons would not be for the purpose of bringing total reconciliation to your relationship and into your life.

You didn't say and do something Eve didn't say or do in the garden. She knew what she wasn't supposed to do and challenged what God told Adam, and she challenged Adam's character, conduct, obedience, discipline, authority, and headship. She listened and heard what Satan was saying to her. And Satan, being more subtle and crafty than any living creature of the field, knew just how to trick, trap, seduce, deceive, appeal, entice her feelings, emotions, and desires (Genesis 3:1–6). Eve was having a conversation with someone who is appealing to her feelings (1–3), getting her emotions involved (4–5), and finally he was able to entangle and entrap her desires, and she gave in (6).

In the end, everyone in the garden that day caused man and mankind to fail and fall. And Satan is still doing the same thing today. He is talking to everyone who will let him talk to their feelings, emotions, and desires. Whenever you start to feel strongly about a conversation, about something or someone, you will then develop some emotions, and you will have an emotional attachment to that matter, moment, memory, conversation, something, or someone. Finally, you will start having desires for that something or someone. On that day, God came into the garden, and he dealt with everyone who had anything to do with man failing and falling.

You have had your hands in causing, creating the atmosphere, and contributing to your relationship failing. Your mouth was speaking poisonous words, and those words came to life, causing, creating the atmosphere, and contributing to the persons and the people you are in that relationship with falling. God holds you personally accountable for the part you played in your failed relationship, and he holds you personally responsible for those whom you caused and helped fall in your relationship. The other person you keep blaming, pointing the finger at, slandering, judging, condemning, and trying to make them look like a bad person is guilty as well. Satan used you, your unbridled tongue, malicious intent, hidden motives, and hidden agenda as a way and as a weapon used to take and break your relationship down.

Don't you think or feel that just because you are not in that relationship anymore, you are free from being accountable and responsible for it failing and falling. You may be delivered from that relationship, but you still need to be cleansed and purged from being a carrier of the compare-and-compete curse. Once that takes place, then God will heal the hole that is in your soul; and finally, he will make your relationship whole and healthy. If you do not get your character, conduct, conversations, and communication cleansed and your personality and integrity purged or all cleansed, you will still be helping the generational cursed and compare-and-compete curse spirit hide.

Carrier of the Curse

If you don't change your words, ways, way of thinking, choice and decision-making process, procedures and principles, behavior, behavior patterns, attitude, etc., and get control over your urges, tendencies, inclinations, intuitions, and instincts, the compete-compare relationship curse spirit can and will continue to lie dormant in your feelings, emotions, and desires. The generational cursed compare-compete relationship spirit can and will lie dormant sometimes for seconds, minutes, hours, days, weeks, months, years, and even decades.

And then one day, when you least expect it and when you are confident, complacent, contented, and you are in a comfort zone, resting quietly and in the flow and rhythm of your life in the flow and rhythm of living, and then that one something is said or done, that one choice and decision is made and that one matter is handled in a specific way, manner, and the compare-and-compete curse show up out of the unseen, unexpected, the unplanned, unknown, unfair, unaware, unsure unforgettable, unexplainable, unthinkable, unbelievable when you least expect it, or you are not even aware that the curse exist.

The compare-and-compete curse spirit can and will manifest itself *in* your feelings, emotions, and desires because that is the strongest and most power-packed, expressed functional part of who you are. Both will also manifest themselves *through* your urges, tendencies, inclinations, intuitions, and through your instincts. Why, it's because once again, those reactions, responses, reactionary responses, parts or pieces of your character, and conduct have an expressed power-packed functional activity flow. Satan and all of his demon and cohort spirits know just when and how to send a signal to your family generational compare-compete cursed feelings, emotions, and desires, causing them to come alive.

Each time there is a breakdown in communication and understanding in a relationship and the truth is being twisted to benefit the selfishness of one or both people that is in that relationship, a message and signal is then sent to your urges, tendencies, inclinations, intuitions, and instincts and to theirs as well, basically placing all of them on high alert. When the temperature, atmosphere, and environment in the room where the discussion, conversation, and communication have broken down and have turned into a heated offensive attack, assault, and assassination of the other person, and there is a defensive struggle, fight, and a war to reject, resist, and refuse to listen and hear what's going on in the room, then a final signal is sent to one or both of the person's involved *self-willed* and *self-effort* driven and motivated unhealthy mind-set, thoughts, train of thought, thinking, way of thinking, mental state of mind, mental frame of mind, mental condition, and mentality.

From that point on, your generational cursed self-effort is in control of the room and your relationship. Satan's assignment and mission is to kill, steal, and destroy your relationship and to do the same to the persons that are in those relationships with you. The same assignment and mission applies to all of those who can and will be affected and effected in any way whatsoever by any means necessary. Your self-effort is powered, driven, and motivated by one central thought, train of thought, thinking, way of thinking, frame of mind, and mentality, and that is "I will do something to get something." The person's mind-set then becomes "I want it the way I want it, how I want it, when I want it, how often or how less I want it, etc.," and the person's mentality becomes "I will say and do whatever I have to do to get what I want."

CHAPTER FIFTEEN

Compare-and-Compete Conspiracy Theory

Just as the spirit of compare and compete has made you its target, you and your relationship are basically marked as well with a target emblem. Every compare-and-compete relationship that comes with a curse will also have or be drawn and driven, pulled or pushed, led or drawn into a satanically caused, created, and devised compare-an-compete conspiracy. A conspiracy is an evil, unlawful, treacherous, or surreptitious plan formulated in secret by two or more persons; or plot or an agreement by two or more persons to commit a crime, fraud, or other wrongful act. So when we are talking about a compare-and-compete conspiracy when it comes to relationships, we are talking about the following:

> ➢ Conduct, conversations, and communication that is deemed to be worthy of comparison, be held equal, appear in a similar standing (compare), and when acted out or spoken, it is done so for the purpose of trying to strive and outdo another for acknowledgement, prize, supremacy, profit, etc., (compete) that is evil, unlawful, treacherous, or surreptitious plan formulated in secret by two or more persons; plot or an agreement by two or more persons to commit a crime, fraud, or other wrongful act (conspiracy).

Other 3T Theories

Now for just a moment let us take a look into some other theories that Satan will always try to hide and disguise so that we cannot see them for what they are. A 3T theory is a theory or theories that are tutored, trained, and taught. It is important to note that once any or all parts of our human outward expression or our self expression have grown, developed and matured properly and it or they are ready to be released each expression goes through the process of being tutored, trained and taught how to function, flow in a way or manner that is conducive to building and establishing or in tearing down a (a) relationship idea or a (b) set of relationship ideas that is intended to explain relationship facts or relationship events. Listed below are some other conspiracies and theories.

1. **Compare conspiracy** is conduct, conversations, and communication that when expressed it is deemed to be worthy of comparison, held equal, and appear in a similar standing that is evil, unlawful, treacherous, or surreptitious plan formulated in secret by two or more persons; plot or an agreement by two or more persons to commit a crime, fraud, or other wrongful act.

2. **Compete conspiracy** is conduct, conversations, and communication that is expressed for the purpose of trying to strive to outdo another for acknowledgment, prize, supremacy, profit, etc., that is evil, unlawful, treacherous, or surreptitious plan formulated in secret by two or more persons; plot or an agreement by two or more persons to commit a crime, fraud, or other wrongful act.

3. **Compare curse** is urges, tendencies, inclinations, intuitions, and instincts that is deemed be worthy of comparison, held equal, and appear in a similar standing with the expression of a profane oath, an evil that has been invoked, a wish that causes misfortune, evil, doom, and trouble that befall a person.

4. **Compete curse** is urges, tendencies, inclinations, intuitions, and instincts that is deemed to be for the purpose of trying to strive to outdo another for acknowledgment, a prize, supremacy, profit, etc., that bring forth a profane oath, an evil that has been invoked, a wish that causes misfortune, evil, doom, and trouble that befall a person.

5. ***Theory*** is defined as a supposition or a system of ideas intended to explain something, especially one based on general principles independent of the thing to be explained. Or it is a set of principles on which the practice of an activity is based, and an idea is used to account for a situation or justify a course of action.

Compare-and-Compete Relationship Theory

When we talk about compare-and-compete relationship theory or theories, we are essentially speaking of someone who is having an abstract relationship thought, or it can be described as the following:

A. A relationship idea that is suggested or presented as possibly true but that is not known or proven to be true
B. A relationship belief, policy, or procedure proposed or followed as the basis of relationship action that produce, prepare, and present a specific and a particular set, kind, or type of relationship principles, procedures, processes, and relationship standards
C. A general relationship principle(s) or relationship ideas that relate to a particular relationship subject
D. A relationship idea or a set of relationship ideas that is intended to explain relationship facts or relationship events

All of which can be used for the purpose of comparing and competing with those of someone else's.

Satan will never create a deceptive something just for the sake of doing so. Everything he creates is deceptively done, and it is always done for the same reason, and that is to deceive, kill, steal, or destroy. When he and all of his foul spirits go after a relationship and the people in those relationships, it is for that purpose. That is not only his purpose, but that is also his plan, and he will never stop pursuing you, your relationship, and the persons and people that you are in a relationship with until he have it and do what he do best with all three.

Get ready, here it is: Satan always will have a way of making it really hard for us to see and really focus on who and what the real problem is in our relationships because he knows how to be deceiving, and he knows how to deceptively get us human beings into his damaging, destructive, and dangerous plan. The way he makes it hard for us to see who and what the problem is in our relationships is to get us over into listening and hearing and then functioning in and out, in accordance with, in agreement with, in cahoots with, flowing, and following the lead of our feelings, emotions, and desires.

Satan knows if he can get our feelings, emotions, and desires worked up or stirred up, he can and will have total control over us, gain access to our relationships, and he will have the freedom to have total control over our rational reasoning capabilities and abilities. So he masterfully and skillfully go about setting up our feelings, emotions, and our desires for failure that in turn will bring our relationships, you, and all of those who share in our relationships down for a fall. And for the most part, we fall for his scheme because Satan knows we are, by nature, emotional beings who has been tutored, trained, and taught to heed and obey our human feelings and to always strive for the fulfillment of our desires.

He knows if and when he get us over into that mode, mind-set, and way of thinking where we become so consciously aware of and in tune with our emotionalism, heeding, and obeying our human feelings and get us locked into passionately pursuing and striving to see the fulfillment of our desires, and he can, at that point, deceptively get that to be not only our mind-set, but also he can get it to be our mentality. Satan can then protect what he have deceptively done from behind the scenes of our relationship. He can then give our emotions the power to plan, prepare, prevent, and protect what he has done.

When the atmosphere surrounding the circumstances, situations, and confrontations that brought you, me, us, and all those who are concerned together for conversation or for communication purposes is changed, then it is emotionally charged with feelings and desires. Satan and all of his secret assassins living, dwelling, and hiding in the unseen will start to bombard those feelings, emotions, and desires with unplanned, unknown, unfair, unaware, uncertain, and unsure of their final end results, weapons of mass relationship destruction. Those weapons are highly volatile, dangerous, destructive, and damaging; and when they hit a relationship, they will produce, prepare, and present the unforgettable, unexplainable, unthinkable, and unbelievable.

You Dropped a Bomb on Me

What are those relationship bombs that Satan uses as a weapon called? Those bombs that he drops on our relationships are highly volatile, and they are (1) fate-filled feelings, (2) fate-filled emotions, and (3) fate-filled desires that are always seasoned with accurate amounts selfishness, self-centeredness, self-righteousness, and self-justification. He will disguise how they manifest themselves, and he will try to deceive you into thinking and feeling your feelings, emotions, desires, and your selfishness is not what your motive, motivation, and hidden agenda is. But in the end, that is what will eventually come out of the whole matter, something that satisfies you and your selfishness. Everything will begin to revolve around the "me-myself-and-I principle".

You will never see how he unveils and unfolds his sneak assault, attack, and assassination because he has got you and everyone in that room, in that meeting, and in that moment all worked up emotionally to the point and place where you and everyone involved have stepped away and is far away from right rational reasoning, and everyone is trying to prove their point.

With no one in the meeting, in the room, in the conversation listening or hearing each other nor is anyone paying any attention to what is really happening, Satan can get everyone emotionally entangled and emotionally entrapped in the moment and into their own hidden motive and unknown selfish reasons for being in the meeting and conversation. And then everyone is drawn, driven, pulled, pushed, persuaded and is being forced into the mode, mind-set, mental state of mind, mental frame of mind, and the mentality where they are locked, flowing and following in harmony with their fate-filled feelings. And from that point and place, they are tricked into trying to initiate and install their deadly, dangerous, damaging, and destructive desires.

Satan will then start suggesting and influencing you to say and do selfish, self-centered, self-righteous, and self-justified things. You and the person in that moment will be caught and then get caught up in the moment. The both of you will try to challenge and confront what is being said and done. When that do not work because Satan is really using that person and people to throw and drop unexpected, unplanned, unknown, unfair, unaware, unsure, word curses, reminders of your past mistakes that they supposedly had forgiven you of and they speak hurtful and spiteful words that have the impact of bombs when they hit you and when they are dropped on you, those are unforgettable, unexplainable, unthinkable, and unbelievable. Your selfish, self-centered, self-righteous, and self-justified reactions, responses, and reactionary responses automatically whisper to your selfish, self-centered, self-righteous, and self-justified urges, tendencies, inclinations, intuitions, and instincts saying, "defend yourself" because the person is becoming more offensive and defensive, and you do so.

What you have walked into in that moment when all of what I have just described is happening, occurring, and is going on is a compare-and-compete conspiracy theory in effect. It's happening so fast and real fast that you can't see it, feel it, and sense it. You have no knowledge of what's happening. Therefore, you can't and won't know how to (1) protect yourself, not defend yourself, and you won't know how to (2) prevent those word curses that have the impact of bombs that are being dropped on you from having any effect and affect on you. You won't know how to (3) position yourself in a spiritual posture so that you can prepare and present a right rational response and not a reaction or reactionary response.

Somewhere in our heart and in the back of our minds or somewhere in our conscience or place of awareness, we are consciously aware of what the Bible says, which are the following:

- "For though we walk, live in the flesh, we are not carrying on our warfare according to the flesh and using mere human weapons" (2 Corinthians 10:3–4).
- "For the weapons of our warfare are not physical weapons of flesh and blood, but they are mighty before God for the overthrow and destruction of strongholds" (2 Corinthians 10:3–4).
- "For we are not wrestling with flesh and blood, contending only with physical opponents, but against the despotisms, against the powers, against the master spirits who are the world rulers of this present darkness, against the spirit forces of wickedness in the heavenly, supernatural sphere" (Ephesians 6:12).

In order to be prosperous, productive, and successful at protecting yourself, your relationship, and those you share the relationship with, your heart, mind, and spirit have to be divinely organized, divinely structured, and in divine order. You will also have to maintain a high level of spiritual obedience. You have to be able to function freely in and out, yield, submit, and surrender to that high level of spiritual obedience, and you have to be free to flow in unselfish agreement with and follow the leading of God's voice in the person of the Holy Spirit. God knows exactly what weapons you will need in order to overpower, overtake, and overthrow the strategic designed compare-and-compete conspiracy theory.

Looking through the Windows of Respect and Reality

One of the most important things I have to tell you and hope, pray, and want you to see and know is Satan and all of his imps and cohort spirits have no love, appreciation, nor respect for you, your life, your love, your relationships, nor the persons or the people who share in those relationships of any kind and to any degree with you. You give Satan respect by not attributing what have gone wrong in your relationship and in your life to him and his behind-the-scenes work. You give Satan respect by not making yourself aware and knowledgeable of what he is and have been doing.

You give him the utmost respect when you do not (1) challenge his methods, principles, wiles, trickeries, schemes, devices, and deceptions, and you do not (2) confront your character, conduct, conversation and communication flaws, weaknesses, and inabilities, and, finally, you give him total respect when you do not, for whatever reasons, make the highly vital and necessary (3) unselfish change and adjustment within yourself and in how you go about being yourself on a day-to-day basis.

You wouldn't respect another person who has clearly demonstrated that he or she does not respect you, right? So why would you ignore and continue to allow yourself to be ignorant of the devil's life and relationship devices? Why would you continue to give respect to that foul spirit by not challenging and confronting him and his devious schemes through making the right personal, private, and public life and relationship change? You have the power and the authority to do so. Satan cannot overpower, overtake, and overthrow your human will and your power of choice without you giving him the right to do so.

You give Satan the right, the power, and the authority to do so when you yield, submit, and surrender to self-will and self-effort plans, principles, practices, and procedures that seem right, feel right, and look right but, in the end results, prove to be all wrong. The reality is you give respect to a demon spirit that does not like nor respect you. Now let us look into the widows of Satan's other compare-and-compete conspiracy theories.

A. **Compare conspiracy theory** is conduct, conversations, and communication that, when expressed, is deemed to be worthy of comparison, be held equal, and appear in a similar standing that is an evil, unlawful, treacherous, or surreptitious plan formulated in secret by two or more persons; a plot or an agreement by two or more persons to commit wrongful act against another *that is*, in reality, a supposition or a system of ideas intended to explain why they're expressed and demonstrated acts, actions, deeds, conversations, communication, etc.

Or it is conduct, conversations, and communication that, when expressed, is deemed to be worthy of comparison, be held equal, and appear in a similar standing that is evil, unlawful, treacherous, or surreptitious plan formulated in secret by two or more persons; that in its end results, it ends up *being* a plot or an agreement by two or more persons to commit a wrongful act(s) against another that is based on a set of *selfish, self-centered, self-righteous, self-justified* principles on which the practice of a relationship activity is based, and an idea is used to account for a relationship situation or justify a course of relationship action.

B. **Compete conspiracy theory** is conduct, conversations, and communication that is expressed for the purpose of trying to strive to outdo another for acknowledgment, a prize, supremacy, profit, etc., that is evil, unlawful, treacherous, and a surreptitious plan formulated in secret by two or more persons; plot or an agreement by two or more persons to commit a wrongful relationship act *that is*, in all actuality, a selfish, self-centered, self-righteous, self-justified supposition or a system of ideas intended to explain something, especially one based on general principles independent of the thing to be explained. Or it is a set of selfish, self-centered, self-righteous and self-justified conduct, conversation, and communication principles that, when expressed, is deemed to be worthy of comparison, be held equal, and appear in a similar standing that is evil, unlawful, treacherous, or surreptitious plan formulated in secret by two or more persons; that, when made manifest, clearly reveals it is a plot or an agreement by two or more persons to commit wrongful act(s) against another on which the practice of an activity is based and reveals the person's *selfish, self-centered, self-righteous, and self-justified* idea(s) used to account for a situation or justify a course of action.

C. **Compare curse theory** is urges, tendencies, inclinations, intuitions, and instincts that is deemed to be worthy of comparison, be held equal, and appear in a similar standing with the expression of a profane oath, an evil that has been invoked, a wish that causes misfortune, evil, doom, and trouble that befall a person *that is*, when it *unveils and it unfolds*, reveals it is nothing more than a *selfish, self-centered, self-righteous*, and *self-justified* supposition or a system of ideas intended to explain the cause and reason(s) for the curse, something, especially one based on general principles independent of the thing to be explained.

Or it is a set of urges, tendencies, inclinations, intuitions, and instincts principles on which the practice of a *self-willed* and *self-effort* conceived, birthed, driven, and motivated relationship activity is based, and a *selfish, self-centered, self-righteous*, and *self-justified* relationship idea used to account for a relationship situation or justify a course of relationship action.

D. **Compete curse theory** is urges, tendencies, inclinations, intuitions, and instincts that is deemed to be for the purpose of trying to strive to outdo another for acknowledgment, a prize, supremacy, profit, etc., that eventually can and will bring forth a profane oath, an evil that has been invoked, a wish that causes misfortune, evil, doom, and trouble that befall a person *that is* a *self-willed and self-effort*-led supposition or a system of ideas intended to explain something, especially one based on general principles independent of the thing to be explained that once it is *unveiled and it unfolds*, it cannot be mistaken for nothing more than something that is derived out of the person's selfish, self-centered, self-righteous, and self-justified mind and mind-set. Or it is a set of urges, tendencies, inclination, intuition, and instinct principles on which the practice of a *selfish, self-centered, self-righteous, self-justified* act, action, deed, and activity is based, that once it is *unveiled and it unfolds*, shows it is just an idea used to account for a *self-willed and self-effort*-filled situation or justify a course of action

Compare-and-Compete Conspiracy

What exactly is Satan's compare-and-compete conspiracy when it comes to your life, relationships, and when it comes to those who make up those relationships? A compare-and-compete conspiracy is an evil, unlawful, treacherous, or surreptitious demonically influenced and suggested relationship plan formulated in secret, in the unseen, in the unexpected, in the unplanned, in the unknown, in the unfair, in the unaware, in the uncertain, in the unnoticed, in the undetected by Satan and all of his cohort spirits for the evil purpose of committing a relationship crime, relationship fraud, or a wrongful relationship act that, when prosperous, productive, and successful, it will bring about a given relationship ending result.

The weapons Satan and all of his cohort spirits use to carry out the conspiracy against you, your relationships, and against all of those who are, have been, or desire to be in a fairy-tale or fantasy relationship with you is the weapons of compare and compete. The conspiracy consist of Satan using unlawful, treacherous, and surreptitious created compare-and-compete methods, moments, memories, techniques, words, images, information, instruction, ideas, inspirations, insights, and ingenuities that is unfolded and unveiled in a concurrent action or in a combination that will eventually bring about the result of overpowering, overtaking, and *overthrowing* your relationship. Not only does he use the method of unveiling and unfolding the unsure, unseen, unexpected, unplanned, unknown, unfair, unaware, uncertain, unnoticed, and undetected, but he also use the weapons of selfishness, self-centeredness, self-righteousness, and self-justification.

The way or manner in which Satan goes about unfolding and unveiling the compare-and-compete relationship conspiracy when he is out to hinder, hold hostage, hold up, distract, detour, delay, and deny you the right to have a prosperous, productive, and successful fairy-tale and fantasy relationship is to badger, bully, block, antagonize, agitate, aggravate, etc., your relationship mind, mind-set, thoughts, train of thought, thinking, way of thinking, your relationship mental state of mind, mental condition/conditioning, and mental frame of mind with unlawful, treacherous, surreptitious, predatory-spirited, unforgettable, unexplainable, unthinkable, and unbelievable compare-and-compete selfishness, self-centeredness, self-righteousness, and self-justification.

He uses the method of compare and compete when unveiling and unfolding the unsure, unseen, unexpected, unplanned, unknown, unfair, unaware, uncertain, unnoticed, and undetected in an unforgettable, unexplainable, unthinkable, and unbelievable that is in concurrence in action and released in a combination of ways and made manifest in and through your selfishness, self-centeredness, self-righteousness, and self-justification the moment when we once again open the door or allow ourselves to get over into handling relationship matters out of self-will and out of self-effort.

Satan's conspiracy when it comes to your relationship, your life, your ability to give love and receive love and when it comes to your fairy-tale and fantasy relationship belief is to overpower, overtake and overthrow it through the use of the spirit of compare and compete.

Compare-and-Compete Theory

Now that you know what Satan's compare-and-compete conspiracy is, let me tell you exactly what Satan's compare-and-compete theory is when it comes to your life, relationships, and those who make up those relationships. Satan's compare-and-compete theory is described as a coherent group of tested general relationship propositions that is commonly regarded as correct, that can be used as relationship principles, processes, procedures, and standards of relationship explanation and relationship prediction for a class of relationship phenomena.

The theory Satan uses when he is out to overtake and overthrow your relationship is to use a coherent group of tested general compare-and-compete-spirited propositions that is commonly regarded as satanically correct that can also be used as misguiding, misleading, and misdirected methods, plans, processes, procedures, and principles of relationship breakdown explanation and relationship breakdown prediction for a class of compare-and-compete relationship phenomena.

The theory that the spirit of compare and compete function, flow, and follow in the path of when it comes to your relationship is to use your self-will, self-performance, and your self-effort in helping cause, create the atmosphere, and contribute to ways in which it can unravel your relationship and then unfold and unveil a particular relationship conception or a view of your relationship and how it can take down, take over, and take out your relationship and how it is to be done and the method that will be used in doing it.

Please Remember

Conspiracy is defined as an evil, unlawful, treacherous, or a surreptitious plan formulated in secret by two or more persons; plot by a combination of persons for a secret or evil purpose.

Theory is defined as a supposition or a system of ideas intended to explain something, especially one based on general principles independent of the thing to be explained. Or it is a set of principles on which the practice of an activity is based and an idea used to account for a situation or justify a course of action.

A *conspiracy theory* is an explanatory proposition that
accuses two or more persons, a group, or an organization of
having caused or covered up, through secret planning and
deliberate action, an illegal or harmful event or situation.

The conspiracy is to (1) overpower you, your life, your relationships, and the persons and people who share in them with you, and then (2) overtake you, your life, your relationship(s) and the persons and the people who share in them with you and finally the conspiracy is to (3) overthrow you, your life, your relationships, and the persons or people who share in them with you. The method Satan uses is the systematic succession of strategic unveiling and unfolding of the unsure, unseen, unexpected, unplanned, unknown, unfair, unaware, uncertain, unnoticed, and undetected in a unforgettable, unexplainable, unthinkable, and in a unbelievable moment and time when we least expect it.

Satan and all of his imps and cohort spirits are highly wicked and volatile. They are demon spirits that specialize in and love initiating the element of surprise. So they have a predator's spirit, and they secretly lie in wait for the right moment when they can surprise, shock, and stun you to the point where your survival senses and survival sensitivity feel the urge, tendency, inclination, intuition, and instinct to take control and say and do things your way, handle matters your way, and make choices and decisions that you want to make, when, where, and how you want to make them. All of what I just describe comes out of, from, through self-will and through self-efforts.

There can also be a self-will and self-effort conspiracy theory. No matter what type of conspiracy theory there is and regardless as to which is used by Satan, they all will have a secret evil purpose, and the conspiracy itself will always have a set of selfish, self-centered, self-righteous, and self-justified principles assigned to them and attached to them that will be the foundational basis and power source in which the practice of a self-willed and self-effort activity is based.

Caught in the "Caught Up"

I want to caution you to be careful and to never leave room for compromise and to never get too contented, complacent, and in a comfort zone in your life, in your relationships, and in and with the people who make up your relationship(s). Be alert, beware, be well-balanced, be temperate, have a sober mind, don't be drunk on what you are getting out of your relationship, which may be that which you need and want. Don't allow yourself to get on such a relationship high that your spiritual senses, spiritual sensitivity, your spiritual guards, and spiritual awareness is let down or dulled.

I want to caution you and challenge you to be vigilant and cautious at all times. Why? For that enemy of yours, the devil, Satan, the one who opposes and hate real and right relationships, Christ centered and created relationships, the wicked one who roams, rule, and wreak havoc in the unseen, unexpected, unplanned, unknown, unfair, unaware, uncertain, undeniable, unsure. He is waiting for the moment when he and all of his host of demonic spirits can torture and torment your life, heart, dreams, faith, and mind with all of its capabilities and abilities.

He is waiting for the moment when he can gain access to your relationship(s) and gain access to those who are make up your relationships so that he can torture and torment and wreak havoc in your relationships with the unforgettable, unexplainable, unthinkable, and unbelievable. That is his mission, and that is the message he wants to send to you and to those you are in a relationship with. He opposes any type of relationship that he did not orchestrate and put together. He and all of his imps and cohort spirits are wicked in nature. They are highly volatile and very dangerous, and that is the mentality and mind-set of Satan, the master relationship deceiver. He wants to keep you blind, ignorant, and deceived when it comes to what he is at work in your relationship.

Satan is there, working behind the scenes of your life and relationships roaming like a lion and roaring in fierce hunger. He is seeking for someone, another life, love, and relationship that he can seize upon and devour (1 Peter 5:8). Satan is looking for any moment and every way he can seize and devour your life, love, and relationship(s) with a compare-and-compete curse conspiracy spirit. Satan and all of his wicked, trespassing, and violating spirits have a fierce hunger for the first thing God created in the Garden of Eden, which was and is relationships.

There are a lot of people in relationships that are caught like a prey in its captor's trap. They are caught in the compare-and-compete conspiracy curse, and they do not know how they got into it and how to get out. And there are those who, without their knowing it in most cases, are and have been caught up in the compete-compare conspiracy curse. They have been for a period, and they are being dominated, manipulated, and controlled with and by self-willed and self-effort urges, tendencies, inclinations, intuitions, and instincts. They have been and they are caught up in making bad and wrong choices and decisions, saying and doing the wrong things the wrong way and handling matters the wrong way. All of which seemingly is consistent in coming out of them no matter where they are, at times when they least or don't expect it, and no matter how hard they try to resist, reject, refute, and refuse not to do so.

When you are just caught in comparing and competing, you are not entangled and entrapped into comparing and competing, and you still have an opportunity, and you still stand a chance of getting yourself free before any real relationship hurt, harm, and damage is done. But when you are already, caught up in the trick, trap, and snare of comparing and competing, you are already entangled and entrapped in it, and it is going to take the power and presence of God to make and set you free from it.

A compare-and-compare spirit is one that your mind, mind-set, mental state of mind, mental condition, mental frame of mind, and your mentality is locked, chained, bound, limited, yoked, in bondage, and enslaved. Your thinking, way of thinking, thoughts, and your train of thought is consistently being conditioned with and, through compare-and-compete senses, being sent and eventually will end up being bombarded with compare-and-compete conspiracy cursed theory curses, compare-and-compete cursed conspiracy creativity, compare-and-compete cursed conspiracy theory cursed images, ideas, instructions, inspirations, information, insights, and ingenuity.

All of which Satan seduces and trick their mind into believing is truth and reality. The final mission, goal, and purpose Satan have for attacking and assaulting you with the spirit of compare and compete is to get you heavily into being a person that is compare-and-compete sensitive. He wants you to become and end up being a person of dangerous, deadly, destructive, and damaging poetic sensibility. He wants to link, connect, and tie all of your spiritual, physical, mental, and emotional senses to the compare-and-compete curse theory, and he wants to keep you consistently drawing all of your life, love, and relationship conclusions out of the compare-and-compete conspiracy. He wants to have the power to dominate, manipulate, and control how your mind and heart function and flow and what processes, principles, procedures, and standards you follow with compare-and-compete theories.

And as a result, your relationship(s), life, day, and years of your life can be, have been, and will continue to be plagued with seemingly uncontrollable, unseen, unexpected, unplanned, unknown, unfair, unaware, unsure, uncertain, undeniable, unforgettable, unexplainable, unthinkable, unbelievable, and at times overwhelming compare-and-compete-conspiracy-theory-led urges, tendencies, inclinations, intuitions, and instincts that have the power to take over and take control of the way you handle matters and will keep you handling relationship circumstances, situations, and confrontations out of your own way out of self-will and self-effort.

When you are caught up, your mind, mind-set, thoughts, train of thought, thinking, and way of thinking have been enticed and entangled, and your mental state of mind, mental frame of mind, mental conditioning, and mentality is and have been deeply entrapped in/ with/by compare-and-compete conspiracy cursed images, imaginations, instructions, and information. Thus, your reactions respond by having reactionary responses that your self-willed, self-effort urges, tendencies, inclinations, intuitions, and instincts interpret.

A person who is caught up in comparing and competing is living in and under the compare-and-compete curse, and without them really realizing it, they will begin speaking and expressing comparing and competing words that have become their cause because they have practiced doing so, and it is a part of their character, conduct, conversation, and it is how they communicate. To the point where they refuse to change or is having a hard time making a right change. It's sometimes hard to challenge and change something that have been a part of who you are and how you have been expressing yourself and how you have been tutored, trained, and taught by and through life, hurtful and painful circumstances, situations, confrontations, negative matters, negative moments and memories as the way to do so. The most dangerous thing that can happen to your mind is getting caught in a compare-and-compete conspiracy mode and compare-and-compete-conspiracy-theory way of functioning and flowing. It is important that you guard and protect your mind and all of its components, capabilities, and abilities caught and then get caught up in the compare-and-compete conversation and communication competition. If you do, your conversations and your communications will be corrupted conspiracy theories.

Compare-and-Compete Conspiracy Cause

To have or make compare and compete as your cause is to make it your principle, belief, idea, goal, aim, or movement. It is to make compare and compete your reason for doing or feeling something. Everything you do when it comes to your relationship will derive out of a compare-and-compete conspiracy mentality, and everything you feel will derive out of a compare-and-compete conspiracy theory mind-set. Because a deep commitment have grown, developed, and matured due to you having practiced compare-and-compete conspiracy theory standards, principles, processes, and procedures for so long, it has become your mind's production pattern. A compare-and-compete spirit will become the central thinking and thought pattern that your mind will consistently formulate, prepare, produce, and present conclusions out of.

And as a result, you are prepared to support, fight, and defend being compare-and-compete minded and compare-and-compete conspiracy theory minded. The next thing that will happen is your feelings, emotions, and desires will draw, drive, push, pull, persuade, and force your reactions, responses, reactionary responses, urges, tendencies, inclinations, intuitions, and instincts into being an advocate for it. Each time you do so, a curse comes because of the cause. What is that cursed cause? It opens the door for your character to be cursed, conduct to be cursed, conversation to be cursed, and communication to be cursed, and all will be filled with cursed words that tear down and not build up.

A modern-day example of what I am talking about is someone who easily gets into the mind-set and mentality where they go off on another person telling them off using comparing and competing conspiracy communication, conversations, and compare-and-compete conspiracy theory words. It doesn't take much for that person to get to that point and place where they easily do so, and they do not feel bad or feel like they are wrong when they do so.

Having a comparing and competing spirit and attitude brings a curse upon your character, conduct, conversations, communication, and choices and decisions, and it will also have profound effects and affects upon your life and relationships. People who are caught up in the compare-and-compete curse have basically accepted, adopted, and applied through and with their behavior and behavior patterns the compare-and-compete causes and curses that comes with it, and they keep causing, creating the atmosphere, and contributing to comparing and competing matters, moments, and memories.

The power of God is the own force that can and will break and destroy all compare-and-compete conduct, conversation, and communication yokes, strongholds, bondages, boundaries, and limitations curses. It cannot happen through human effort or through self-will nor can it happen through self-effort. It is important that you go to God and ask him to

> Deliver you from the desires, patterns, patterns of behavior, connections, ties, etc., of a spirit of a compare-and-compete curse;
> Cleanse and purge your character, conduct, conversations, and communication from being a slave to the suggestive influences of a compare-and-compete cursed cause;
> Heal you so you will not have any remaining residue left over from the compare-and-compete curse, and you will not have any residue left over from the nature of a compare-and-compete curse; and
> Make you whole so that no part of who you are, is, and will ever open to the spirit of compare and compete again.

Until you do so, every correct and right relationship choice and decision will continue to be hindered, held up, and held hostage to comparing and competing. It is important that you really pay attention to what is happening in your relationship, and do not allow it to get caught in the flow acts, actions, and deeds that can and will bring about a reason for a compare-and-compete conspiracy theory competition to be made manifest in it. Do not let what you have to say and do, the way you handle relationship matters, and the relationship choices and decisions you make end up being caught. It is something that you have been satanically set up for that brings about a compare-and-compete conspiracy theory competition effect or a compare-and-compete conspiracy theory competition result.

Captivated Cause(s) and Effect(s)

There is something that can and will happen the moment when a compare-and-compete spirit has its way in a relationship. It can and will have a powerfully profound negative effect and affect upon your integrity and intellect. When the spirit of compare and compete have captivated your *integrity*, Satan is using the broken lines of communication and the dangerous, deadly, destructive, and damaging conversation you and that person have been heavily indulging and engaging in as a way to attract and hold hostage your attention and your quality of being honest and having strong moral principles and moral uprightness.

When a compare-and-compete conspiracy is launched or raised against your integrity, it is a weapon and a secret plan Satan has formed to do something harmful or spiritually illegal against your quality of being honest and fair and against your state of being complete and whole. Satan does not want your mind, mind-set, mental state of mind, mental condition, mental frame of mind, and mentality to be strongly connected, yoked, bound, entangled, and entrapped to a firm adherence to a code of especially moral or artistic values.

The wile, scheme, and trickery of Satan is to find and use some type of deceptive and deceiving device as a way to attract and hold the attention of your spiritual, physical, mental, emotional need, want, desire, hope, dream, and even some kind of financial stability by making the spirit of compare and compete interesting, pretty, rewarding, fulfilling, prosperous, productive, successful, etc. He will use everything that look good, feel good, and feel right, but it's not a weapon. Every person that is close to you, every moment and memory that you have had as a method, motive, motivation and seduce, entice, trick, and deceive you into compromising with the spirit of compare and compete to the point where you are being strongly influenced and dominated by some what looks like a special charm, an art that is being in a compare-and compete-conspiracy-theory-competition mode has.

Satan wants you to think and feel that by having you a compare-and-compete trait. It will place or give you some kind of irresistible appeal. He also wants to get you so enticed, entangled, and entrapped in the spirit of compare and compete you will begin to think and feel you have an irresistible appeal because you have the compare and compete trait, compare-and-compete conspiracy trait and or the compare-and-compete conspiracy theory trait.

The moment when your cause is captivated or your reason for doing or feeling the right something when it comes to your relationship and when it comes to your reason for an action or condition that will bring about a right effect or right result when it comes to you being in a fairy-tale or fantasy relationship is compromised, the compare-and-compete theory or the compare-and-compete idea or set of compare-and-compete ideas that is intended or is used to explain the fairy-tale and fantasy relationships facts and the fairy-tale and fantasy relationship events is released, or they are restored, revived, revisited, and relived.

Satan deceptively takes the right relationship solution and idea that is suggested or presented as true and is possibly true, and he uses anything and anyone he can to challenge, confront, and change that possibly true solution and truth into an image where that solution and truth seemingly is not known or proven to be true. Therefore, the people in that relationship end up halt between two opinions or double minded and eventually blinded and begin to open themselves up to the general compare-and-compete principles or compare-and-compete ideas that relate to any particular relationship subject.

Once your integrity have been breached and compromised, the compare-and-compete curse spirit can and will have the freedom to dominate, control, and manipulate your choice and decision-making processes, procedures, and principles, forcing both into all types of unseen, unexpected, unplanned, unknown, unfair, unaware, unsure, uncertain, undeniable, unstable, unforgettable, unexplainable, unthinkable, and unbelievable circumstances, situations, and confrontations that, in the end, will endanger, damage, and harm the relationship and the people that are in that relationship.

It is at that point, Satan can and will have taken full advantage of your compromised and captivated integrity. When you are in a midst of a compare-and-compete conversation that has suddenly turned into a heated argument or confrontation, Satan will bring forth division, and he will then impair your mental state of mind, mental conditioning, and mental frame of mind so that you cannot and will not be open with the person. You are not being honest with the other person, and you will not be fair with them.

The compare-and-compete weapons you will use to fight with will not be fair ones. Your adherence to relationship codes and moral values will also be compromised and captivated, which will open the door for Satan to push and persuade you to leave the argument in the wrong mental state of mind, mental frame of mind, and mentality so that he can then seduce, suggest, influence, and lead you into getting so mad and upset that you leave the room and end up indulging in urges, tendencies, inclinations, intuitions, acts, actions, or deeds that you normally would not.

When you cannot and will not be honest and fair, you will not be strong enough to stand and be firm in your adherence to your relationship codes, standards, and principles. To have you compromise your relationship code, standards, and principles can and will open up the door for the spirit of compare and compete to manifest itself in and through your thoughts, train of thought, thinking, and thinking.

Captivated Intellect

The spirit of compare and compete will also have the power to captivate your *intellect* when you and that person are in disagreement, and your conversations and communication have turned into word weapons. When that happens, Satan has seized the opportunity to use you and the person you are in a relationship disagreement with, or he will use some other person that will be the one to start a compare-and-compete cursed conversation and communication. The cursed, corrupt, competitive, conspiracy-filled compare-and-compete conversation and communication that is introduced is done so for the reason of attracting and holding the attention or holding the interest of the person's power or faculty of the mind by which they are able to know or understand as distinguished from the power to feel and to will.

As that attraction and attention holding distracting, detouring, damaging, delaying, and denying demonic suggested and influenced compare-and-compete conversation and communication is going on, the power of the person's mind that is involved in the breakdown in conversation and communication and the faculty of their mind by which they are able to know or understand what the other person is trying to share, what is happening in the room and in the atmosphere, and what Satan have set them and their relationship up for is suddenly drawn, driven, pulled, pushed, persuaded, and forced into a satanic understanding yoke, a satanic understanding stronghold, and a satanic understanding bondage.

The person's mind and their ability to discern, decide, determine, and distinguish what is right and wrong understanding is being held in a satanic and demonic lock down. Compare and compete and relationship truth and reality is able to penetrate and give power to their understanding. As the heated conversations and communications continue and the person(s) are being heavily enticed, entangled, and entrapped in compare-an-compete words, the person's capacity for thinking and acquiring conduct, communication, and conversation knowledge, especially understanding that is of a high or complex order is severally hindered, damaged, and disconnected.

The Master Mental Manipulator

When the person's mental capacity, capabilities, and abilities have so many understanding boundaries and limitations and all is so halt between opinions, the person will not be able to know or understand as distinguished from that by which the person is not sure how they feel and that by which neither is not able to will. Satan is the master manipulator of your will and your feelings, emotions, and desires. He also can and will end up being the master manipulator of your intellect if you let him do so. Satan is out to use the two that are in disagreement to cause, create the atmosphere, and to contribute to ways in which he can distract, detour, delay, detain, or delay their understanding and to distract, detour, delay, detain, and delay their faculty of thinking and acquiring knowledge of a high complex, order, and mental capacity.

Satan wants to place a block, hinder, hold hostage, kill, steal, and destroy the capacity you have for relationship knowledge. He will challenge, confront, battle, and beat down your mind until he can break it. He does not what to have the freedom and the ability to think in a local way when it comes to your relationship. He wants to keep you in a mental state and in a mental frame of mind where you keep asking God, "Why me, why this, and Why us?"

That sounds like it's a good thing, right? It would be if the question is left open to receiving and applying the solution. But in this case, that is not what is happening. The one who is asking God the question "why me, why this, and why us" is so emotionally charged, and their feelings really tore up to the point they are not able to listen, hear, and fully comprehend what God is saying to them. They are not able to clearly articulate what he is saying because of a lot of emotionalism, and the person have been driven, drawn, pulled, pushed, persuaded, and forced too deep off into their personal feelings.

If he can break down your mind, your mental state of mind, your mental condition/conditioning, and your mental frame of mind and get you so full of compare-an-compete emotionalism and get you heavily into following your compare-and-compete-filled feelings, he will not be challenged and confronted when he steps in and begin the process of captivating your intellect. Being seduced, tricked, trapped, and under the suggestive influence of a compare-and-compete spirit will always severely impair your ability to become and end up being a very smart relationship person.

As a result, you will continue to experience and even encounter all types of relationship frustrations, discouragements, and disappointments. Your ability to accept, adopt, and apply God-given, power-packed relationship principles, processes, and procedures will continue to be met with compare-and-compete restrictions and restraints. Once your intellect is captivated, caught, and caught up, it is then held a captive because of compare-and-compete relationship restrictions and relationship restraints opening the door for relationship compromises. The other thing that happens when your intellect is captivated by, with, and because of compare-and-compete relationship restrictions and compare-and-compete relationship restraints is those restraints and restrictions will begin to flare up in your capacity for rational relationship or they will flare up in your capacity for relationship intelligent thought just like firewalls do in a computer.

This is especially the case when your capacity for rational relationship wisdom, knowledge, understanding, and capacity for relationship intelligence is highly developed. The good, the real, and the right that drives you and your relationship along with your relationship ambition and your relationship motivation will end up being stagnant or stalled. Please remember, all of what I just shared with you and what I have just exposed is a behind-the-scene satanic movement, and what I have shared and exposed is a revealing of his methods when it comes to his compare-and-compete setups.

Captivated Cause

Once Satan has set you and the other persons and the people in your relationship up for failure by using a compare-and-compete-curse-captivated intellect and integrity, he will then move into using a compare-and-compete curse spirit to captivate your *personal and private* relationship *cause*. A person who has a captivated relationship cause is someone who has not clearly recognized the reality that Satan is using and have used their corrupt compare-and-compete conversation and their corrupt compare-and-compete communication as a weapon and a way to attract the reason(s) and hold the attention or interest of a person and their heart and mind for good or sufficient reasons or motives they have for their human actions.

In other words, you and the persons and the people in your relationship have not only allowed yourselves to be captivated and then caught in a compare-and-compete conversation, communication, and conduct, but you have also allowed yourself to get caught up in a compare-and-compete conversation, communication, and conduct. You have opened yourself up to yielding, submitting, and surrendering to the way Satan will use your feelings, emotions, and desires as a way to seduce you into selfish, self-centered, self-righteous, and self-justified compare-and-compete principles, compare-and-compete ideals, compare-and-compete goals, or compare-and-compete movements.

As that happen, Satan will have you believing, feeling, and thinking you have or had good and sufficient reasons and motives for the way you acted while you were caught, and then you were caught up in your corrupt compare-and-compete conversation, communication, and conduct. He will have you believing, feeling, and thinking you had good and sufficient reasons for the atmosphere you help create and for the actions you demonstrated because they were for your personal welfare and not because of your selfish concerns.

Don't Get It Twisted

No matter what you do and no matter how strong of a person you may be, Satan will never respect you or your relationship(s). He is always working behind the scenes in your relationship. While you are asleep in your comfortable bed, he is walking around the outside of your home, and he is walking around your neighborhood, seeking out a way he can captivate you, contaminate your character, conduct, conversations, and communication and then bring about a corrupt cause by using compare-and-compete cursed methods.

CHAPTER SIXTEEN

When Opposites Attract

We say it or we have heard it said that opposites attract, but do we really know what it means? Some may think it means something like this: "I found out why opposites attract when I met you. It's because everything I'm not, you are, and the pieces fit together perfectly." This basically is the thinking behind that statement. The thought is a person is attracted to someone who is nothing like themselves or is totally the opposite. In everyday life, we see this theme played out in the lives of so many. For instance, he may be someone who loves rap music, and she may be someone who loves the opera.

They are different, totally the opposite, but they are in a relationship, or they are married, and they love each other. All of us are different in so many ways, and we are the same in a lot of ways. What is it that really attracts us to someone? Is it where we are different, or is it where we are the same? Is it our differences that is attracted to each other, or is it where we are the same that is attracted to each other? No matter which we choose to look for, where we are different or where we are the same, there is still some part of you that is the total opposite of the person you are or was in a relationship with. And it is that one little something that keeps you attracted to and in a relationship with that person.

The way we verbalize the opposite attraction is by saying, "I love the way he/she say and do that. It's different from the way I would say and do it." What exactly is it that we are drawn to when we choose relationship partners? We probably could debate that for a long time and still never come to a right or wrong conclusion. Most people actually look to be in a relationship with someone who is a lot or a little different from the way they are. Others look for someone who is a lot or a little the same as they are. A few people look for someone who is a little of one and a lot of the other.

No matter which we choose, there is something that drive, draw, push, pull, persuade, and at times, it seems like there is something that forces us into the path of someone we never ever thought or dreamed we would be in a relationship with. One may be tall; the other short. One may dress preppy, and the other may wear jeans with holes in them, yet they both have a somewhat-good relationship. It really depends upon what that opposite is that have attracted you to the person you are and have been in a relationship with. Society and the media have basically tried to dictate, determine, and decide who we are compatible with, and if and when we let them do that, they basically have taken the relationship power of choice right out of our hands. Society, the media, and our family and friends have stepped in and have told, suggested, or influenced us into a few, if not all, of the relationships we are or have been it.

We all have different things we look for in a person when we decide to get into a relationship. Our power of choice and our right to choose when we get into a covenant relationship with is the one thing Satan wants to take away from us. He is always behind the scenes, trying to suggest to us and trying to influence who we get into a relationship with. He never stops working, but we stop watching. For a moment, I want to get you to take a behind-the-scene look into those words, "opposites attract." I want to get you to take a look at those words from another perspective. I'm sure it is a perspective that you probably have never thought about nor have ever heard. Let me start by giving you some background history and set up the scene for the perspective that I am about to lead you into seeing.

The first scene: It was the beginning of time and the beginning of creation for your family and their bloodline. The *very first person* in your family's genealogy was about to come into this world. This first person would be the one who would set the standard and principles for how your family and all of its generations would live by. That very first person would be the one who would have your family's spiritual, physical, mental, emotional, character, conduct, conversation, communication, intellect, personality, etc., DNA in him or her. In that person's DNA would be all of the faults, failures, flaws, and weakness everyone in your family would have. Everything that has to do with you and your family would be found in this one person's genes, DNA, and bloodline.

The second scene: Satan wanted to get his hands on some genealogy, and he had to figure out a way to do so. In the beginning, when God was creating mankind, Satan did not have any access to man. So he had to find a way to have his say when it came to the creation of families and their generations, and he wanted to have his say when it came to determining what type of nature they would have. He found the one person who would give him access to your first family member, and that was through Eve, the moment she ate the forbidden fruit in the garden. That day and at that moment, Satan has gained access to mankind and to your first family member. In the Garden of Eden, there were no curses, sin of any kind, and there was no satanic and demonic presence or activity of any kind. Your family's generational bloodline was safe, secure, clear, and clean up until that moment.

The third scene: When Eve gave him access to the world's generational seeds, he took advantage of the opportunity. Now here is my version. I want you to see it real clear. Satan took out his syringe and needle that contained the curses he wanted to plague you and your families generations with, so before your very first family member was to be conceived, birthed, and born, Satan, working behind the scenes in the unseen and in the unknown, *injected* your first family member that was to be born into the *natural* realm with the curses he wanted your family to be plagued with. Once he was successful in injecting the generational curses, you now have in your bloodline, into your very first family member, your family's whole DNA that would be *infected*, and you and your family members would be *affected*.

Right after that injection was successfully administered, he stepped once again behind the scenes into unseen and into the unknown. He was successful in talking Eve into being disobedient by way of the serpent. That act not only opened man's eyes, made him wise, gave him the opportunity to be like God, knowing the difference between good and evil and blessing and calamity, but there was also a more *sinister* plan being unveiled and unfolded. Satan didn't have human beings under his command. He only had fallen angels (Revelation 12:7–12), so he had to find his way into the natural realm, and he had to position himself so he could gain access and enter into the bloodline, genes, and genealogy of man. Satan wanted to have his chance at tutoring, teaching, and training mankind and your very first family member his interpretation and definition of what it means to be like God. He also wanted to make sure mankind and your very first family member knew what his definition and version of them knowing good and evil and blessing and calamity was, is, and would be. Once that apple was eaten by Adam and Eve, Satan not only gained access to your family's generations, genealogy, and genes, but he also gained access to everyone else. Are you with me? Now let's make what I just shared with you real.

Satan the Puppet Master

We live our everyday lives just like we are puppets. Our choice and decision-making process and procedures are consistently dominated, manipulated, and controlled by images, instructions, and information that are injected into our minds, mind-set, your thinking, your way of thinking, your thoughts and your train of thought, mental state of mind, mental frame of mind, mental conditioning, and mentality. Everything for the most part in our everyday function and flow of life is sent directly or indirectly through some source of media.

Satan uses the media, games, anything, and anyone he can use to help suggest and influence our choice and decision making even when it comes to whom we covenant with in relationships. Everything about us and everything that have to do with us, Satan is behind the scenes, injecting, effecting, and affecting. He is behind the scenes using everything and everyone he can to help take away our *power of choice.*

Now before I go any further, let me state some questions that we need to focus on and examine and find answers to. As we go along, I am going to answer each question for you. The following are the questions:

1. What would you say is the other perspective, version, and behind-the-scene look into the phrase "opposites attract?"
2. Where did the phrase "opposites attract" come from?
3. What happens when opposites attract?
4. What do we really mean when we say "opposites attract?"

The fourth scene: Let's go back to the beginning of your bloodline, when your first created family member was in the creation place and was being created. The moment when Satan took out a syringe and needle and injected specific curses in your bloodline, he knew it would have an everlasting and eternal effect and affect upon your families bloodline, genes, and genealogy. He would be the one who would introduce what would be known as a generational curse. Once the curse was successful in being administered in your family's bloodline, Satan then stepped into the role of a puppet master, and he would, from that place, would begin to work his sinister, evil, and wicked plan to overpower, overtake, and overthrow your family and any relationships they would try to get into.

With Satan knowing your family's generational curses and the family generational curses of everyone and anyone you would get into a relationship with, he would send the phrase "opposites attract" into the earth realm through someone who thought it was a good way to explain why and how two people who really have nothing in common or maybe a few things in common could and would be attracted to each other. Sounds good and right so far, right? Maybe the intention of the first person who came up with that phrase thought it was good and right, but if you really look behind the scenes of what was said especially in relation to relationships, you will find that there was a deeper and a more significant meaning. Let me give you another insight into what was else was happening when that phrase was being birthed into the natural realm.

The fifth scene: We see someone that appeals to us, and for some reason we feel like we have to get to know that person. And after a certain period, we just feel like we have to have that person, and we want to be with that person in a relationship. Even though we really are not sure why we are drawn to that person, we still stay with them anyway. And even when we can sense there is something about that person, and we just can't put our finger on what it is that is really different almost in a mysterious way. We get into a relationship with that person anyway, and every now and then, we begin to see some things that have to do with that person or something they may say, do, and the way they handle certain matters, and some of the choices and decisions they make are a little awkward, strange, different, etc.

But even in spite of those things I just mentioned and many more you may start to see, there is also still something that keeps you attracted to that person. You and that person are as opposite as day and night, but you enjoy each other's company, etc. Over the course of time, you have learned to overlook the things about that person that is too opposite of the kind of person you are. So one day you and that person are engaged in what you see as a normal conversation. Nothing out of the ordinary has happened. Or maybe there is something you feel is important that you want to share with that person or talk to that person about.

You and that person start talking in a normal tone, and before you know, it the spirit of compare and compete has gained access to the conversation, and you and that person have engaged into a heated argument. And before you know it, that person or you have said and done something that you never had said and or done or imagined you or that other person would ever say or do to each other. You and that person are shocked and stunned, and you are experiencing hurt, and you are in some kind of pain.

The sixth scene: What happened and why? Satan working behind the scenes of your relationship already knew the generational curses that would be and still is in your family, and he knew the generational curses that would be and still is in the other person's family. And those generational curses in your family and the ones in the other person were not the same. They were the opposite. How and why you and that person met had to do with those family generational curses. Satan was behind the scenes, and he knew just what it would take to get you and that person with opposite generational family curses to meet. And so he set things in motion with your help, the other persons, and maybe with the help of some others. No matter how you and that person met, the attraction, meeting, and connection was made.

But what really drew you, pulled you, pushed you, persuaded you, or forced you into the path of that opposite person was the opposite family generational curses from your family and the generational curses from that of the other person's. Here's an *example*: if you are female and in your family generational cursed bloodline Satan has injected a being battered curse. You can look back into your family history and see where all or most of the women in your family have been battered. It may have skipped a generation of women and landed on you and in your generation. So you are with the person you have or had an opposite attraction to and in his family generational cursed bloodline Satan had injected being a batterer in his bloodline.

It was information you nor that person didn't have any knowledge of. Or maybe you heard of or had seen certain family members going through being battered, or one of your family members was the batterer, and you overlooked it, and you looked at it as just their problem.

The seventh scene: So what was in your generational bloodline and what was in his or hers was attracted to each other. If they were the same, they would have rejected, resisted, and refused each other. Just like two magnets have to attract at opposite ends, so do family generational curses. Just like the negative end of a magnet is attracted to the positive end of a magnet, the same applies to family generational curses. The family generational curses that is in your bloodline is attracted to and attach themselves to another person's family generational curses that's not like itself or they are not like yours. Another way for you to see this picture clearly is the bad-negative in your inherited family generational curses attracted the bad-positive in the other person's inherited family generational curses. So you have the inherited generational curse of being battered attracted to the inherited generational curse of being a batterer. Because you were so caught by the outer look of that person and then you got caught up in the relationship and in the person you did not inquire into the other person's family history to find out what type of generational curses they inherited.

The attraction has to be based on one person's generational curses being stronger and more dominant, manipulating, and controlling than that of the other persons. The other person's inherited generational curses have to be of a weaker pedigree that is easily dominated, manipulated, and controlled. That weaker person may be one who procrastinate, hesitate, one who question themselves and God and second-guess a lot. Another example would be a strong drug user being involved with a non-drug user. The non-drug user family members have a history of people in their family getting involved with someone who is the opposite from them, and they, one day, end of saying, doing, and acting like the person they are nothing like or they are the total opposite of.

You really wanted to be with that person to the point that you did not pay attention to what was right in front of your eyes. There were times when you were around their family and saw certain negative things being said, done and handled and sometimes you heard some of the other persons family members you were in a relationship with talking about their family and some things that was going on with them and you didn't pay any attention or you chose to ignore what you were seeing and hearing. When your relationship started to change or collapse and the bad, wrong, hurt, pain, and brokenness was the end result, no matter if it was verbal or physical, you had a chance to look into that person's family generational curses. Someone from that other person's family you had met would have told you what type of generational curses existed in their family if you would have taken the time to ask.

The eighth scene: So you are attracted to that person, and you are in that relationship, and things are going good. You didn't know it, but it was your family and the other person's family generational curses that really made and had the attraction. As the relationship goes on, that attraction turns into something that is dangerous, destructive, and damaging. That attraction turns into a connection. Which means no matter what either one of you say and do to the other that is hurtful, painful, and brings brokenness, you manage to work things out, and you and that person somehow end up back together. Why? It's because both you and that person that's in the relationship opposite family generational curses were attracted, and then they got connected, and that is when the unseen and unknown chaos and confusion started brewing. Once connected, those two opposite attracted generational curses in both of you was set by Satan on a course where they would collide with each other.

It was the connection that brought and would bring about the curses colliding. What you have to see, know, and understand is Satan know what family generational relationship curses you inherited, and he knows the same about the person(s) you are or is still in a covenant relationship with because he was the one who injected, if you will, your first family member with them. Satan knows your generational curses and he knows the generational curses of the person(s) you have been in a relationship with and he knows they are not the same, and that is the only way they can collide. So the opposite attraction brought about the connection and the connection will be that which will and shall bring about the character collision, conduct collision, conversation collision, and communication collision. Whenever something goes really wrong in a relationship, it is because the opposite generational curses have collided.

Curse Collision Course

What happens when both opposite-attracted and connected family-inherited generational curses collide? When that collision happens, it often ends up producing a lot of collateral damage, and that type of damage is the hardest of all to repair and restore. Just imagine two vehicles traveling at a very high rate of speed headed straight toward each other with no letting up on speed. When the curse collision happens, both people in the relationship are so hurt, and they are experiencing so much pain and brokenness that they spend a lot of time to themselves usually trying to find the reason(s) to explain what happened, and they are looking for the cause of the collision. While they are doing this, they are also trying to find their way back to where they were before the collision occurred.

My point is, behind the scenes of any and all relationships, Satan is at work making sure the opposites in both of your generational curses are attracted to each other, and at some place point and time, they end up colliding. There are a lot of things happening behind the scenes when it comes to relationships that the human eye cannot see and cannot hear. It is very important that when you decide to get into a covenant relationship with someone you know, the other person's family history, you know what type of generational curses is in their bloodline so you will know how to plan and prepare for a relationship with that person.

When the opposites in your inherited generational curses and the inherited opposite generational curses in the other person is attracted to each other and then that opposite connection is made, it is just like two opposite attracted magnets that are forcefully pulled, persuaded, drawn, and driven to each other. The attraction is a strong one and will take a lot of human strength, depending on the size of the magnets, to pull them away from each other. That is the way those generational curses are when they are attracted to each other and they get connected.

It will take a lot to pull those two people apart because the generational curse attraction and the generational curse connection or bond is so strong. So much so that the people in the relationship have a hard time staying away from each other even when the relationship curse collision brought about an unseen, unexpected, unplanned, uncertain, undeniable, unknown, unfair, and unaware surprise. What is left from those curse collisions are two people who are left with an unsure, unforgettable, unexplainable unthinkable, and unbelievable moment and memory of what happened that is so shocking and stunning that neither one can fully recall how the curse collision happened. That is because they both did not have the knowledge and the understanding of how powerful, dangerous, damaging, destructive, and demoralizing generational curse are.

Generational curses are volatile in nature, and they are potent, and they are loaded with enough venom to kill, steal, and destroy even the strongest of relationships. When one or both persons in that relationship yield, submit, and surrender any part or all of their will to the generational curses they inherited, Satan uses those family generational curses as a weapon and a tool he can use to get the persons and the people in that relationship over into self-effort motives, self-effort motivation, and into self-effort hidden agendas. Satan is always trying to find ways to exploit and bring a damaging, dangerous, and destructive explosion in our relationships.

He knows the generational curses that he has injected in our family generational character, personality, integrity, intellect, images, imagination, and generational instructions that we receive. Every time we are being enticed with the belief that we will get some kind of entitlement of any kind, Satan will always be the one who will suggest, influence, and place that desire within us to pursue that desired entitlement because he has set us up to bring about entanglement and entrapment. If we do not challenge those curses and then change our course and correct our cause, we will end up caught and then caught up in a vicious-cycled opposite-attracting generational curse experiences and encounters.

The other thing that happens is the person who has the strongest generational cursed gene is always attracted to someone who has a weaker generational cursed gene. We have to stop allowing ourselves to become, be, and end up being puppets for Satan, who is the puppet master. And because he is the puppet master and he knows our family generational curses, he is always working to get us over into our generational cursed feelings, emotions, and desires because they are also his puppets that he can and will dominate, manipulate, control, and maneuver.

You Can't See for Looking

Now you know why you and that person you were/are in a relationship with had a strong attraction to each other, and you ended up getting into a relationship with them. What you have to understand is one day, without you or that person expecting or knowing it and without any advance warning, you and that person can and will end up having a conduct collision, conversation collision, and communication collision, and that collision could and will end up causing some type of physical, mental, emotional, or relationship hurt, harm, or danger. It is really important that you not allow yourself to get caught and caught up in the generational curse game.

You cannot and will not win when you play that game. I want you to also remember Satan is always working behind the scenes in your relationship, and he is going to make sure your inherited family generational curses that isn't the same as the person you were/are in the relationship with end up colliding and exploding, bringing about all kinds of relationship damage. This is a fact, and you must face this fact. It doesn't matter how good things may be going in your relationship thus far. Satan is always relentless in his endeavor to make sure the totally opposites in every person's relationship, character, personality, integrity, intellect, images, imagination, interpretation of instructions, principles, processes, and procedures find a common cause connection.

You and that person's inherited family generational curses are seemingly and correctly connected, and for a period, things between you and the person whose inherited family generational curses that was the opposite of yours was going really good. Both of you were having fun and getting what you felt and knew you needed out of each other and out of a relationship. It was a fairy-tale and fantasy relationship that came true. It was all good, and you proudly displayed your relationship with that other person for all to see. You and that person knew the both of you were really the opposite in a lot of ways. You knew you were the opposite even in your mind-sets, thinking, way of thinking, thoughts, and train of thought.

But it really wasn't something that neither one of you were really concerned with as long as your relationship was working like you hoped and prayed it would. When you saw some displayed acts, actions, deeds, behaviors, and behavior patterns that were the opposite of yours, you knew that your mental state of mind, mental frame of mind, and mentality was the opposite from the other person you were fellowshipping with, friends with, married to, and in a covenant relationship with. But you didn't think much of it and tolerated it even though at times you got agitated and aggravated.

Sure, there might be some good opposite attracting human being relationships that work. When they do it is often because both people in that relationship

(1) have learned about the things I am sharing with you in this book, and they have accepted, adopted, and applied the solutions, principles, process, and procedures they have learned or that I have outlined

(2) work hard on eliminating any and all type of satanic and demonic interference because they are always consciously aware of the reality that Satan will consistently try to find ways to get into their relationship or try to find ways to get to one or both of them and

(3) have a high tolerance level for the things they do not like nor appreciate that shows up in their relationships In this case, a lot of sweeping things under the carpet takes place, or one or both have low relationship expectations, and one or both have a passive personality

I'm not talking about the kind of relationships and attractions that are stated above. Those are exceptions to the rule relationships. I am talking about the attraction that your family generational curses and the other person's family generational curses have that is the opposite, and they are a damaging, dangerous, destructive, and demoralizing opposite attractions that Satan has set you and the other person up without you even knowing it. Satan secretly matched your opposite generational curses in the unseen and in the unknown when your first family member was not even a thought. The day when your first family member became a thought in the mind of whomever the opposite other person would be that would help in bringing him or her into this world, Satan was instrumental in making sure he (a) matched the two opposite generational curses that was in the both of them, he (b) matched how and what would attract them to each other, he (c) matched when and where those opposite generational curses would meet so that they could and would get attracted to each other, and Satan (d) matched who would be the other person that would have the other attracted-opposite generational curse seed within them and in their family generational cursed bloodline.

My point is, long before your first family member was even conceived, birthed, and born and long before your very first family member became an embryo and a fetus, the opposite-attraction generational curse appeal was placed within them. When your first family member was actually born into this world, they were born with your family generational curse within them, and they were born with the opposite gene that would attract and then attach itself to the other generational cursed opposite-attracting match. Why is it that we don't know about this behind-the-scene working of Satan?

The Answer to the Question

There are four main reasons why you do not know about Satan working behind the scenes of your relationship, and they are the following:

(1) The puppet master, your adversary, the one who hate you and your life and relationships and all those who are in covenant with you. He is the God of this world, and because of that, he wants to keep you in a state, mind-set, and mentality where you have a worldly view of your relationship.

(2) He has blinded your unbelieving minds to what I am sharing with you about your life, yourself, and your relationships.

(3) He wants to make sure you do not discern the truth when it comes to what's been hindering and holding your relationship back. He knows if you are able to discern, it will make and set you free to war a good warfare against whatever is hindering and holding your relationship back.

(4) He wants to make sure you do not remove whatever it is that is preventing you from seeing the illuminated relationship light.

The truth is, your life and your relationships are supposed to be lived in, out, through, and in accordance and in agreement with the manifested revealed Gospel of the glory of Christ, who is the image and likeness of God. Are you still struggling to see what I'm sharing with you?

If so, you can't see for looking! Your mind had been blinded up until you read this book. And Satan wants to keep you locked into being an unbeliever of this opposite attraction inherited family generational curse truth so that you cannot see the illuminated opposite attraction generational curse relationship light. It all comes down to you having eyes, and you cannot see with them. You have ears, and you still do not, have not, and cannot hear and perceive and understand the compare-and-compete, opposite-attract generational curse sense that I have been sharing with you.

Satan wants to keep getting the advantage over you, over your life, over your relationships, and over those who are or have been in relationships with you. He want to keep being the puppet master, and he wants our lives and our relationships to be his puppets so that he can easily dominate, manipulate, control, kill, steal, destroy, damage, and bring all types of hurt, pain, and brokenness into them. You need not reject, resist, and refuse to acknowledge, accept, adopt, and apply what I am sharing with you in this book. If you choose to do so, you will not continue to be ignorant of his opposite attraction generational relationship curse wiles, trickeries, devices, deceptions, and intentions.

Where Did the Term "Opposites Attract" Come From?

The term is derived from the nature of magnetism. When you hold two magnets together and you try to put the two ends that have the same matching poles together, either positive or negative, they will repel each other. The reason is it's because they have the same pole, either positive or negative. But when you put opposite poles together, a negative pole and a positive pole… they attract. Hence, opposites attract.

CHAPTER SEVENTEEN

Twisted Thinking

It's hard to believe that there are those who believe, expect, think, feel, and would even go as far as to say they know something wrong is going to happen in their relationship. In fact, they will spend a lot of their time expecting and waiting for something to go wrong. It's true. I know it sounds really unreal, but it's absolutely true. It's hard for someone who thinks and feels like they won't ever be happy to believe they can and will be in a good, strong, healthy relationship where they are getting everything they need and even want and nothing major or relationship threatening happens. If something bad or something negative do not happen within a certain time frame, that person starts feeling urges, have tendencies, and inclinations, and, out of intuition and out of pure instinct, will begin to cause, create the atmosphere, and contribute to something going wrong.

The tools they use to bring about something going wrong in that relationship is always the destructive weaponry tool of selfishness, self-centeredness, self-righteousness, self-justification, self-will, and self-effort. Those who have this type of mind, mind-set, thoughts, train of thought, thinking, and way of thinking have tutored, trained, and taught their mental state of mind and mental frame of mind to easily accept, adopt, and adapt and even live with something going wrong. People who have this kind of mentality are also individuals that cannot handle nor accept being in a relationship where things go right, but they can accept being in a relationship where things go wrong.

In fact, people who have been conditioned to be in this type of mode impatiently wait for and expect the negative unseen, unexpected, unplanned, uncertain, unknown, unfair, unaware, unsure, undeniable, unexplainable, unforgettable, unexplainable unthinkable, and unbelievable to show up; and when those negatives do show up, the person knows how to conduct themselves and abide within the flow of those negatives.

They also know how to work in agreement and in direct harmony with those negatives. I have seen it firsthand, and I am giving you a personal account of what I actually witnessed. When I first met a person who thought and felt like that, at first I thought they just needed someone who spoke positive things and would speak positive things into their life and day, and they just needed to be around positive people. I wanted to be that positive person that would help take away all of the negatives they had been tutored, trained, and taught to accept, adopt, and adapt over the course of their life. After hearing and seeing how they went about life and living and after listening to their conversation and how they communicate and watching how they went about being themselves, I quickly recognized and then realized I had met someone who really expected and believed something bad or negative was going to happen in any relationship they would get involved in. I was shocked, stunned, and really taken by surprise. It's really hard to believe that there are people who actually function and flow better when there is chaos, confusion, and drama going on in their relationships. The more chaos, confusion, and drama that would be going on in their relationships, the better they were are at functioning and flowing in that relationship. The other thing I noticed was when there was no chaos, confusion, and drama going on, that person acted like they were a fish that was out of water. People who think like that can only exist in that relationship for a short period before they get uncomfortable and begin to demonstrate a nervous like reaction.

How did they get into that kind of mind-set, mental state of mind, mental condition, and mental frame of mind? How and why did they end up adopting, accepting, and adapting to a "something have to go wrong, be wrong with this relationship?" How and why did they allow themselves to be seduced, tricked, trapped, deceived, led, enticed, entangled and entrapped into a "this is just too good to be true and this has never happened to me before," in a relationship mind-set and mentality?

3T Stimuli

In order for me to answer the questions I asked, I have to take you on a journey. Long before that person met you, they were in an abusive relationship where they were being spiritually, physically, mentally, emotionally violated and sexually abused and molested. They were being battered, neglected, rejected, used, taken advantage, taken for granted, and made to feel like they were insignificant and unimportant, and they don't matter. All of what I just described and much more may have come at the hands of family member(s), friends, neighbors, mentors, enemies, or someone they trusted, looked up, or were in some kind of relationship(s) with.

Satan was behind the scenes of that person's life and relationship using the person and those people they felt they trusted and could confide in to basically say and do whatever it was that was said and done to them. They willingly participated in saying and doing what Satan had put in their minds and in their lust-filled, selfish-appetite-driven desires to do to the person you are with. At the time when they were being targeted for the negative things that happened to them, they may or may not have been an innocent target. No matter which happened, the person you are in a relationship with or you just met, it was their first painful and hurtful experience.

They either got away from the violator, abuser, and batterer so it would not happen again, or they stayed and suffered through more of the same until it would break their spirit, kill their will to win, steal their drive and motivation, and destroy their self-worth, self-confidence, and self-esteem. For the person who feels he or she got away from the abuse when it first happened, that was a good move; but if that person don't seek out and get spiritual, physical, mental, and emotional deliverance, cleansing, purging, and healing so that they can be made whole, the I've-been-abused-battered-neglected-etc. spirit lies dormant in them. It's still there because they are running from what has happened to them. They feel so ashamed that they, without knowing it, begin to protect what happened to them so that others cannot see, hear, nor gain any knowledge of what happened to them, and they have not confronted and dealt with it.

As a result, the spirit that attracts them to the people Satan have control over that is locked in those vicious cycles, or it may be someone he is trying to force into a vicious cycles, do not know, haven't recognized or realize that spirit is still lying dormant within them. They keep running from place to place, relationship to relationship, and not confronting, dealing, getting completely delivered, and then cleansed and purged and then healed and finally made whole from all of what happened. The spirit of what happened to them and the moment and the memory of it all or the residue from what took place is still inside of them. In order for that person to receive freedom and victory over it all, they have to speak and exercise total forgiveness and confront and face their fears and flaws with faith as their weapon. Forgiveness and faith are the only two weapons that can be used that can and will defeat the spirit of the memory, the spirit of that moment, and the symptoms that moment brought about.

You can be a runner or one who tries to pretend like it never happened, etc., or you can be one who tries to block out what happened to you. Whatever bad and wrong you have suffered through that keeps showing up in your life and day is a family generational curse. It is something that is right out of your genealogy, or it is something that is right out of the genealogy of the one who was the abuser, batterer, and violator. When you met that person, you were either a magnetic attraction for what was lying dormant in them, or you were just a target, and you became the target. When you have a badgering and bullying generational curse spirit pursuing after you, the worst thing and the wrong thing to do is to run from it, try to hide from it, and try to avoid a head-on collision with that spirit.

You are not dealing with some amateur, lazy spirit. I hope you can clearly see what it is that Satan does not want you to see and how he wants to keep your mind, mind-set, thinking, way of thinking, thoughts, train of thought, mental state of mind, mental frame of mind, mental condition, and mentality drawn, driven, pulled, pushed, persuaded, seduced, enticed, yoked, in bondage, enslaved, in a stronghold, and limited because of you having adopted, accepted, and adapted, and you have been applying a twisted way of thinking.

That spirit will stay in hot pursuit of you, and it will not give up nor give in until it has cornered you in a relationship and have used your past or some part of you to stir up the wrong things in the person you are with. Don't set your own self up for failure, stand up, face your fear, fight it with your faith, and fight the feelings, emotions, desires, urge, tendency, inclination, intuition, and the instinct to be a target and or a carrier of an abuser and abused person's spirit. The spirit you are running from is going to find a way to corner you, captivate you, and then it will finally capture you.

Make sure you don't set yourself up for abuse, neglect, being battered, molested, being deceived and then tricked and trapped into the wrong type of activity, corrupt conversation, and communication that will bring you hurt, harm, danger, cause you to be taken advantage, be taken for granted, used, be broken, cause you to change your right behavior patterns, conduct, conversation, way of communication, and your right way of thinking. To be honest, most of the time we are our own worst enemies.

When we look into the life, heart, spirit, mind-set, mental state of mind, mental frame of mind, mental condition, and mentality of a person who feels uncomfortable, unsettled, and unnerved when they are in a relationship that they can finally feel safe and secure in, and it is one that is strong and stable, we see a person whom the spirit of fear is tormenting, torturing, reigning, ruling, dominating, manipulating, and controlling their self-confidence, self-esteem, and self-control. We see a person who cannot and is not able to live their life. The only thing they are able to do and the only thing they know is to exist in their very own life and stay in a survival mode. The wounds, scars, and bruises they have are deep, painful, and very much so personal and private. This is even more so true if what they have suffered through was played out in public. Now let me answer the questions that I asked you earlier, which were the following:

1. Why do people end up thinking they can only exist in a relationship for a short period before they get uncomfortable and demonstrate a nervous reaction?
2. How do they get into that kind of mind-set and metal state of mind, mental condition and mental frame of mind?
3. How and why did they end up adopting, accepting, and adapting to a something-have-to-go-wrong-be-wrong-with-this-relationship, this-is-just-too-good-to-be-true, this-has-never-happened-to-me-before mentality?

The answer is they have been indoctrinated with and have accepted, adopted, adapted and have applied the 3T stimuli. A stimuli or stimulus is something that excites an organism or part of a functional activity. In the case of those who get over into the mode and mind-set where they believe, expect, think, feel, know, anticipate, and wait for something to go wrong in their relationship along with number's 1, 2, and 3 above, all is due to the first person Satan used to break their spirit and their heart and wound them deeply, batter, violate, neglect, reject, degrade, etc., them. That person ended up being the one who tutored, trained, and taught (3T) them to be in that mode and mind-set on a consistent basis.

That person Satan used to kill, steal, and destroy your drive, ambition, motivation, will to win, self-confidence, self-esteem, faith, hope, belief, and confidence kill, steal, and destroy some part of the person you are involved with, in a relationship with, etc. Whatever sick and twisted demonic methods, tactics, wiles, trickeries, schemes, delusions, deceptions, distractions, and devices that the first person in the life of the person you are in a relationship with used worked to satanic perfection.

Why would I say this? Whenever you get into a new relationship or maybe you are already in a new relationship, whatever survival mode, mind-set, reactions, survival mind-set, fear mode, fear mind-set, and fear and survival mentality you were tutored, trained, and taught to get into when you were in the very first abusive relationship you were in, it is the same mode and mind-set you bring or have brought into a new relationship. You have been tutored, trained, and taught how to get into, how to flow with, how to follow, how to work in agreement with, etc., a twisted way of thinking.

Let me dig a little deeper. Remember a stimuli or stimulus is that *something* that incites to action or exertion or quickens action, feeling, thought, etc., something that excites an *organism* or part to *functional activity*. Let me break it down for you.

- That *something* would be whatever it was that Satan suggested and influenced the first person in your life who hurt you to bring you pain, brokenness, deceive you, abandon you, batter you, rape you, verbally abuse you, etc.
- An *organism* is defined as any living thing. The living thing in reference to what we are talking about would be your survival mode, self-effort mode, selfish mode, your enticed, entangled,

and entrapped urges, tendencies, inclinations, intuitions, and instincts.

- Your *functional activity* would be described as the way you react/reactions, respond/responses, your acts, actions, deeds, choices, and decisions, the way you say, do, and handle things, your moods, feelings, and emotions.

Let me dig just a little deeper: Satan suggested and influenced the first person in your life who hurt you and brought you pain and brokenness to use deceiving you, abandoning you, battering you, raping you, verbally abusing you, neglecting you, molesting you, etc., as that something that will always incite to action, quicken an action, feeling, thought, etc., and excite an organism within you.

Once that happened, Satan would then use deceiving you, abandoning you, battering you, raping you, verbally abusing you, neglecting you, molesting you, etc., as that something that would not fail in inciting to action, quickening an action, feeling, thought, etc., and exciting your survival mode, self-effort mode, selfish mode, your enticed, entangled, and entrapped urges, tendencies, inclinations, intuitions, and instincts.

After that took place, Satan would then use deceiving you, abandoning you, battering you, raping you, verbally abusing you, neglecting you, molesting you, etc., as that something that would consistently incite to action, quicken an action, feeling, thought, etc., and excite the way you react, respond, your acts, actions, deeds, choices, and decisions, the way you say, do, and handle things, your moods, feelings, and emotions.

3T Stimuli Views

View number 1: Satan suggested and influenced the first person in your life who hurt you, who brought you pain and brokenness to use deceiving you, abandoning you, battering you, raping you, verbally abusing you, neglecting you, molesting you, etc., as that something that will always incite to action, quicken an action, feeling, thought, etc., and excite your self-performance mode, self-will mode, survival mode, self-effort mode, selfish mode, survivor patterns, survivor behavior patterns, excite your enticed, entangled, and entrapped urges, tendencies, inclinations, intuitions, and instincts, and it would be that which would excite the way you react, respond, your acts, actions, deeds, choices, and decisions, the way you say, do, and handle things, your moods, feelings, and emotions.

View number 2: With that being said, the part(s) of you Satan want to tutor, train, and teach (3T) to be attracted, accept, adopt, adapt, and apply the 3T stimuli principles, processes, and procedures as its function, flow, and the pattern it would follow was and is your mind, mind-set, mental state of mind, mental condition, mental frame of mind, and mentality. He wanted to tutor, teach, and train them to be attracted, accept, adopt, adapt to you being deceived, you being abandoned, you being battered, you being raped, you being verbally abused, you being abused, you being neglected, you being molested, etc., as the method and the motivator that would constantly and consistently, without failing, used that would incite to a negative, bad and wrong action, quicken a negative, bad and wrong action, feeling, thought, etc., and would excite your survival mode, self-effort mode, selfish mode, your survival patterns, survival pattern of behavior, your enticed, entangled, and entrapped urges, tendencies, inclinations, intuitions, and instincts and excite the way you react, respond, your acts, actions, deeds, choices, and decisions, the way you say, do, and handle things, your moods, feelings, and emotions.

Setup for the Stimuli

Long before you and the person you are in a relationship/marriage with was born, met, was attracted to each other, decided to get together, decided to get to know each other, decided to do whatever it was that you did and you then got into a relationship, Satan wanted to make sure he had access to messing up your life, dreams, hopes, desires, fairy-tale and fantasy relationship belief, faith, and confidence. So he, working behind the scenes of your life and relationships before you stepped into them, came up with the 3T stimuli/stimulus plan, syndrome, illness, patterns, behavior patterns, behavior, process, procedure, and principle. From that day forward, he began trying to set you up for the stimuli.

He had the stimuli/stimulus, he had the stimuli plan, stimuli syndrome, stimuli illness, stimuli process, stimuli procedure, stimuli pattern, stimuli pattern of behavior, and stimuli/stimulus principle, but what he didn't have was a person who would be the carrier, instigator, initiator, and the one who he could use to inject the stimuli. He had to come up with a way and a method that he could use that would not be highly noticeable and recognizable but could quickly be damaging, destructive, and would bring about instant deception, depression, delusions, and would even bring about a person being disoriented to the point of being self-destructive.

The day when he was in the Garden of Eden in the form of the serpent and he saw the selfish desires that was inside of Eve, he then knew he had found a way to get his stimuli into mankind. He approached Eve and told her what was her desire was even before she had a chance to verbalize it herself (Genesis 3:1–2). But when he did so, he twisted her selfish desire so that it sounded good and right to her; but all along, he was going to steal her selfishness and twist it so it would fit his devious stimuli plan. Eve took the bait and ate, and then she helped Satan gain access to Adam when she got Adam to eat the apple. That fall in the Garden of Eden is what Satan needed in order to use and get man to fail in his relationships. Satan then would inject, if you will, every generation of mankind with a curse.

He had his man, and he had his motive. He had his motivation, and when he and one-third of the angels were kicked out of heaven, he entered into his madness mode. And the last thing he did was come up with a method. The method he would use since he had access to man was to get him into a twisted way of thinking when it came to the power and the authority he had. He knew he couldn't really get to him and suggest and influence him into using his power and authority in a twisted way, so he once again went to the one person he knew he could count on that would get man into abusing his power and authority. That one person would be his comrade and coconspirator—Eve.

He would prey upon and use the same approach he used in the garden and that was to appeal to her selfishness and appeal to her selfish desire for something no man in his right mind would give her, and that would be power and control over him and what belongs to him, and no man would make a woman his God. He would unveil, unfold, and use the provoke method. He would get the woman over into pride, stubbornness, and heavily into selfishness. And that plan has worked since the beginning of time.

Fast forward, and the time is now, and it's your first really serious relationship. The others prior to this real one have been immature love and nothing really serious. You are involved with the first guy, man that you fall in love with for the first time in your life. It would be that first guy you said you fell in love with, and you gave all of yourself to that would be the one that would teach you his version of what a relationship is. You were so in love, so vulnerable, and so into that person. He/she could do no wrong. For a while, things went really great. Nothing serious really happened, just the usual relationship things. But one day all of that changed, and before you knew it, everything went wrong. Satan had decided it was time to introduce his 3T stimuli into your relationship, and it was time to get you and your first love enticed, entangled, and entrapped into unveiling it, introducing it to each other, and getting each other to be a partaker of its principles, processes, procedures, and standards.

How did Satan do it?

Satan has consistently suggested and influenced you into wanting to tell him what a man is, teach a man how you think he should go about being a man, and teach him your version of what you think or feel a real man is. You also want some kind of control over him, and you want to have authority over him, which is totally the opposite of what 1 Timothy 2:12 states. Pride, stubbornness, selfishness, and being anti-submissive have become the tool Satan is using to get the woman over into provoking, pressing, and pushing the wrong behavior patterns out of man. Provoking him, that is her new apple. Every day Satan is making sure her heart and mind is being deceived, seduced, tricked, and trapped so that he can use her for the purpose of trying to entice, entangle, and entrap a man into partaking of her new apple.

She gets loud, boisterous, and takes on a badgering and bullying spirit when she is provoking him. And then she starts saying, daring, and provoking him to hit her. When and if he tries to leave her, she grabs him and won't let him leave. From that point on, all of the wrong things happened. Afterward, Satan sat back and laughed. He was happy.

Why? He used *you* to provoke that person into introducing you to the 3T stimuli.

View number 3: You were set up for the 3T stimuli, and your mind and all of its capabilities and abilities were set up for the 3T twisted thinking stimuli. Satan suggested, influenced, and let the first person in your life who hurt you, who brought you pain and brokenness into tutoring, training, and teaching you how and when to demonstrate you have a twisted way of thinking by keeping you connected, tied, linked, yoked, in a stronghold, and enslaved to remembering and reliving every detail of the day and moment that first person deceived you, abandoned you, battered you, raped you, verbally abused you, neglected you, and molested you. Whatever the wile, trickery, scheme, device, deception, and method that was used, it can, will, and still is that same stimuli or stimulus that will always

- o   excite your mind, mind-set, mental state of mind, mental frame of mind, and mentality into a twisted thinking action, quicken a twisted thinking action, twisted feeling, twisted thought, etc.;
- o   excite your self-performance mode, self-will mode, survival mode, self-effort mode, selfish mode, survivor patterns, survivor behavior patterns;
- o   excite your enticed, entangled, and entrapped urges, tendencies, inclinations, intuitions, and instincts; and it would be that which would
- o   excite the way you react/reactions, respond/responses, your acts, actions, deeds, choices, decisions, the way you say, do, and handle things, your moods, feelings, and emotions in a wrong way, negative way, and in a twisted-thinking-based way.

A Picture-Perfect Twisted Thinking

Are you ready? Here it is: The *first* thing that happened is Satan was/ is working behind the scenes of your life, knowing what type of family generational curses that is in your bloodline, placed you in the path, in the same place, and used someone you were attracted to. However it happened, he designated that person as the one who would introduce you to a twisted way of thinking. You met that person and you got involved with the person that Satan set you up by way of the methods he used.

The *second* thing that happened is Satan used the first person or whomever it was that came into your life and was your first love, first person who took away your innocence, etc., as the one who would also be the first one to hurt you, bring you pain, brokenness, deceive you, abandon you, batter you, rape you, verbally abuse you, etc., and through all of what happened to you and even those times when what happened took to you occurred on more than one occasion. You were, at that moment, being tutored, trained and taught what to do, how to respond, react, what to say, how to say what you were saying, etc. Your feelings, emotions, desires, conduct, conversations, communication, understanding, mind with all of its capabilities and abilities were being tutored, trained, and taught the difference between what a right or wrong 3T Stimuli reaction, response, or reactionary response is.

The *third* thing that happened with will excite an organism. When what you have been through, what happened to you in that first, second, third, last relationship started happening to you again in a new relationship, or it *looked like it was but it wasn't*. Your twisted thinking based mind, will, and emotions told you to do something, and you, out of fear and being fearful, *excited* your survival mode, self-effort mode, selfish mode. That in turn *excited* and then enticed, entangled, and entrapped your urges, tendencies, inclinations, intuitions, and instincts.

The *fourth* thing that happened was a part of functional activity was *excited*, which would be the way you reacted, responded, your reactionary responses, your acts, actions, deeds, choices, decisions, the way you say, do, and handle things. Your mind, mind-set, thinking, way of thinking, your thoughts, train of thought, mental state of mind, mental frame of mind, and your mentality were all excited. And when all of your functional activities were excited, you made your move.

Let me say it again: A stimuli or stimulus is something that excites an organism or part of a functional activity.

Let's look at this from this perspective: (1) He/she/they said or done *something* that reminded you of something you had been through before in your past (the stimuli or stimulus), and when that reminder showed up, (2) before you knew it, that stimuli or something *excited* your memory and remembrance of the person and the hurt, pain, brokenness, being deceived, abandoned, battered, raped, verbally abused, molested, rejected, etc. (an organism or a living thing, event, moment, or memory), that he/she/they put you through, and you remember all of what happened to you and how it happened more than once (3) and that remembrance **excited** the old torturing and tormenting feelings of *fear,* fearful driven emotions and being so fearful that it *excited* your survival reaction, survival response, survival reactionary response, survival mode, self effort mode, selfish mode and *excited* your survival mode enticed, entangled and entrapped urges, tendencies, inclinations, intuitions and instincts (functional activity).

Can you see it? It only takes one stimuli or one something that can and will have the power to excite a past living thing, event, moment, or memory of yours, and that will in turn excite your survival-driven and motivated reactions, survival-driven and motivated responses, and survival-driven and motivated reactionary responses. That in turn will excite your survival urges, survival tendencies, survival inclinations, survival intuitions, and survival instincts. The stimuli or stimulus can be a person, place, thing, similar circumstance, similar situation, or similar confrontation.

All of what I just stated will have the power to excite and seduce your mind, mind-set, thinking, way of thinking, thoughts, train of thought, mental state of mind, mental frame of mind, mentality, feelings, emotions, desires, self-will, self-effort, selfishness, self-centeredness, self-righteous, self-justification into twisted thinking.

CHAPTER EIGHTEEN

Fear-Driven Twisted Thinking

When Fear Is the Stimuli

*A stimuli or stimulus is something that excites an
organism or part of a functional activity.*

When the spirit of fear or the fear factor is the stimuli or it is that
something that is doing the exciting, that person's sensibility, senses,
sensitivity, sensations, and sensuality have been tutored, trained, and
taught to connect with something that is soothing to all of them. In
most cases, that something soothing is sexual, or it can be something
that is superficial. The stimuli fear excites that person's sensibility, senses,
sensitivity, sensations, and sensuality by torturing and tormenting them.

The point being, whatever the stimuli is, that person's excited
organism and their functional activity have been tutored, trained, and
taught how and when to excite and deliver the right responding and
corresponding urges, tendencies, inclinations, intuitions, and the right
responding and corresponding instincts. Keep in mind fear tortures,
torments, and twists truth, and then it tricks, traps, and triggers the
person's mind, mind-set, thinking, way of thinking, thoughts, train
of thought, mental state of mind, mental frame of mind, mental
condition, and mentality into going into a protective mode where it will
automatically begin to reject, resist, refute, and refuse. That protective

mode is dangerous, deadly, and destructive because it can and will also protect that person's mind and all of its capabilities and abilities from receiving the truth. The questions I now have for you are the following:

1. Who or what is it that tutored, trained, and taught your mind, mind-set, thinking, way of thinking, thoughts, train of thought, mental state of mind, mental frame of mind, mental condition, and mentality?
2. Who and what is it that is or have tutored, trained, and taught your urges, tendencies, intentions, intuitions, inclinations, and instincts?
3. Who and what is it that can, will, and have tutored, trained, and taught your reactions, responses, and reactionary responses to automatically flow into and function in a survival mode?
4. Who and what is it that have tutored, trained, and taught your feelings, emotions, and desires?
5. Who and what is it that can, will, and have tutored, trained, and taught your images, instructions, ideas, imaginations, and ingenuity?
6. Who and what is it that have tutored, trained, and taught your choices and decision-making process, procedures, and principles?
7. Who and what is it that have tutored, trained, and taught you your relationship standards and principles?
8. Who and what is it that have tutored, trained, and taught your character, conduct, conversations, and communication?
9. Who and what is it that have tutored, trained, and taught you how, when, and where (the physical place) you should be hurt, be in pain, and have brokenness?
10. Who and what is it that tutored, trained, and taught your feelings, emotions, and desires how, when, where, and why they should receive that which would trigger a reaction, response, and reactionary response?

As I stated earlier, fear being used as the stimuli can and will torment and torture the person's mind and all of its capabilities and abilities to the point that the person's mental state of mind, mental condition, and mental frame of mind is so shocked and stunned that it will send the person's mood, mentality, and attitude into a twisted thinking mode. When a person ends up in this mode, they cannot and will not have the ability to accept, adopt, apply, grasp, comprehend, nor understand the conversations and communications of others because they are disoriented, and they are in a disconnected state.

When we talk about fear being the stimuli, we are talking about an unpleasant emotion caused by the belief that someone or something is dangerous, likely to cause pain, or a threat that excites an organism or part of a functional activity. It can also be described as a distressing emotion aroused by impending danger, evil, pain, etc. Whether the threat is real or imagined, the feeling or condition of being afraid excites, entangles, and entraps your behavior and behavior patterns into dangerous, deadly, destructive, devastating, demoralizing, deceptive, and damaging acts, actions, activities, deeds, purposes, or tasks that the person is not aware of that they are engaging in.

When a person is drawn, driven, pulled, pushed, persuaded, and forced into a what-look-like-and-feel-like-I-have-seen-been-through-heard-this-before moment or memory, it can and will stir up your negative reactions, responses, and reactionary responses that will seduce the person's self-effort-filled, driven, and motivated urges, tendencies, inclinations, intuitions, and instincts, tricking and trapping them all into something that do not, cannot, and will not function and flow in their favor.

Fear stimuli fact 1: In order for fear to be, become, and end up being successful and affective and effective as a stimuli it will need the cooperation of your mind and all of its capabilities and abilities and the cooperation of your feelings and your emotions and desires.

With that being said, you must clearly understand fear can only torment and torture your moods, feelings, emotions, attitude, and mind with all of its capabilities and abilities successfully, producing a fearful-intended result whenever the person adopt, accept, and apply past hurt, pain, abuse, neglect, being battered, bruised, beaten, violated, molested, abandoned, rejected, etc., principles, processes, procedures, and patterns and begin to work and operate in and through them.

When fear have access to tormenting and torturing your mind, feelings, emotions, and desires, it will send invisible shock waves into your memories, mind-set, thoughts, train of thought, thinking, and way of thinking that in turn will bring forth an outward affect and effect that is visibly seen and manifested and then showing up in a person's mood, attitude, expressions, acts, actions, deeds, choice, and decision-making process and procedures.

The fear stimuli is only successful, potent, and powerful when it can place the person's past in a yoke, bondage, stronghold, make it a slave, and is able to keep their past bound and limited to producing a demonically designated, directed, and desired intended result and when it can do so without being challenged and confronted. The other thing that is an important truth, fact, and reality when it comes to the fear stimuli is it will always be prosperous, productive, and successful when it can easily have direct access to shocking and stunning your mental state of mind, mental condition and conditioning, and mental frame of mind. That in turn will produce the fulfilling of the person having to go through a vicious cycle of satanic and demonic suggested and influenced tests, trials, tribulations, and temptations.

Fear stimuli fact number 2: Fear can and will always fight your faith, and fear will always work in cahoots with its best friend, which is fate. The *first* person in your life who introduced you to fear, what it is, what it does, how it acts, what its actions and deeds are was successful in doing so because you, at the time, had no knowledge of what fear was, its nature, and origin. As a result each time that tutored, trained, taught, and learned first fear feeling, first fear memory, first fear moment, first fear remembered circumstance, situation, confrontation, first fear remembered matter, and first fear emotion is revived, restored, revisited, and relived, it shows up in your urges, tendencies, inclinations, intuitions, and instincts. It produces and sends a specified unseen, uncertain, undeniable, unexpected, unplanned, unknown, unfair, unaware, unsure, unforgettable, unexplainable, unthinkable, and unbelievable potent and powerful power surge into the function and flow of your moods, feelings, and attitude.

When fear is the stimuli, it is something that causes feelings of dread or apprehension. There is the anticipation of the possibility that something unpleasant will occur, and that anticipation excites their mind, mind-set, thinking, way of thinking, thoughts, and train of thought, which in turn stir up the person's functional activity. When there is something a person is afraid of, that fear can and will cause, create the atmosphere, and contribute to phobias, terror, fright, horror, concern, anxiety, alarm, panic, agitation, trepidation, dread, consternation, dismay, and distress.

As you look back over your life and what you have been through, like all of us, there are some events that took place in your life that is really unforgettable. Like the first time you heard someone say they loved you and your first kiss from that person that you really liked. Maybe it was your first trip outside of the state you lived in, or maybe it was that first time a dream you had come true. No matter what has happened to us and regardless as to the impact our most precious moments and our most treasured memories had on our lives, in some kind of way, some part of who we are were affected and effected.

Life has only one guarantee, and that is we all are going to die. And that thought often strikes fear in a lot of people. Why? Because feel they haven't lived their lives in the way they wanted to, and the thought of leaving this world with unfinished dreams often bring about a lot of anxiety, frustration, and fear. From the time we came into this world, there were things that was assigned to us and attached to our lives. You and I had no way of knowing exactly what was attached and what was assigned to our life, love, dreams, hopes, desires, and relationships. It wasn't until we began to grow, develop, and mature in who we are and in what we thought and felt we were to do in this life did we begin to see the path that we would have to take.

Fear is a dream, hope, and desire stealer. It can shorten our life span and cause you to fall into a deep state of depression. Fear is a dangerous, destructive, deadly, and damaging stimuli spirit that can leave your mental state of mind, mental condition, and mental frame of mind in a destitute state. Each time you experience or have an encounter with caused feelings of dread or apprehension, it is always because what you anticipated and that which you have connected with is the possibility that something from the past that is unpleasant will occur, take place, or show up in your present.

That feeling will eventually produce a change in what you say, what you do, how you act, which direction you will go in, how you conduct yourself, and how you perceive yourself due to that feeling being a direct result of an unseen, unexpected, unplanned, unknown, uncertain, unfair, unaware, undetected, unsure, unforgettable, unexplainable, unthinkable, and unbelievable consequence of an action.

It's hard to believe that from the time you were in your mama's womb, Satan was putting together a sinister plan that included sending someone into your life and placing someone in your pathway. Be that person a family, friend, or foe, that person's assignment, charge and mission is and was to grow, develop, and mature you into receiving, reacting, and responding and having a reactionary response to what would one day be your past unpleasant emotions. Those past unpleasant emotions were caused by the belief that the first person that tutored, trained, and taught you what fear was and the method they used to tutor, train, and teach you the true meaning and concept of what fear is would end up being that which is likely to forever cause you pain.

That pain-filled fear you were tutored, trained, and taught to look for and expect have caused, created the atmosphere, and contributed to you having wrong relationship flashbacks, setbacks, and experiences while you are in a right relationship. Each time you demonstrate you have those fear-driven and motivated flashbacks and setbacks Satan is always behind the scenes using both as something that he can use to excite your behavior and your beliefs in a negative way, stripping both of their ability to produce, prepare, and present the right end results. Satan knows using an unpleasant emotion that is caused by the first person who hurt you and didn't help you can be dangerous and cause you to have feelings of dread or apprehension. Why? It's because your mental state of mind, mental condition, and your mental frame of mind is anticipating the possibility that you will have to remember, revisit, and relive something that is and was unpleasant, and you will end up believing and expecting it will occur again.

God did not create us with a fear-factor mode. He did not give you a spirit of timidity or cowardice, of craven and cringing and fawning fear. He created us out of his love, and he gave us a spirit of power and of love and of calm and well-balanced mind and discipline and self-control (2 Timothy 1:7). When we are not able to have a sound mind or a calm and well-balanced mind and make strong, safe, sound, and stable choices and decisions that will help us to feel secure in our relationships, it is always due to that first person in our life being dominated, manipulated, and controlled by the generational curses they inherited.

That person engaged in an unpleasant emotional act, action, and deed that was caused by the belief that you, the person, were that someone who had something in your character, conduct, conversation, and communication that posed a dangerous threat to their mind-set and mentality and would likely cause, create the atmosphere, and contribute to them receiving hurt, pain, and brokenness.

The day we came into this world Satan had assigned generational curses and assigned people to our lives that he knew he could use to challenge us and change how our lives would function and flow and change what type of principles, processes, and procedures we would follow. As a result, every person that have had a negative impact of some kind and to some degree upon our lives is someone that was also tutored, trained, and taught the fear factor that would negatively excite the wrong behavior and behavior patterns in their lives.

Our twisted self-truths and twisted relationship truths was and have been able to grow, develop, and mature because we had been tutored, trained, and taught by the first fear-teaching teacher that was and is in our lives to accept, adopt, adapt, and apply fear factors and then function, flow, and follow unhealthy and unpleasant emotions, feelings, and desires. Once we did, we were to allow dread and apprehension-filled urges, tendencies, inclinations, intuitions, and instincts the freedom to dominate, manipulate, and control our behavior and how we behave ourselves.

Every person who allows an unpleasant emotion that is caused by the belief that someone or something that is in the unseen, unexpected, unplanned, unknown, uncertain, unfair, undetected, unaware, and unsure is dangerous also believes it is possible that something that is really unpleasant enough to excite the unforgettable, unexplainable, unthinkable, and unbelievable.

CHAPTER NINETEEN

My Brokenness

Brokenness is that indescribable feeling you get when you have said or done something that directly or indirectly hurt someone that you really deeply love and care for, and you never ever intended to hurt them. And after you have said and done that something to hurt that someone you never intended to hurt, there are no words to describe how you feel. You can find yourself standing or staring into a place I call utter disbelief at what has just transpired. What took place wasn't something you planned, prepared for, nor was it something that was premeditated on saying and doing. What took place was an in-the-moment-something that happened and occurred that not even you saying sorry is enough to make up for what happened.

Offering an apology is what you should do, and it is the right thing to do, but it still does not seem like it's enough. Saying I'm sorry is the right thing to say, but it still cannot mend the brokenness that one can and will feel especially if the person who caused the brokenness is a caring, concerned, compassionate, and loving person who is really trying to do their best, and they were not trying to hurt or hinder anyone. I attribute the brokenness I have felt inside me to what I had done to bring my relationship(s) to the end they came to and not because I was ending a relationship with that someone. I could let go of the relationship if I had to or needed to because it was time to do so, but to have to let go because I made a bad and wrong choice and/ or decision that caused, created the atmosphere, and contributed to my relationships ending would really hurt me. I had been married for over seventeen years, and it took a lot for me to fight through all that I had been through just to bring an end to that marriage. It wasn't easy for me to do so, and in fact, it was downright hard.

Being Broken

What took place at the end of that seventeen-year marriage and the events leading up to the end of it was a moment and a memory that took me a while to overcome. I had to forgive the person who allowed the enemy to use her to get to me, and I had to forgive myself for a negative reaction that I demonstrated. That negative reaction that I demonstrated was not something I had a history of nor had I ever demonstrated it before. It's true you don't hit, hurt, or hinder the person you love. If and when you do so, you are also doing it to yourself, that's if you really love that person and care about them.

For days, weeks, and months, I could not shake the thought of what had transpired between us, and my mind kept replaying it. Each time my mind replayed what took place, I could only shake my head in disbelief and feel my heart breaking into what seemed and felt like a thousand pieces. I had never had anyone who had pushed me to my breaking point. I had never had anyone who knew how to bend me to my limitation until that one day in September of 2013. I was already under a lot of stress and pressure. I had been trying to better myself by trying to find a good job.

I had been walking all over Clayton County, Riverdale, Georgia and Atlanta, trying to get gainfully employed because I had not had a consistent job in a few months. I was under so much stress and pressure, and I was really filled with months of built-up tension. At the end of every week and month, I was faced with the same needs, and add to those consistent old needs, the new ones that would show up. It was a very tough time for me, and I didn't know how or where the provision was coming from.

The last three years of my marriage wasn't good, and my marriage was on a steady decline. There was so much going on in my relationship with my then wife and with myself, and there were a lot of unbelievable things that were taking place. I wasn't getting the help from the one I was married to, and because of that, things was just hard and tough. I was constantly faced with choices and decisions, pressure, stress, tension, and I still had to stay in my role and handle my responsibilities as a husband, father, and provider. And to make things worse, I was dealing with negative feelings I was having about myself. I was having marital problems, money problems, and I still hadn't had time to mourn all of the real close family members I had buried. I would on more than one occasion cry silent screams that no one but God and I could hear.

Painting the Brokenness Picture

I often found myself speaking words that no one could and would hear. When you are filled with so much silent frustration, hurt, and pain, that hurt so bad, and it's so intense that you can't and don't know how to scream because that silent hurt and pain is so excruciating. The only thing a person could do is mime what's going on in the inside. I didn't feel good about myself, my life, and my marriage. I wasn't where I wanted to be, and I wasn't doing what I wanted to do. I was struggling in all areas of my life and struggling to overcome and struggling to survive. Every day and every moment, minute, second, hour, month, and in every New Year that came brought more of the same. I couldn't and didn't relax because I really didn't know how to. Every day I was fighting an enemy that I couldn't see or touch. The pressure the enemy was applying would come through circumstances, situations, confrontations, matters of the heart, and through people. It was a never-ending battle. I had begun to see so many different and consistent satanic and demonic manifestations showing up right in the midst of what I just described to you. Eventually, I just got into a mind-set and a frame of mind that kept me fighting to survive, fighting to win, and fighting to overcome.

The ironic thing about being in a fighting mode or mind-set all of the time is everyone began to look like and sound like the unseen enemy that you had programmed yourself to wake up to and go to sleep fighting. That is not a good mode to be in. All I knew to do, could do, and had to do was to fight, and that's the attitude and mind-set I got into without even knowing it. Not only did everything and everyone begun to look like my enemy, but also every request and demand sounded like the whisper I had heard in the dark. I kept hearing a voice that was telling me it was going to kill, steal, and destroy me. Sometimes it was hard for me at times to get and have clarity on what I was hearing.

Every uttered request, demand, need, and want that was made coming from those I cared for and had to provide for registering in the wrong place within me. Their words landed in my fight and not in my faith. I was under so much intense pressure that I just wanted it to stop. I wanted those whom I was to provide for to stop putting and adding more pressure on me and to stop placing unrealistic expectations upon me, but they didn't. I just couldn't and didn't understand why the person I was married to and the people who were close to me hear me and help me. Why didn't they come to my rescue? I was always there when they needed me.

Why weren't they there for me when I needed them? I was a husband, a father, a provider, and I was dealing with the way I felt about myself. The pressure, tension, frustrations, and discouragements that I was feeling were mounting up and adding up day by day. I found myself fighting to stay cool, calm, collected, and under control. I was really hurting and hurt because I had this one person who is supposed to be for me, with me, and helping me, but instead she was sticking her selfish agendas and selfish motives in my already-silent frustration, in my pain, pressure, tension, and stress. Instead of her giving, she was taking away the little that I had and I needed for myself that kept me together. She kept pushing me and taking from me.

The more I tried to stop her, the more she kept coming at me drawing, trying to pull from me, and then put more on me. I was trying to be strong, be a man and man up and handle it; but in the end, I only ended up becoming a volcano waiting to erupt. And to make things worse than what I just shared with you, I had family members that were/are close to me that suddenly started doing things I had no control over that would, in the end, have an effect and affect upon me, the man, the husband, the father, and the human being.

Silent Assassin Celebration

The things I was trying to handle was just handling me and hindering me. Somewhere in a place unknown and unseen to my human eyes, Satan and his demon spirits were preparing to throw a party. They were getting ready to celebrate their masterfully designed carried-out plan to assault and then attack and finally assassinate who I was and where I was trying to get to. He was after my character, conduct, conversation, communication, integrity, personality, dreams, hopes, desires, my faith, etc. Satan would stoop so low as to use my own wife, helpmate, etc., to help carry out his plan, and she compromised and then cooperated. She no longer looked like and sounded like my wife, lover, friend, helpmate, etc. She sounded like the silent assassins that were living in the unseen and orchestrating the unknown.

I could hear, see, and feel their assaults and attacks of the silent unseen assassin's bullets. Every weapon he was forming against me was hitting and hurting some part of me, and I knew Satan was trying to find ways and weapons he could use that would penetrate the very core of my faith and my being.

I could see those satanic assassins celebrating and partying because they just knew they had me. They had successfully used the one person who was the closest to me to say and do things they knew should, could, and would destroy me. I got to the point and place where I got into the mind-set and into the mentality without even knowing it or without even trying to, where I just woke up, went through my day, and went to sleep fighting everything and everyone Satan was using. Every time those silent, unseen assassins fired a weapon at me, my will to win, my desire, my ambition, my motivation, etc., I could feel the sting from the hit.

I felt hurt and pain and I knew I had to fight back without any rest just so that I could survive. In the end, I ended up doing something that I know I wouldn't have ever done if I wasn't dealing with so much and if I wasn't under the constant assault of those silent unseen assassin's attack. If I was at peace, had peace, and had those who was close to me spiritually aware of my welfare and was standing by me and with me in the fight, nothing that happened in the end would have taken place.

In the end, I found myself trying to fight a spiritual battle with carnal means. When Satan used her to hit me with something I never expected her to say and do without me even knowing it, I reacted in the wrong way. I was tired of Satan using her to hurt and hinder me. I got tired of her yielding, submitting, and surrendering to him using her to tear me down. I just wanted her to stop what she was doing. I wanted her to stop badgering, provoking, pushing, daring, challenging, and trying me. I was really hurt even more because the person who was supposed to be helping me was the same person who was just screaming and shouting real loud in my ear and wouldn't stop.

Every day, all day the only thing I heard was complaints, demands, insults, and her saying and doing sneaky things, doing dirty, underhanded, selfish things she knew was wrong. I knew I was standing alone and hurting, but I was still holding my own against the assassins. I knew it was wounded but still willing to fight, beat down but not broken, battered and bruised but still trying to be, become, and end up being victorious. I was still helping others, but I couldn't help myself. That one last time she stepped into my years of silent frustration, hurt, pain, wound, discouragement, and disappointments, etc., I did what I had tutored, trained, and taught my mind, mind-set, thinking, thoughts, and mentality to do, and that was to come out fighting.

The mode I was in said, "Don't think about it, no plan, no preparation, just fight." Don't let nobody or no one take me down and out. My fighting became instant and automatic without me thinking a reaction. The person I was in a relationship with really wasn't the target. The things she was saying and doing and the negatives that she was drawing out of me that she and I both knew I didn't like—that was the target. I wanted those things that she was saying and doing, how she was acting out, what she was demanding, that I couldn't deliver, her badgering me, pushing me, challenging me, provoking me, etc., to stop. I was trying to stop those things.

My reaction, my attempt was to stop her from putting her foot, selfish, self-centered, self-righteous, self-justified motives, desires, needs, wants, dislikes, etc., in my way and to remove her and them out of my face, out of my space, and out of what I was already dealing with. The more I shouted stop, the more she kept coming at me with even more. I was provoked and pushed to my breaking point, and without me thinking about it, I hit back. In the end, I found myself in utter brokenness. I was beaten up, battered, bruised, and bent but not broken. I was just in a place of brokenness.

Set Me Up for Failure

After it was all over, I just sat in a place in my mind I called emptiness. I couldn't believe what had transpired and what took place at my hands. I just shook my head in disbelief and just asked God, "Why? How? Why me, and why this?" I bowed my head, and I was feeling like the lowest of the low. I had a lot of different feelings going through me, and none of them were good at that moment. I tried to replay what happened and how things ended up like they did. The only thing I could do was still shake my head in disbelief, feeling worthless, empty, ashamed, embarrassed, downtrodden, and downright broken into a thousand pieces inside. I was hurting in a place within me that I really couldn't describe, and I really couldn't describe how I was feeling. There were no words. I just sat there. I could hear people talking. I could see faces in the room where I was, but I was in a place where there was silence and me still asking God, "Why? How? Why me? Why this Lord?"

Let me try and paint this picture: It was like silence had come into the room and had taken that moment and surrounded it just like you would wrap something up, and once silence had surrounded that moment, it was then isolated and pulled away from all of the activity that was going on in the room. Once the moment was isolated, silence had wrapped my mind up in the middle of it all, and the only thing I could see and hear were the replays of what happened. It was almost like being in an unconscious state, condition, or frame of mind, but you are conscious. I was consciously aware of what took place, but I was unconsciously aware as to how things got into that place and to that point.

Everything happened so fast, it felt like I was rationally talking and trying to reason and then some unseen force pulled me into a reactionary response mode. As I sat there after everything had happened, I remember having this feeling of being isolated from everything and everyone. That isolated feeling brought about total and complete isolation with my mind and all of the things it wanted to replay on its own. Each moment my mind would replay was surrounded with what had happened, and they were blanketed with silence. My reality became, once again, the forces in the negative unseen, unexpected, unplanned, unknown, undeniable, unfair, uncertain, unaware, and unsure had once again set me up for an unexplainable, unforgettable, unthinkable, and unbelievable moment.

Misdirection Play

Once again, without me knowing it and without me knowing what was going to happen on that day, what circumstances, situation, and confrontation was going to develop, those unseen forces had set me up for failure, and I had failed and was in my fallen state. If I had any clue as to what Satan was setting me up for, I never would have allowed myself to get caught up in the midst of his diverted delusional deception. He had set me up and had got me caught and caught up in a misdirection play. A misdirection play is one where it looks like everything is going one way, but in reality, that which is really happening or is really going to happen will be moving in the opposite direction.

When you are caught and you are caught up in a misdirection play, you are busy going in the flow of what is happening, taking place, or being said and done. You are drawn, driven, pulled, pushed, persuaded, forced, enticed, seduced, captivated, tricked, and trapped into flowing and following in line and in agreement with the direction the conversation is going in. No matter how hard you try to get out of that flow and following, you seemingly can't. And when you least expect it and never saw it coming, the conversation all of a sudden turn from moving in what you thought and felt was a positive or a right direction; and before you know it, Satan has caused that conversation to make a quick unsuspecting turnaround, and the conversation start going in the wrong direction.

And you are so close upon and you are so connected, locked into the moment and the conversation your mind and all of its capabilities and abilities is captivated because of the conversation, your attitude, and your attention is deeply involved. Without you knowing it, Satan has you conducting yourself as if you are a slave to being engaged in the conversation. In that moment, you can't and don't recognize and realize another force have taken control of the moment, circumstance, situation, confrontation, and conversation, and that unseen and unknown force is dominating, manipulating and controlling it all.

Once again, my enemies, my adversaries, and my foes living in the unseen, unexpected, unplanned, unknown, uncertain, unfair, unaware, unsure had showed up in a way that I didn't see or hadn't seen before and had drawn some part of whom I was that I didn't realize had not been totally and completely delivered, cleansed, purged, healed, and made whole, drawn into a unexplainable, unforgettable, unthinkable, and unbelievable act. As my mind would replay what had took place over and over again, I still came to the same question that I would over and over again cry from the deepest depths of my shattered, broken, wounded, torn spirit and soul to God, "Lord, why me, and why this, how?" I asked God, "Where did what I had done come from"? I had no history of such an act.

Wherever it came from, I knew I didn't want it, and it had to be removed and rooted out by any means necessary. It was an indescribable moment and an indescribable place to be. I never considered myself a victim nor was I trying to make any excuses for what had taken place at my hands. I just wanted to know why me, why this, and why would it happen to us. We all are different, and yet we are the same, and we do not get into relationships of any kind because of our differences. We get into relationships based on where we are the same and how we can connect same and then take them and turn them into something or turn them into prosperous, productive, and successful fairy-tale-fulfilling something's.

Everything that day happened so fast, and I didn't get a chance to express my deepest regrets for what had taken place. In and through my brokenness, I kept asking God to forgive me and to give me the right words of apology for the person I had hurt. I didn't want anything for myself nor was I expecting anything. I just wanted to say I was so sorry and ask for forgiveness. For days and weeks and months after that awful moment in my life, I was still trying to find a way to live through and live with that moment and the memory of it all.

I had to live with myself, look at myself, and look at the person I had hurt, and I had to find a way to live through and live with that moment and memory. When I finally got a chance to offer my apology to the person I had hurt, I said I was sorry and asked for forgiveness even though I felt like my apology wasn't enough. At that time, my heartfelt, sincere apology was all I could offer; but in my heart of hearts, I felt it just wasn't enough for me. The day's following that moment wasn't easy for me. I didn't feel sorry for myself, and I made no excuses nor did I offer any type of explanation for my actions. I just didn't know why, and I didn't understand why that happened to me and to us.

Broken and Contrite

Time after time, I had walked away from being drawn into a scene like that. On more than one occasion, I could see, sense, and even feel the presence of those enemies of my soul trying to bait me, lure me, and set me up for what had eventually happened, but I never gave in. On that particular day and in that particular moment and with that particular circumstance, situation, confrontation, conversation, and argument, what I intentionally avoided happening would happen. What I thought and felt I had been avoiding was an argument that would lead to us not communicating and not being able to move forward in our relationship. I never fathomed in my mind, thought, or felt what I had been avoiding when we got into heated disagreements and arguments would be what eventually happened.

It was something that never crossed my mind. It was that one particular moment, discussion, conversation, and argument, *not* the others, but this one particular ones that brought out the wrong reaction. What was the difference with that one? I really didn't know. It took me some time to get past that. I did a lot of soul-searching, praying, working on myself, changing me and my way of thinking, my way of saying, doing, and handling things and matters. I went to God in my brokenness, seeking deliverance, cleansing, purging, healing, and wanting to be made whole.

I knew I had to find the root cause of what had brought me into that low frame of mind and moment, and when I found it, I had to get rid of the root cause. I didn't need nor want a fix. I needed a root removal. The thought that I had hurt someone with my hands really hurt me more. I knew I wasn't that kind of person. Yes, I'm guilty of doing what I had done. I couldn't and wouldn't deny that. Even though I know that's what I done, that is not and was not who I really am.

I spent a lot of days and weeks just crying and hurting for the person I had hurt. That was all I could do. I would cry for the person I had hurt and cry for the people who would be directly hurt behind my actions. I would cry for the person and the people who would be indirectly effected and indirectly affected by what had happened. No matter how hard I tried to walk away from that scene and that person, and no matter how hard I begged and pleaded with that person to please stop provoking me and pushing and pressing their selfish issues and agendas at me, they just wouldn't stop. It was a consistent badgering, provoking, pushing, and pressing, being loud, boisterous, agitating, and aggravating with their conversations, comments, accusations, and assumptions.

The person I was in this relationship with did not care and wasn't concerned with what I was already dealing with. They just wanted things to go their way. It took some time before my spirit would be lifted up. I had to learn how to get to the place and point where I could forgive myself. I knew God's grace and his finished works on the cross had already provided and paved the path that would lead to me forgiving and releasing myself from all of my past, present, and future mistakes, failures, and moments when I would fall. I had seen his mercy show up on my behalf when judgment was imminent and due. I had to fight through Satan assaulting and attacking me with feelings of self-condemnation and his consistent efforts in trying to assassinate the power of God's forgiveness and the power of self-forgiveness.

Fighting against Failure

I had to fight against all kinds of negative self-feelings, and I had to stay in the place where the power of God's word and the power of his presence would flow freely into the very core of my being. As long as I stayed in that type of atmosphere, it would bring deliverance, cleansing, purging, and healing, and I would be made whole. I needed an encounter with the power of God's deliverance, cleansing, purging, healing, and being made whole power, and I wholeheartedly sought and pursued after it. My heart would break and be filled with brokenness at times and moments when I didn't expect it to, and I would weep bitterly out of my brokenness.

Every time I found myself in that state, condition, and frame of mind where I was encountering brokenness, I would go to God with my sacrifice and fruit that is consistent with repentance so that my life, conduct, conversations, and communication would prove I had a change of heart (Matthew 3:8). I would crawl up to his mercy seat in my brokenness and with my sacrifice, which were a broken spirit and a contrite heart. I could feel the hurt, pain, and brokenness of the person I had hurt, and I could feel the magnitude of their hurt, pain, and brokenness I had caused her on the inside of me. You should never hurt the person and people you love, and if and when you do, you should *never* just walk away and leave them in that state, condition, and frame of mind.

I was broken down with sorrow because of what I had done, and I was humbly and thoroughly penitent. I wished all of what happened that day never happened, but it did, and I just didn't know why me, how, why us, and why this that happened. Not that I would want anything worse to happen, but to someone like myself who really have love, care, has concern and compassion for those I'm in any type of relationship with, I have a heart, and I have the heart of God living inside of me. I wouldn't intentionally allow myself to do what took place that day in September. If I only would have known or had some kind of highly visible, noticeable, recognizable, and undeniable clue or witness, I *never* would have allowed myself to get caught and then caught up in that matter and in that moment.

Yes, it happened and all of those who stand on the outside looking in do what they always do. They judged me and labeled me and left me broken and in my brokenness. I was stoned, and when you are in that place, you can see and hear people whispering, pointing their fingers at you, and you know they are talking about you. In my brokenness, those who judged and condemned me, not judged and condemned my act and action, felt like they were better than me, and they would look down on me because they had not done what I did not intentionally try to do.

That day in September, when all of the wrong things happened, my heart and mind were clear and clean. My motives and intentions were clear and clean, and my conversation and what I wanted to communicate that day were also clear and clean. I wanted to get her to see what we were doing to each other and see what she was doing to herself, me, and us. I wanted us to stop and get out of the dangerous, destructive, and damaging mode we were in. I was hurting, and I knew she was hurting. I only wanted to get her to see how two wrongs don't make a right. We don't do evil for evil, and we should get out of demonstrating childish ways and get out of demonstrating childish thoughts, train of thought, thinking, way of thinking, childish acts, actions, deeds, choice, and decision making, etc.

All of which would, in the end, lead to us having a childish and immature mind-set, mental state of mind, mental condition, mental frame of mind, and mentality about things. I wanted her to see that we both were being set up for failure and for a fall. I wanted to get her to see how Satan and demon spirits, in a place somewhere that our human minds and our human vision could not see nor even conceive, were there working behind the scenes of our relationship, and they were launching at us and our relationship unseen, unexpected, unplanned, unknown, undeniable, and unfair family generational curses.

That once they were successful in their assault, attack, and assassination assignment would catch us unaware of what was happening and lead us to being unsure of what we should and could do next. Once this has been accomplished and achieved, Satan, the enemy of your soul, your relationship adversary and opponent, would then set you, me, and us up for an unexplainable, unforgettable, unthinkable, and unbelievable moment like the one that took place in September.

I'm Coming Right at You Now

What God has shown me was, that day even though my motives and intentions was clear, clean, and pure while I was trying to hold a conversation and communicate how I was feeling about some important matters that was hurting her, me and us; and being in the right spirit, speaking with the right tone of voice and talking with her for all of the right reason(s), she wasn't where I was. She was heavily over into her selfish-driven and motivated feelings, emotions, and desires. Satan had somehow *distracted* me and distracted my thinking, way of thinking, thoughts, train of thought, *detained* my mental state of mind, mental condition/conditioning, and mental frame of mind, and he then *detoured* my conversation and then *delayed* what I was wanting to communicate with her and then *derailed* my once-sound, safe, stable, and secure mind, mind-set, and mentality and finally my *power of choice* was *denied*, and my right reasoning was *disconnected*.

Not only was I hurt, but now my mind-set, mental frame of mind, mental state of mind, mental frame of mind was also being held hostage, hindered, and bombarded with hurt. As all of this was unfolding, Satan and all of his imps and demon spirits started assaulting, attacking, and assassinating that whole moment with unseen, unexpected, unplanned, uncertain, unknown, unfair, unaware, unsure, undeniable, unexplainable, unforgettable, unthinkable, and unbelievable generational curses that they knew would kill, steal, and destroy my relationship.

The door for distracting happened when the person I was talking to went into a selfish protective mode and begin to reject, resist, refute, and refuse me and what I was trying to share. When Satan was able to pull, push, persuade, seduce, trick, force, lead, and trap her thinking, way of thinking, thoughts, train of thought and lead them over into a selfish mode where she would begin thinking and feeling her selfishness was in danger of being overthrown, tested, tried, threatened, tormented, and tortured.

Deep into the Ds

As she was being deceived into thinking and feeling her selfishness was in danger of being overthrown, tested, tried, threatened, tormented, and tortured, her self-survival and her self-protective-custody mode kicked into high gear. In that moment, Satan was about to launch his master relationship deception plan. As she was locked into what she was thinking and feeling, her self-centeredness kicked in automatically and provided the detour, and then her self-righteousness would kick in automatically and provided the delay, and then her self-righteousness finally kicked in automatically and provided the derailing for the whole moment, conversation, and communication. Her self-performance then kicked in, automatically providing the distraction; and then her self-will kicked in, automatically providing the detour. Finally, her self-effort kicked in and automatically provided the disconnection that they both felt in that moment.

This whole demonic and satanic assault, attack, assassination process was quick, automatic, systematic, and strategic. Neither one of us really didn't have time to think about what was happening. It was like that ball rolling down a steep hill. Before we knew it, our three worst enemies of any relationship showed up for the party, and they are the following: (1) your feelings (2) your emotions, and (3) your desires. If and when all three of these are powered by selfishness, self-centeredness, self-righteousness, and by self-justification, all of that person's power to discern, detect, and do right reasoning is disconnected.

Anytime a person get over into their feelings, emotions, and desires, they will automatically be connected, linked, tied, enslaved, yoked, in bondage, in a stronghold to an attitude, a mood, and a mode where they automatically have the overwhelming and undeniable urge, tendency, inclination, intuition, and instinct to demonstrate self-performance, self-will, and self-effort.

Unhappy and Unhealthy

If a person already has damaged and unhealthy feelings, emotions, and desires that came from a previous relationship that they were in, and they have not taken those feelings, emotions, and desires to God, asking him to deliver, cleanse, purge, heal, and make them whole from those same unhealthy feelings, emotions, and desires, they can and will get infected and infested with the spirit of control, and they will then become, be, and end up being control-powered feelings, emotions, and desires. In other words, the person's feelings, emotions, and desires are so strong they dominate, manipulate, and control that same person's character, conduct, conversations, and communication abilities.

They don't know it, but that is how they come across when they are expressing their feelings, emotions, and desires. The listener feels like the person who is sharing their feelings, emotions, and desires is being controlling when they are expressing their feelings, emotions, and desires. Thus, the listening person will begin to feel intimidated and think they are insignificant. We live in a world where opposites attract, and that is exactly why this type of scenario happens. One person in the relationship is dominant because they have stronger feelings, emotions, and desires, and the other person do not.

Every now and then, that same person who does not demonstrate they have strong feelings, emotions, and desires may step up and try to demonstrate they do, and that only happens when they feel pushed and pressured or feel like they are just a doormat in that relationship.

As the person is sharing how they feel, those feelings are secretly powered with control, and that power is expressed in and through the sharing person's emotions, and those emotions being secretly powered by control is expressed in and through the person's desire(s) that brought them into the conversation with the other person. When there is unhealthy feelings, emotions, and desires dominating, manipulating, and controlling, one or both people in that relationship becomes unhappy. Unhealthiness always conceives and births unhappiness.

Satanic and Demonic Opportunists

The door was opened, and Satan and all of his demons, imps, and cohort spirits are opportunists, and they are wicked, dangerous, destructive, damaging, and violent. They showed up, and they brought everything right out of both of our family generational curses into that moment we were in and into that conversation we were having without us realizing it. They were using us to hurt each other and using us to tear down a relationship we had both invested a lot of time, hard work, and prayers into building without us even knowing it. It happened, and it hurt. At the time I didn't see any of this that I'm sharing with you. It took some time before my spirit was lifted up. I had finally got to where I had forgiven myself, and God gave me his strength made perfect in my weakness so that I could get up and get out of my brokenness and could start all over again and get back into life and living.

Months later, after being divorced and finally getting to where I was really feeling good about myself and about my life, I met someone that I wanted to get to know. I wasn't seeking to get into a committed relationship at the time. I just wanted to start with a friendship. I was thinking I would find someone I could hang out with and really get to know first that could and would one day become a committed relationship. The person I met I didn't know at the time had a hidden agenda and selfish motive, and there was a lot from her past that she had not been delivered, cleansed, purged, healed, and made whole from. Seven months later, I found myself dealing with the same things I had fought to get past, and I found myself in the same place I had been while I was in a place of brokenness.

CHAPTER TWENTY

The Brokenness Formula

The Formula for Brokenness

Brokenness is not a place where a person will eventually end up and they find self-pity. It is not a place where you end up viewing yourself as a victim, but It is a place up end up at when you really feel three things, and those three things are the following: (1) remorse, (2) regret, and (3) repentance. When you really feel godly sorrow or godly grief in your heart for what you have said or done to hurt someone, it is not a hopeless sorrow or grief. It is a sorrow that produces the right things while you are in the midst of your brokenness. When God is able to direct his grief or sorrow into your heart, it will bring you to a place of repentance.

Sorrow and grief are two other words that have a significant meaning when it comes to feeling brokenness. To feel sorrow is to experience mental suffering that is caused by loss. To feel grief is to feel or experience and then encounter intense emotional suffering that is caused by a loss. Those two words are often used interchangeably a lot of times. A person really have to feel remorse and regret for what they have said or done that was wrong in order for them to have what is needed that will lead them into having a repentant heart and spirit.

Brokenness seemingly shatters your personality, and it allows or brings embarrassment and shame to your character, conduct, conversation, and communication because those are the pieces that make up your personality. Your character consists of your distinctive individual qualities that are considered collectively. Those who watch will know what kind of character you possess when they see it being expressed through your conduct, conversation, and through your communication.

The brokenness I felt came as a result of the way I felt about myself after what I had done. Brokenness happens when what you never intended to happen end up happening. When others know what you have done to bring about brokenness, they like to stand on the outside and judge you and not your action. They want to picture and portray you as some horrible person. They love to pass judgment and initiate some type of retaliation instead of looking at the person and judging not according to appearance, but to judge the righteous judgment. When a person is in a state of real true godly brokenness, they have regrets and a repentant heart.

Yes, the act that was committed is and was wrong, but that doesn't make the person who done the act useless, worthless, or the worst person on the face of the earth. Brokenness brings about a different kind of hurt and pain, and it has a feeling of its own. When God deals with you in and through you being a broken person with a broken spirit, it is far more painful that the judgments and indictments that is passed on you, and it is more painful than the hurt that can come at the hands of others.

When a person is in a state and frame of mind where they feel brokenness, they are also experiencing or encountering mental suffering and emotional suffering. Your mind keeps replaying the incident that happened, and you are feeling emotionally entangled and entrapped in that moment as if it was just happening all over again. You can feel so much brokenness at times that you will begin to feel so many different emotions that end up causing and contributing to you becoming emotional. Each time your emotions are stirred up, they will always end up preparing, producing, and presenting strong feelings of some kind.

A person who really has godly or God-fearing sorrowful brokenness is someone who clearly knows and understands the magnitude of what they have done, and they know they have hurt God, the other person, and themselves. So there are a lot of ingredients that bring a person to a place of God-fearing brokenness. The most important fact that remains true is when a person really feels brokenness that is accompanied by a broken spirit and a contrite heart they can't and won't try to explain why they did what they did. They do not have an explanation nor will they try to make excuses for the wrong they did. With that being said, let me give you the formula for a godly sorrowful brokenness, which is

- a broken spirit;
- a contrite heart;
- being remorseful;
- having regret
- having a repentant heart

Every person that have a repentant heart, do not want to repeat what they have done. To have a broken spirit is to have a broken life principle. To have a contrite heart is to show deep sorrow for having done wrong. To show remorse is to feel a torturing sense of guilt for your actions. To have regret is to feel sorry for your acts. To have a repentant heart is to feel sorrow for a wrong you've done and to not only feel sorrow for the wrong that you have done, but also to be in touch with the affect and the effect the wrong done will have on others. All of these words are ingredients that go into bringing a person to a place of godly brokenness or God-fearing brokenness.

Hurt

God heals hurt, and God gives peace when and where there is pain. Brokenness is something that God have to mend within a person. Hurt is accompanied by feelings of being injured, harmed, offended, and hurt in its finished work and produces and causes pain and indescribable emotional-driven feelings of being damaged. Pain is accompanied by feelings of being in a state or condition of physical and mental suffering in its finished work, and it produces injury, anxiety, grief, and all kinds of fears. When a person is hurt, they feel like they are damaged. When a person is in pain, they feel physical and mental hurt that causes them to suffer with thoughts and feelings of fear. Hurt *attacks* your feelings and emotions so much that one will end up being driven and constantly drawn, pulled, forced, pushed, persuaded, seduced, and led into an emotional state of being so damaged that they will begin to think and feel they are really not someone that is really desired. When you or someone is really hurt, you and that person need to go to the healer, Jesus, and let him make you and that person well and healthy again so that you can function and flow as you should and need to.

When a person is deeply hurt, they are severely hindered, and they cannot help anyone or anything. They can only be, become, and end up being a handicap that in turn will cause them, their feelings, emotions, desires, and willingness to help to end up being and becoming a distraction. That distraction will lead the person's feelings, emotions, desires, and willingness to help into and onto detours where there are a lot of delays, denials, and ultimately, death and destruction. Remember, when a person is hurt, they cannot give you something they do not have within for themselves.

A hurt person's heart is held hostage to what has been said or done to hurt them. A hurt person cannot see or feel feelings of happiness because their feelings, emotions, and right desires are constantly being attacked with what sometimes seem like and feel like is overwhelming and unbearable relived moments of being harmed, offended, injured, and damaged. A person that is really hurt will begin to live *out of* that hurt. Every choice and every decision they make is driven by their hurt, and every time they step into a specific direction, it is a direction that has been and is consistently drawn out of the hurt they have endured.

There are people who actually believe and feel that if what they are saying, doing, or whom they are with do not hurt or bring them some kind of hurt, they cannot and will not feel good about themselves, and they will not feel good when it comes to the person they are with. Just imagine someone you are with and you are in a relationship with basically counting down the days leading up to the day and moment when they would be hurt. All of who they are, their whole psyche, bodily functions, reactions and responses, what and how they think, feel, what they need and want, what they beg for and crave have been tutored, trained, and taught to look and expect some kind of hurt to come their way. It's almost like the person can't and won't be happy or let me say contented, complacent, or in a comfort zone until the hurt has been administered to their feelings and emotions.

The Hurt-Haven Principle

Can you picture in your mind someone intentionally setting themselves up for some kind of pain? It happens, and I have seen it for myself. I have been in a relationship with someone who was addicted to hurt and pain. That was the first time in my life that I had met someone who lived in the hurt haven. What is the hurt haven? The hurt haven is a sheltered and protected place within a person that they are used to going to after they have received the hurt, harm, injury, pain, and damage they feel they deserve. It is a place where they shelter and protect the hurt they set themselves up to receive, as if the hurt is some kind of prize, reward, or priceless treasure.

The person who is addicted to the hurt-haven principle is someone who, in some kind of way, will push, pull, force, persuade, entice, seduce, and trick an innocent person, usually someone who is trying to do good, do right, live right, be right, etc., into delivering some kind of harm, injury, pain, or damage to them. Deep down within this kind of person, they are saying, "If you really love me, care about me, want me, need me, etc.," then hurt me. They can't go to long in life and in a relationship before they will intentionally say or do something that they know can and will bring them some kind of hurt. If you are really paying attention to the person, you can almost clock or calendar the date and day when they will self-destruct. They are not used to having a hurt-free relationship.

Who Are You?

A hurt-haven person can be someone who is always saying or doing something someone has asked them not to do. Most of the time, what the person say and do that bring them hurt are things they know the person they are with do not like, but they say and do them anyway. A hurt-haven person is someone who has discovered what will, as we say, push a person's buttons the wrong way or know just what to say and do to get to you in the wrong way. It can be someone who is trying to see how far they can push you, how far they can go in taking you for granted, and how far they can go in using your kindness for weakness. It can be someone who have been hurt in a previous relationship and have become so immune to the hurt, without even knowing it, their feelings, emotions, and desires have been tricked and deceived into believing they are supposed to be harmed, offended, injured, and/or damaged.

The first person they were with or someone they were with had tutored, trained, and taught them and their feelings, emotions, and desires to be a target for and to accept any type of hurt they receive. An example of someone whose feelings, emotions, desires, and mind, mind-set, thoughts, train of thought, thinking, way of thinking, mental state of mind, mental frame of mind, mental condition, and mentality that have been tutored, trained, and taught to be a target for pain is the person who, from past experience, knows they get to talking too much or, as we say, running their mouth excessively in an argumentative, combative, bullying, badgering, rude, disrespectful, hostile, and provoking way. The person has asked them to not be that way, but they continually do anyway, thus offending the person and pushing them to the extreme.

It can be a person who knows how to and when to cross over into the other person's space, boundary, or limitation without demonstrating any respect for the line the person has drawn when it comes to space invading. Another example of a hurt-haven person is someone who haphazardly and without any regard for what they are saying or doing, get loud, hotheaded, arrogant, etc., and, in a badgering way, dare the person to hurt them. There are so many ways a person can be a hurt-haven person.

Every man, every human being has their boundaries and limitations, and they should be adhered to and respected. Hurt-haven people will get up in your face, go off on you, degrade and belittle you, dare you to do something, and intentionally invade your space and your personal things just to see how far they can go with you and just how much they can get away with.

The Message of the Hurt-Haven Principle

The hurt-haven principle states that if you really love that person and you care about them, say and do something that will hurt them. The mind-set becomes, if you love that person like you say you do, why are you delaying, hurting that person? It also states that in order to love that person who is, for some reason that you really can't understand, is always pushing the wrong buttons with you, the right reaction is to cause that person pain, injury, harm, offend, and damage. And when you do so, make sure it is said and done in a way that the person believes, feel, and know the hurt you are administering at their urging is and will become a fundamental truth and law that will govern the relationship they have with you. Sounds twisted right?

A person who is this state of mind and in this frame of mind will continue to press, push, and provoke you until they are sure you get to the place and point in your thinking and in your way of thinking where you will begin to make sure, when you are administering hurt to them, you do so without procrastinating, hesitating, questioning, and second-guessing. Each time they are pushing, testing, and trying your patience and self-control, it is for the purpose of tutoring, training, and teaching you what a hurt-haven principle is.

The message's that Satan wants you to learn from a person like this is how to do the following:

(1) Make a learned hurt principle something that you will use *to base and build your other relationships on* and to also make sure you delivering hurt become a rule of conduct for you.

(2) Make sure the person you are with and everyone that comes after that person know you have had someone who have pushed and provoked you to the point where you hurt the one you are with/love, and that new person must adhere to the "hurt you" rule that the person before them have set the precedent for.

(3) Make sure you involve yourself with people and get in relationships with people who will push you to the point and place where you consistently compromise your integrity by administering hurt to the people or person in your life who knowingly can or will or *might* push you to your breaking point.

(4) When you deliver the hurt to the person who keep provoking you and pushing you to your breaking point after you have asked, begged, and pleaded over and over with that person to leave you alone, stop talking, and have tried to walk away and they wouldn't let you, automatically get into the mind-set and in the mentality where you make hurting them a scientific hurt law that explain your natural action and reaction.

(5) And finally, make sure the hurt haven principle is the method of operation your hurt-filled feelings and your hurt-filled and driven emotions get used to.

(6) Make sure the hurt-haven principle is the driving force and the empowering force that your urges, tendencies, inclinations, intuitions, and instincts function, flow, and operate out as its standard of operation.

The person that is receiving the hurt has made hurt their place of refuge when happiness, joy, fulfillment, personal satisfaction, a satisfied feeling, and other good and positives want to and try to show up.

Pain

Pain *assaults* your physical and mental frame of mind, mental state of state of mind, mental state of being, mental condition, and mentality. Pain targets your mind, mind-set, thoughts, train of thought, thinking, way of thinking, mental state of mind, mental frame of mind, and mental condition. Once pain hit its target, the goal then becomes to kill, steal, and destroy your self-confidence, self-esteem, will to win, right desires, hope, belief, and faith. In order for one to be free of pain, God will have to provide you with inner peace, peace of mind, peace in your heart, peace within your spirit, and peace all around you.

When God gives you peace where there has been pain, he is giving you freedom from the war that is within you or that is taking place within you mind and all of its components. There is basically an agreement that is being made to end the war that is going on within you and your mind. Once the agreement has been made or reached through the power of God's word, truth, presence, power, and anointing, the Holy spirit and through you receiving God's word and truth and mental law and order is restored.

Your mind, mind-set, thoughts, train of thought, thinking, way of thinking, mental state of mind, mental frame of mind, mental condition, and mentality is brought back into harmony and one accord, which in turn births and bring your mind and all of its components, capacity, creativity, and capabilities into a flow where there is serenity and quietness. When a person is in pain, they live *in* their pain, and they cannot and will not be able to enjoy the pleasures that loving and living may bring.

No matter how positive they may be and regardless as to what God has been doing and is still doing in their life that should and would encourage, help, and motivate them, the power of what has brought them pain acts as the stimulus that feeds their mind and all of its capacity, components, creativity, and capabilities. You cannot and should not rely or count on a person whose life, day, mind, mind, mind-set, thoughts, train of thought, thinking, way of thinking, mental state of mind, mental frame of mind, and mental condition is consistently being bombarded with pain because they cannot and will not have the ability to plan, prepare, and produce the right provision that you need to help you get where you are trying to get to.

It's a truth and a well-known fact that just like a person can get addicted to pleasure principles, a person who is in pain can get addicted to the pain principles.

The Pain Principles

Exactly what are the pain principles? Before I tell you what the pain principles are, let me first tell you the pain principles dominate, manipulate, seduce, and then trick and trap the person's mind, mind-set, thoughts, train of thought, thinking, way of thinking, mental state of mind, mental frame of mind, and mental condition into being controlled by deceptive and deceiving fundamental distorted and dangerous false truths and laws upon which the person's mentality will begin to base its rule of conduct that it uncontrollable adheres to. Those same pain principles becomes a basic part of what the person's integrity is based and built upon and deceives the person into explaining their natural wrong reaction that seems and feels so right.

Those times when there should be completeness, unimpaired condition, and when there should be soundness freely made manifest and revealed in and through who the person is, when they need to and have to make tough choices, when they face tough challenges, and when they need to make a tough change has been infected with the pain principle. Their mentality will eventually become *affected* and will end up being *effected* to the point where the person cannot demonstrate honesty and sincerity.

The person's mind, mind-set, thoughts, train of thought, thinking, way of thinking, mental state of mind, mental frame of mind, and mental condition has been assaulted so much with the wrong stimulus, that their mentality has produced and consistently presents the wrong type of integrity for the person. The person's integrity or the place where there should be completeness, an unimpaired condition, and soundness in the total makeup of who the person is has been compromised, therefore making the person's honesty and sincerity suspect.

The pain principle basically states, suggest, influence, deceive, declare, and decree to the person's mind, mind-set, thoughts, train of thought, thinking, way of thinking, mental state of mind, mental frame of mind, and mental condition into believing if the tough decisions and choices that need to be made when it comes to the challenges and when it comes to the change that need to and have to be made, if it doesn't bring negative and painful feelings, and emotions that take the person through *changes*, then something is wrong. And the final conclusive tough decisions and choices that they were about to make and the conclusion that they arrived at when it came to the challenges and the change that needed to be made had to be wrong.

Thus leading the person to make the wrong decisions, choices, and, in turn, cause, create the atmosphere, and contribute to more challenges and changes instead of a change. Basically, the person's mind, mind-set, thoughts, train of thought, thinking, way of thinking, mental state of mind, mental frame of mind, and mental condition is dominated, manipulated, and then tricked, trapped, and deceived into functioning and flowing in and out of what seem, feel, and look right but, in all actuality, is all the way wrong. And what seems, feels, and looks to be all the way wrong is actually right.

A person whose mind, mind-set, thoughts, train of thought, thinking, way of thinking, mental state of mind, mental frame of mind, and mental condition has been enticed by and is entangled and entrapped in and with pain is always halt between two opinions and is double minded, and their mind can never arrive at the right understanding of a matter.

The pain principle will keep the person's mind, mind-set, thoughts, train of thought, thinking, way of thinking, mental state of mind, mental frame of mind, mental condition, and mentality expecting something bad, negative, wrong, and injurious to be said or done that will cause that person some kind of physical or mental suffering, disease, grief, or anxiety. The pain principle is and will eventually become the method that the person's mind, mind-set, thoughts, train of thought, thinking, way of thinking, mental state of mind, mental frame of mind, mental condition, and mentality is tricked and deceived into operating in and out of. It's really something when you can just sit back and watch someone set themselves up for what they know will bring them pain, injury, physical or mental suffering, disease, grief, and anxiety and not be moved or flinch when the pain come.

CHAPTER TWENTY-ONE

The Hurt and Pain Prosecutor

When you have an encounter with a person who has been hurt and they are in pain, they are not the person you are physically looking at, the person who said they loved you, cared about you, forgave you, etc. They are not the person you thought you knew and had decided to get into a relationship with. Satan is at work behind the scenes of their life, transforming their nature and personality and changing their spirit into that of a *prosecuting* attorney, who, without you knowing it, have been keeping a record of the wrong you have said and done in and over the course of your relationship with them.

That spirit had your friend, your wife, your lover, etc., keeping a record of your wrong. From the first day you met him or her, that spirit had them building their case against you. That non-surrendered, non-delivered, non-cleansed, non-purged, non-healed, and not made whole past hurt, pain, and brokenness that you didn't know was still living and hiding within them and knew, at some place at some time and at some point in the course of your relationship with that person, something would go wrong. How did the spirit of the past hurt and pain know that? It had been working behind the scenes in a place called the unseen, unexpected, unplanned, unknown, undeniable, unfair, uncertain, unaware, and unsure working diligently and making sure it sets you and your relationship up for failure, hurt, and pain and set it up for unforgiveness.

So from the first day that something inside of you was attracted to that something inside of the other person, Satan and all of its wicked, trespassing, deceiving, disrespectful, dangerous, and destructive spirits came alive and began to put in motion ways to draw, drive, force, push, pull, persuade, and deceivingly lead you and that person into circumstances, situations, and confrontations that you and that person had not ran into, thought, knew, dreamed, or felt that would ever happen to you, that person, and to your relationship. That same spirit of past unforgiveness, a non-repentant heart that one or both of you had lying dormant inside of you, which could have been just some of the residue of unforgiveness and a non-repentant heart from a past relationship, Satan knew was still inside of one or both of you, or it was still lingering around you, and he and all of his wicked spirits had to come up with and develop a hidden agenda, hidden-motive-filled secretive and masterfully disguised way to bring to life, activate a flashback of some kind.

Satan and his demon spirits knew just when and how to bring to life that which was lying dormant inside of you. He knew he had to use someone you both knew or didn't know and was close to or a stranger to one or both of you as the one to carry out his plan. Satan and all of his wicked spirits stand against and highly oppose, resist, reject, and refuse to allow you, me, us, and anyone of us the right, power, and the authority to get into a rewarding, fulfilling, prosperous, productive, successful, Christ-centered and based, dreamed of, hoped for, prayed for that glorify God relationship; he knew it had to use you and the person you were in a relationship with as a weapon formed against each other and as a weapon it would use to form against your relationship.

Here's the Plan(s)

Satan would use you, the person you are in a relationship with, family, friends, enemies, acquaintances, people you associate yourself with, people, places, and things as tools that would bring you into the flow the path and to the point where you are on a collision course with an I-thought-I-had-been-healed-from-that past hurt, pain, brokenness moment and memory flashback. He had to in a sneaky, conniving, deceiving, hidden agenda, hidden motive way, find a strategy, trickery, scheme, and device he could use that without you and the person you were in the relationship with knowing it, use them, use you, and use the person you were in a relationship with to carry out his attack and assault.

He chose to use someone that you really loved, cared, needed, wanted, desired, look up, believed, finally trusted, relied, opened up, gave all or the part of you that you had never given anyone else as the one that would cause, create the atmosphere, and contribute to your own relationship and your relationship with each other failing and being damaged beyond repair.

Satan and all of his dangerous, destructive, and highly confrontational driven and motivated spirits were at work in the unseen, unexpected, unplanned, unknown, unfair, unaware, and unsure, hidden from human eyes, using whatever and whomever it could to be the initiator and instigator that he could use to scrub and scrape any and all matters, memories, and moments that was in your past with the goal of trying to find some residue from an old vicious-cycled, devastating, resentment-filled, bitterness-filled, vengeance-filled and led, anger-filled, stalker- and fatal-attraction-filled relationship. The goal was to find something from your past that you had a hard time letting go, getting over, moving forward from and use it against you.

If Satan could use whatever and whomever he could to find some old relationship residue living, dwelling, abiding, lingering, and lying dormant inside of you or the person you were in the relationship with, he would bring alive the spirit of it or the spirit that led and surrounded that matter, moment, and memory that was so hurtful and painful and kept you so broken it almost killed, stole, and destroyed you spiritually, physically, mentally, emotionally, and even financially. To the degree where you got on a self-destructive path and you got into a self-destructive point in your mind, mind-set, thinking, way of thinking, thoughts, and train of thought that had begun to kill, steal, deceive, and destroy your mental state of mind, your mental state of being, your mental condition, and your mentality.

Right, Right, Wrong

Satan was trying to bring about ways he could bring up the spirit of your past and the spirit from your past that was so beyond what you could have thought of or imagined that the spirit of and the spirit from your past would have enough power and drawing power that it could and would lead you away and get you off your strong, safe, stable, and secure spiritual path and foundation that you had worked hard to find and build and get on. Once you were led into that compromising place because of the spirit of and from your past, the plan Satan would then put into effect and put in motion was and is to make sure you and the person you have worked hard to get into and build a satisfying and fulfilling relationship with would get and stay connected to each other in all of the wrong places.

What that would mean is when you needed and wanted that person, they will never be where you wanted and needed them to be, and they would continually and at times consistently say and do all of the things that bothered you, agitated you, aggravated you, frustrated you, and discouraged you. They would never or every now and then be in the right place at the right time. Their timing was not in sync with yours, and they could not find, flow, and function with you on the same level. Satan could do all of this because he knew how hard you were fighting against and guarding yourself from the spirit of and from your past, and the person you were in a relationship with did not know, did not want to hear and know, totally gave utter disregard to, and/or ignored what you had been through, downplayed it, and discounted it.

Satan had that person focused on what they could get out of you, what they wanted and needed out of and from you, how they should and could keep others from getting to and having any part of you. Why? It's because you and that person was not and would not be connected in the right places with each other. The end results would be that person would bring out the worst in you and not the best in you. Satan would also work behind the scenes, making sure the other person you were in a relationship with saw, viewed, interpreted, felt, believed, analyzed, and perceived your spiritual, physical, mental, emotional, character, conduct, conversation, communication, integrity, intellect, and financial strengths as things about you that make them feel inferior and less, that dominate, manipulate, and control.

Satan would come up with ways to use all of what you had worked so hard to gain and what you have done that would make you a strong person for all of the right reason(s); and he would use what you changed in your way of thinking, changed about yourself and your life, changed in your choice and decision-making process and procedures, changed in the way you say, do, and handle things, what you have worked diligently and consistently hard to change about yourself as the change that which he would use to take the person you were/are in a relationship through changes. As that would happen, it would bring out feelings of insecurity within the person that Satan will then use to batter, beat, bruise, and beat down their already-low self-esteem, lack and loss of drive, motivation, ambition, passion, and self-confidence.

All of this and much more are vicious-cycled methods that Satan kept hidden from us in the unseen, unexpected, unplanned, unknown, uncertain, unfair, unaware, undetected, and in the unsure. When he gets ready, he and all of his demon spirits, generational-curse-carrying demon spirits that know the areas/places you have not been delivered, cleansed, purged, healed, and made whole in are also knowledgeable about you, me and us and our past; those same wicked and foul spirits Satan has empowered so that they can and will have something they could use to drive, draw, pull, force, persuade, seduce, entice, trick, entangle, entrap, and lock up our relationships.

The reason Satan and all of his imps and cohort spirits are at work on your relationships in the way I just described is for the sole purpose in making sure your relationships cannot be or end up in a prosperous, productive, and successful manner. They want to make sure your relationship will not flow and function and be, become, and end up being able to accomplish, achieve, acquire, and accumulate all of that which God says your relationships can and will. If your relationship is able to do so it will in the end make your relationship filled with his glory, and it will function and flow in Gods goodness.

The person you are in a relationship with was someone you felt, believed, and thought would be the right person who would stand by and be with you and would be there for you when you needed and wanted them. They were the right person at the right place, and when a wrong matter, moment, circumstance, situation and, confrontation came about and you needed and wanted their help, they clearly demonstrated on more than one occasion they the wrong go-to person.

Let me paint the picture: It's like when you know, thought, felt, believed, was confident, etc., that which you would need would be in your right pocket/in the right place because you had worked hard to put it/them there. You always are consistent in putting what you need, that something in the same place and pocket. The day and moment came when you needed that something, and when you put your hands in that pocket to get that something out when you needed it, for some reason, it would not be where you put it. Instead of being in the right-front pocket/in the right place where you would consistently put that something, it's not there. Instead, it is in the right-left pocket or in the left- or right-back pocket.

Essentially, the person you are in a relationship with is always or most of the times connected to you in the wrong places; and as a result, they end up in the wrong place, saying, doing, handling, and making choices and decisions that do not help you. Instead, their acts, actions, deeds, etc., end up bringing more unwanted and unwarranted challenges to what is already a tough matter, circumstance, situation, confrontation, and moment. To have that happening in turn will bring about or lead to you having to go through more unnecessary changes. He or she is the right person, and they are at the right place and time to help you, but what comes out of them is all wrong.

The Function and Flow of Flashbacks

When a person has been hit unexpectedly and without them seeing, knowing, thinking, believing, feeling, expecting, and being able to have time to plan, prepare, and position themselves for that hurt and pain in the course of their relationship with you, that unexpected hurt and pain they receive in turn can and will cause, create the atmosphere, and contribute to them remembering, reliving, and reminiscing what they had been through that is still an open wound, or that place is still a wound that is in the process of being healed. That old relationship wound being relived again ends up getting the relationship scab or relationship covering painfully removed, and it starts to get infected all over again. Which means this wound or that new unseen, unexpected, unplanned, unknown, unfair, unaware, undetected, uncertain, and unsure relationship hurt, pain, and brokenness is deeper, greater, and more excruciating than the ones before.

All of what I just shared took place because the hurt and pain that came about was what they had or hadn't experienced or encountered before. The hurt and pain may have been the same kind or type, or it could have been similar to relationship hurt, pain, and brokenness that was similar or just like what they have been through in a relationship(s) before you came into their life. But this time, this new unexpected hurt and pain is not only deeper, greater, and more excruciating than the ones before, but both will also have a more profound, deeper, and more traumatic affect and effect.

The thought and feeling suddenly becomes "I can't believe this is happening to me again" with or at the hands of this person. Because the new hurt and pain comes at the hands of someone, that one person you never expected it to come from, not only do it bring a new, greater, deeper, and more excruciating hurt, pain, and brokenness, but there is also that unsuspecting state of being so stunned and shocked beyond belief that the person goes through a triggered transitioning character, conduct, conversation, communication, integrity, intellect, personality, and image change right before your eyes.

Triggered Traumatic Transitioning Transformation

As the triggered traumatic transitioning is going forth, it will lead to the hurt person and their character, conduct, conversation, communication, integrity, intellect, mind, mind-set, thoughts, train of thought, thinking, way of thinking, mental state of mind, mental frame of mind, mental condition, mentality, and personality being transformed from being clean and pure and honest into the flow, function, image, and expression of one who is now a prosecuting attorney.

Satan is triggering this traumatic transitioning and transformation in the unseen, unexpected, unplanned, unknown, uncertain, unfair, unaware, undetected, and unsure. It is happening in a place that your human eyes can't see and at a pace that your carnal mind cannot conceive and you can't and won't believe. You and that person may start out holding a conversation that is filled with communication and understanding, and before you know it, their whole mind, mind-set, thinking, way of thinking, thought, train of thought, mental state of mind, mental frame of mind, mental condition, and mentality suddenly change, and you can't and won't know it if you are not spiritually aware, mature, and in tune. Their tone of voice, body movements, and facial expression suddenly change as well as everything that is within them. Their feelings, emotional state and condition, and desires will suddenly change as well.

What's happening is that person is in that moment being hit with strong, deep wounding, painfully indescribable doses of past feelings, past emotions and past desires. You can't see it and feel what they are feeling. There are doses of faith breaking, confidence shaking, havoc wreaking, "I don't understand why this is/has happened to me again, what did I say and do to deserve this", shattering, "why is this happening to me again", shame bringing, "I'm still recovering from my past" truths and realities. With every dose they are hit with, they powerfully force that person's personality, character, conduct, understanding, intellect and feelings of being safe, secure, and stable with you and in your presence to be challenged and changed. Their entire mental state of mind, mental frame of mind, mental condition, and mentality is suddenly being transitioned from being deeply rooted in understanding to being traumatically transformed into one that is filled with chaos and a lot of confusion.

The person is then in and at a place and point within their mental makeup where their mental capabilities, mental abilities, and mental capacity have taken so much doses of indescribable shock, stress, tension, hurt, pain, and broken thought and thinking patterns that it is leading and keeping them at a place and point where they are and will be, become, and end up being locked, yoked, in bondage, enslaved, bound, and limited to being halt between two opinions, double minded, unstable, unreliable, and uncertain about everything they think and feel.

This transitioning from having a strong and stable mind with secure thoughts and thinking into being traumatically transformed into being in the state and condition of having two minds that is so compromised, that it is consistently hesitating, dubious, and irresolute you can't see with your human eyes. But it is happening, and it is taking place right before your eyes.

As I stated before, you are talking to that person who you have intentionally or unintentionally hurt, and they start out communicating with you, and understanding was flowing between the both of you. And in a moment and before you can blink your eyes, another personality has emerged, and now you find yourself in the presence of a person who is flowing and functioning out of the spirit of a satanically wicked, nasty, highly smart and intelligent, manipulatively deceiving, and unclean spirit. That person who is filled with unexpected hurt and pain at your hands in the moment I just described is operating in the spirit, nature, and personality of a cold, calculating, and controlling prosecutor or attorney.

Once the person you once felt close to, made love to, shared your life, made memories and moments with, been there for, shared your day, fears, faith, dreams, hopes, and desires with, etc., Satan has transformed their nature and personality and changed their spirit into that of a *prosecuting* attorney who, without you knowing it, is that same person you was so proud to show off to your family, friends, and even flaunt before your enemies in a proud manner and way and now have turned against you.

The ultimate purpose and plan Satan uses flashbacks for is as weapons he can use to draw, force, pull, push, persuade, seduce, entice, deceive, and trick a wounded, hurt person into remembering, and reliving the former things and considering things of old. All of which, once indulged in, can and will distract, detour, delay, and even deny the hurt person their God-given right to be delivered, cleansed, purged, healed, and made whole again,. It can and will hurt, hinder, and handicap their relationship. Flashbacks relived can and will restore anything that is old, good or bad, happy or sad, right or wrong.

The Three Pain Prosecutors

When it comes to knowing who the recorder is or was of your pain or the pain that you have caused someone else, it was the three pain prosecutors. The three pain prosecutors for that hurt, pain-filled broken person is and will be their feelings, emotions, and desires. As you are listening, hearing, and talking to the person you have hurt or have been hurt, you hear them say they have forgiven you, and deep down inside that may be true. But it is still that person hurt, pain, and brokenness-filled feelings, emotions, and desires that have kept a record of the wrong that you have done or that have been done to the hurt person.

While you are listening, hearing and talking to the hurt person and as the hurt person is listening and talking to you, the three pain prosecutors are quickly at work bringing back to *remembrance* the face of the last person who caused the person you are talking to and you are trying to reach out to and reason with to feel hurt, pain, and brokenness. Once the remembrance is brought up, then those three pain prosecutors will stimulate a *replaying* of what took place and what were the circumstances, situation, and confrontation that led up to and that brought that hurt person the hurt, pain, and brokenness they feel.

There is also a replaying of every moment from the beginning, to the middle, and to the end of what took place, how it took place, when it took place, where it took place, why it took place, an image of who was the initiator and who was the instigator, what led up to, etc., in very vivid detail. Some or most of the actual events and how they really were unveiled and unfolded may be distorted and twisted. The next thing those three pain prosecutors will do is bring about a *reliving* of the very moment when the hurt, pain, and brokenness was occurring.

As the person who was the target of the hurt, pain, and brokenness is being pulled, pushed, persuaded, drawn, driven, and forced to remember replay and relive what led up to bringing them the hurt, pain, and brokenness they had to endure through, the hurt person's mental state of mind, mental condition, and mental frame of mind will begin to react, respond, or have a reactionary response to the record that is being remembered, replayed, and relived.

Everything that I just described to you was and will be happening and occurring at a very fast pace. You can't physically see it with your human eyes because what's going on is taking place in the unseen, unexpected, unplanned, uncertain, unknown, unfair, unaware, undetectable, and unsure. The hurt person's nature, personality, character, intellect, and integrity is being transitioned and placed into a hurt, pain, and brokenness-filled person's protective custody. After this happens, the three pain prosecutors will stimulate the hurt person's mind, mind-set, and mentality into going into an offensive and then defensive mode.

When in the offensive mode, the hurt person will begin to assault, attack, and assassinate. When in the defensive mode, the person will demonstrate unconcern, a nonchalant attitude, hostility, anger, bitterness, resentment, forgiveness, sorrow, and they will sound like they are halt between opinions or they are hesitating, dubious, irresolute, unstable, unreliable, and uncertain about everything they are thinking, feeling, and deciding.

All the while these things are taking place, the person's thoughts, train of thought, thinking, and way of thinking is entangled and entrapped into consistently releasing reflections and scattered images of the danger, damage, hurt, pain, and brokenness each moment brought as well as the wounded feelings, the emotional scars, and the destitute desires that are and will forever be unforgettable, unexplainable, unthinkable, and unbelievable. This is why it will take some time for the person who has been hurt by you or someone else to recover from the wrong they have suffered through. The person as a whole is not hurt, just their feelings, emotions, and desires are. It is also the person's feelings, emotions, and desires that is keeping record, remembering, replaying, and reliving the hurt, pain, brokenness, abuse, neglect, being battered, rejected, abandoned, violated, etc., they have suffered.

Recognizing the Recorder

Just like a real court have a court reporter, which is someone who records everything that is said in a courtroom and can recall what was said at any time when requested to do so, there is a part of you that records and can recall and replay everything that has ever happened to you. Be that good or bad, happy or sad, right or wrong, it is still recorded and remembered. The part of a person that is/have recorded and kept the record of your wrong will also always be that hurt person's fate-driven feelings, fate-powered principles, fate-positioned past, fate-filled hurt, fate-filled pain, fate-filled brokenness, and fate-filled feelings as well as their damaged, dangerous, destructive, deadly emotions and desires and not their heart.

The process: The person's recorder, which would be their feelings, emotions, and desires, act as messengers. They send a *first* message to the part of that hurt person's feelings, emotions, and desires that have the power to remember, telling them to replay the memories, moments, and matters that brought about the wrong done. And then a *second* message is sent, telling those remember-your-wrong-recording feelings, emotions, and desires to replay and relive the end results of the wrong that was done to them in the past and present.

Once the person's recorder, their hurt feelings, emotions, and desires have remembered, replayed, and relived, the matters, memories, and moments that led up to the final end results, a *third* message is sent from the person's recording recorder of the-wrong-you-done feelings, emotions, and desires to that person's remembrance, telling their power of remembrance to get in a protective I-can't-I-don't-know-if-I-can-live-with-trust-love-open-up-to-you-again mode.

Once the recorded recorder-of-the-wrong-you-done message have been sent by and through the hurt person's feelings, emotions, and desires, a protective survival mode order demand is sent into and through the person's power to remember. The *final* thing that happens is the person's mind, mind-set, thoughts, train of thought, thinking, way of thinking, mental state of mind, mental condition, mental frame of mind, and mentality begin to reject, resist, refuse, rebuke, refute, and react and respond to the messages and images the person's fate-filled past hurt, past pain, past brokenness, and past broken feelings, emotions, and desires have sent. No matter what took place and regardless as to who initiated what took place your fate-filled, damaged feelings, emotions, and desires is always recording what happened.

It's amazing what the human mind and body can do and the signals that it can send to any and every part of your body, and all parts of your body will react, respond or cause, create the atmosphere, and contribute to a reactionary response to take place. To have a person's hurt and broken-filled feelings, emotions, and desires acting as the pain prosecutor or acting as the pain-prosecuting, assaulting, attacking, and assassinating attorney is just like having an eyewitness account of the wrong that was done. A person's pain is usually accurate and, in a lot of cases, can be tainted with accusations and assumptions. It's really hard to stand in a room with a person who is so hurt and broken. They are allowing their past or present pain to persecute and then prosecute you. In that moment, the person you once felt connected to, cared for, have concern for, and have compassion for is no longer the one that you are talking to and listening to.

It's almost as if the person have transitioned or transformed into the image and spirit of someone else. One of the most important facts and truths that you must clearly understand is from the first moment you meet a person and eventually get into a relationship with them, their feelings, emotions, and desires are recording everything that take place in your relationship with that person.

Your mind, with all of its capabilities and abilities, is the recorder of the images of the wrong that was done to you or that person. Your heart records, remembers, and replays the wrong, hurtful, and painful words that were spoken because your heart is easily affected and easily effected. But your feelings, emotions, and desires are the actual recorder of the wrong that was said or done to you. Your hurt and your pain-filled broken feelings, emotions, and desires is what actually record, remember, replay, relive, and experience that which have been restored, and then there is a revisiting of the actual feelings that's associated and connected to the blunt-force-trauma hit of the wrong that was said or done.

The dangerous part about all of this is, at times, you can be talking to or trying to talk to someone who is experiencing some type of hurt, pain, and brokenness, and they will not be showing it. But the moment when you inadvertently and unknowingly step over into their place of pain, they, without any warning, will begin an aggressive assault and attack at trying to assassinate who you are. At times we can encounter and have an experience(s) with people who are protecting their past and present pain and they are pretending to be okay, but in all actuality, they are just a problem that is waiting to happen. These kinds of people who have that kind of deceptive and deceiving spirit upon them are always perpetrating a facial fraud.

Fact: The most dangerous, deadly, destructive, and damaging pain is the one that is deceiving, and it is very deceptive in its mode and in its manifestation. It stays hidden, and with speed and pinpoint accuracy, it quickly hits and strikes an unsuspecting person, causing that person's will to win, power to overcome, and ability to exercise their authority to end up being in a incapacitated state or condition. You do not want nor need this kind of pain acting as a prosecutor, and you do not want to have any type of experience or encounter with this kind of pain acting as a prosecutor.

CHAPTER TWENTY-TWO

In the Court of Hurt and Pain

Here's the picture: Out of innocence and out of you really feeling remorse, regret, and having a repentant heart and spirit that demonstrate and show you are and have been in a mental state, mental condition, mental frame of mind, mind-set, and mentality where you have felt nothing but a deep brokenness, all of which will cause you to feel everything within you that makes you strong and stable as a person has been shattered into a thousand pieces. The person you are trying to humbly apologize to and try to share your repentant heart with and show you really do care about what happened cannot and, in most cases, is so blinded by what you have said and done and by your choices and decisions and the way you handled what they had to say to you, the way you handled that matter, circumstance, situation, and confrontation that, in the end, would bring them some unsuspected deeply wounding hurt, pain, brokenness, shame, embarrassment, etc., is now demonstrating the spirit of a prosecutor who have a lion's spirit and a lion's tenacity.

Without you knowing it, you have been moved from being in a conversation where there was communication and understanding, and you have been moved or transitioned into the court of hurt and pain. The person you had children with, met, and wanted to spend the rest of your life with, traveled and had a lot of good times with, been there with through thick and thin, through better and worst, in sickness and in health, when you were rich or poor, thought forgave you because they said they did, wanted to reconcile, etc., is not the same person you are talking to in that moment. That person and their heart and spirit have left the room and can't be found.

All of a sudden, the charges against your character, conduct, conversation, communication, choices, decisions, image, intellect, integrity, personality, promises you made, and everything you have ever said, promised, made a commitment, and vowed are being read against you by the same person who, in earlier conversation, was open to you, listening, receiving, and hearing you and your apology, etc. That person has suddenly and once again without you knowing it, is being used and have been used to draw you into a vulnerable, open, honest and sincere, compromised place and point with them. And when you are at that point, that is when you will begin to see and feel their vengeful, mean-spirited I-want-you-feel-and-know-what-and-how-I-feel-and-I-want-you-to-feel-and-know-what-you-have/are-putting-me-through spirit. That person's right and rational reasoning have been disconnected, and they are allowing their self-survival urges, tendencies, inclinations, intuitions, and instincts to force them into yielding, submitting, and surrendering to demonically suggested and influenced self-performance, self-will, and self-efforts that will be the driving force behind their acts, actions, deeds, conversation, communication, conduct, ways, thoughts, and mannerism in that moment.

The Hurt and Pain Judge

The judges that have power, authority, and the final say when you are in the court of hurt and pain will be that hurt person's mind, mind-set, and mentality, mental state of mind, mental condition, mental frame of mind, and mental mode. The hurt and pain judges' responsibility is to shut down any attempts you make to defend yourself and to make sure every and any kind or type of heartfelt, sincere desires and attempts you try to make in order that you can reach out and touch the heart of the person you have hurt is overruled. Every time you think or feel you have something to say that would vindicate you, the court of hurt and pain judges will suddenly, abruptly, and even rudely interrupt you and shut you down.

The person's mind being twisted and tainted is receiving satanically strongly suggested and intense influenced images, ideas, instructions, inspirations, information, insights, and wicked ingenuity that Satan has dominated, manipulated, and controlled by Satan himself. He is basically filling that hurt and pain-filled person's mind, mind-set, mentality, mental state of mind, mental condition, mental frame of mind, and mental mode with chance gusts of relationship teaching, changing wind of relationship doctrines with relationship cunningness and relationship craftiness.

All of which will keep the hurt- and pain-filled person's mind, mind-set, mentality, mental state of mind, mental condition, mental frame of mind, and mental mode wavering with and wavering in every shifting form of relationship trickeries that is constantly and consistently being an easy prey to being seduced, tricked, trapped into being enticed, engaged, engulfed, entangled, and entrapped in inventing relationship errors that mislead.

The end results will end up being the person's mind, mind-set, mentality, mental state of mind, mental condition, mental frame of mind, and mental mode staying in a state and a condition where it is consistently being tossed to and fro due to being bombarded with deceiving, distorted, damaged, delusional, depressing, damaged, incorrect, and inaccurate relationship images, ideas, instructions, inspirations, information, insights, and ingenuity.

Because Satan have the hurt- and pain-filled person's mind, mind-set, mentality, mental state of mind, mental condition, mental frame of mind, and mental mode loaded and locked into his relationship strategies and locked into his relationship deceits, none of them can function, flow, and follow sound relationship doctrinal teachings. Their mind, mind-set, mentality, mental state of mind, mental condition, mental frame of mind, and mental mode will always be entangled and entrapped in hesitating, dubious, irresolute, unstable, unreliable, and uncertain about every relationship thing or matter.

The job and the responsibility of the mental judges is to make sure everything the hurt- and pain-filled person think, feel, or decide when it comes to the relationship they have been hurt in and when it comes to the person who has hurt them and caused them pain is to overrule, overpower, overtake, and overthrow any type of rational right relationship reasons and reconciliation of any kind and to any degree.

The other responsibility of the mind, mind-set, mentality, mental state of mind, mental condition, mental frame of mind, and mental mode judges whose reign and rule is in the court of hurt and pain is to make sure the hurt- and pain-filled person is deceived enough so that they can, without procrastinating, hesitating, questioning, and second-guessing,

❖ refute right rational relationship reconciliation arguments;
❖ refute right rational relationship reconciliation theories;
❖ refute right rational relationship reconciliation thoughts, train of thought, thinking, and way of thinking;
❖ refute right rational relationship reconciliation plans, purposes, processes, principles, and procedures; and
❖ refute right rational relationship reconciliation reasons

The Two Statements

Here it is now up close and personal. Are you ready? You have been led as a sheep ready for the slaughter into their court of hurt and pain. The person you hurt, damaged, hindered, let down, felt you lied and deceived, can't believe you hurt, used, abused, neglected, battered, rejected, abandoned, raped, molested, sodomized, dominated, manipulated, controlled through spiritual deception(s), violated, etc., have got your attention, and they have you where they want you. It is now time for them to bring the hurt and pain to you. You have been caught, and now you are caught up in their court of hurt and pain where they are the prosecutor, witness, jury, judge, and they are the law enforcer that will carry out your sentence.

Well, what about them saying they forgave you? That was just one of those "i'm-not-feeling-the-hurt-pain-brokenness-and-the-sting-of-what-you-done-right-now" stated agreement and not an I-have-been-delivered-cleansed-and-purged-healed-and-made-whole-from-all-of-this signed agreement. A stated agreement is a statement that is made or spoken out of the mouth of a person but not necessarily out of their heart, that essentially gives them the right as a hurt person to say one thing and do another without thinking about it and without you knowing it. A stated agreement is broken or breached or triggered the moment when that person feels or relives any part of or all of what has happened to hurt them.

A broken or breached stated with the mouth agreement is still subject to the person who made it an interpretation. They can challenge or change any part of it whenever their demonically pressured hurt, pain, and brokenness lead them to. You will never really know when that happens. When that person will snap, flip the script on you, and become a persecutor and a prosecutor, you are just led like a sheep ready for slaughter and easily led into its web of deception at any time and no matter where you are.

A signed agreement is one where the person has really forgiven you, and that forgiveness-stated statement came out of their heart or came as a result of them seeking out and getting delivered, cleansed, purged, healed, and made whole from being hurt, in pain and brokenness, abused, neglected, battered, abandoned, rejected, violated, etc. A signed agreement is one that is made not just in theory or in speech, but is also made, shown, and demonstrated in deed(s) and in truth, in practice and in sincerity. The person can talk to you about how you have hurt them and brought them pain and brokenness, how it affected and effected them, and it don't and won't hurt anymore.

There are no matters, moments, and memories that they pull up and relive as if it were still alive. Their signed agreement-spoken forgiveness is demonstrated with and accompanied by actions that speak louder than their words. A signed forgiveness agreement cannot be broken or breached. Why? It cannot be broken or breached because it was made in and came out of a clean and pure heart. It was an agreement that came out of a heart that God had touched, and he has delivered their emotions from the sting, cleansed and purged their feelings from the stench, healed their thoughts/thinking from being entangled as a result of it, and he has made their will whole so that it can't and won't be entrapped due to what they have been through. A signed forgiveness agreement is sealed in truth that makes all free, and it is delivered in God's unconditional love.

Secret Indictments

The person who has been hurt, that's acting in the spirit of a prosecuting attorney, is someone who has a vengeful and spiteful spirit upon them and is so hurt they are existing in pain, and they are filled with brokenness. And that is their reason for having you in their court of hurt and pain. The next thing that happens is they will begin to open up secret sealed indictments that they have formed against you. This person you befriended, helped, stood up for, changed, or rearranged your whole day and life for was in some kind of relationship with had been keeping a record of the wrong you have said and done in and over the course of your relationship with them.

And they hid their record, keeping from you in sealed indictments; and in that moment, when they are feeling, experiencing, and encountering a lot of often-overwhelming and excruciating hurt, pain, and brokenness, they open up those sealed secret indictments for the purpose of using them as a weapon formed against you. They don't care if you feel like you have been lied and misled, or they betrayed your trust by saying they forgave you. Every time they are hit with that overwhelming and excruciating hurt and pain that bring them into a state and condition of pure brokenness, they will retaliate and will engage in trying to tear and take you down so the spirit that is upon them and is leading them can take you out.

Every wrong that you have every committed over the course of your relationship with that person who has the nature, personality, and spirit of an assaulting, attacking, and assassination-minded prosecutor will, in that moment, end up being read. Their severely damaged, hurt, and pain-filled feelings, emotions, and desires have kept an accurate record of the wrong you have done to them, even if the things you said, done, matters you handled, choices and decisions you made were at that time in their best interest, and they benefited from it.

The fact being, in some kind of way, they ended up being offended, hurt, mad, angry, and upset and they never showed it or told you. Every time you helped them, it ends up hurting you, but they did not want to see or hear that. And even though you talked about, agreed, had good lines of communication and a good understanding of what was to take place, the cause and reason for such choices, decisions, and change or changes, the person you had feelings for, trusted all that you have with, etc., will be out to use everything they did not like, did not feel comfortable with, didn't tell or talk to you about, couldn't dominate, manipulate, and control when it came to you, couldn't get to change for their own personal benefit.

They didn't care if the change they were demanding you to make was the wrong one. It doesn't matter if what they were demanding could, would, and did have bad, wrong, and negative collateral damage, never-ending consequences, and a lot of negative repercussions. They still demanded and tried to force you into meeting their selfish demands. And when you didn't feed them what they selfishly desired, it led to their hurt, pain-filled, and broken feelings, emotions, and desires, issuing a vengeful, spite-filled secret sealed hurt and pain-filled personal indictment being formed against you, and now you stand accused. I know what I'm sharing is hard for you to believe.

After all, this is the person you looked up to, respected, supported, made personal sacrifices for, made compromises for, stopped hanging out with your closest friends for, stood up for even when you thought or felt they really wasn't all the way right when they said or done something, made a choice and a decision, handled a matter a certain way, dealt with a specific personal, private, or public circumstance, situation, and confrontation in a particular way or manner, etc. And that same person is now trying to use your mistakes as a weapon they can persecute and prosecute you with.

Answering to the Charges

In their court of hurt and pain, you have no voice. You have not been warned or notified so you can prepare, and you have not been given the time to properly produce evidence so you can present a defensive strategy. The person you were in the relationship with read the list of things you said and done, handled, made choices, and decisions that they feel was wrong in your relationship with them. And to your surprise, the record of your wrong seen through their eyes and seen from their point of view were things that you had said and done, matters you handled, choices and decisions that you made you know, and knew was, at that time, the right ones.

There was visible produced evidence and noticeable right end results to help prove that you made the right choices, decisions, and handled things the right way. You are being persecuted at times, and at times, you are being prosecuted and already found guilty before any evidence is presented. It's really hard being in that place with that person you really love and care for. It's even tougher when you are hearing the things that you are being accused of and the only thing you can do is listen and shake your head in disbelief.

As the person you were in a relationship continues to pull up record after record of the wrongs you are accused of committing that, in all honesty, is and was in direct opposition to what they, out of being selfish, self-centered, self-righteous, self-justified, out of past hurt, pain, brokenness, negative experiences, could not force you to comply with and be controlled by will continue to deliver twisted accounts of things that happened in your relationship. They are being satanically led into believing and feeling they are right in having you as their hostage in their court of hurt and pain. When you try to challenge what they are saying, challenge any of the accusations, assumptions, and presumptuous weapons they are trying to use against you, they then change their role from that of a prosecutor to that of a witness against you.

The Switch-Out Witness

All of the things they never talked to you about on a day-to-day basis, things that you really didn't know or was aware of, are allowed to be freely spoken in their court of hurt and pain. All of the mistakes you made are the only things that are brought up. There is no mention of the good things you said and done, and there is no mention of the good choices and decisions you made and of the good way you handled matters that they benefited greatly from. The switch from being a prosecutor to being a witness against you is quick and fast. You can hear them as they say things like, "I know. I was there, and I had to put up and live through those days/times you put me through."

You can also hear them say things like, "I didn't keep a record. I went through it with you every day." Not wanting to sound like you are being argumentative or sound and appear to be defensive, you are still trying to and you still want to be sensitive to their pain, brokenness, hurt feelings, emotional and mental state, condition, and mental frame of mind, you just listen. The only thing you or one can say out of the right spirit and for all of the obvious reasons is, "If the wrong I have said and done in our relationship and to you outweigh the good I have done, we don't need to be together, and this conversation we are having is not necessary."

Before you know it, he or she transforms back into a prosecuting attorney who will then begin to bring up more indictments raised against your willingness, your ability to listen and hear, your willingness to admit you are wrong and guilty of all that you are being charged and accused of. The prosecutor in him or her says, "See, that's what I'm talking about. You always…"

The Hurt and Pain Jury

Just when you think you are on the right path in presenting a defense, he or she then transforms into a jury foreman that has finally reached the verdict, and they quickly cut you off from talking and says, "The wrong you did most definitely did outweigh the good." Anything you say to defend yourself, Satan will make sure he use that person to belittle and degrade you in an effort to entice, seduce, draw, pull, push, persuade, and force you into initiating another vicious-cycled assault and attack against that person. The hurt, pain, brokenness, past abuse, neglect, being battered, rejected, victimized, and everything negative, bad, or wrong that has ever happened to that person will use that person as a prosecuting attorney.

The Hurt and Pain Prosecutors Closing Remarks

In that hurt and pain-filled persons closing remarks, they will make a mockery out of who you are, who you say you are, the image you try to portray, your human flaws, mistakes, weaknesses, vulnerabilities, compromises, your efforts in trying to clean up what you messed up, and you trying to change and make things better. Whatever it is that you wholeheartedly have set your heart and mind to when it comes to demonstrating you are not the person you once was, will end up being scrutinized, scrubbed and scrapped for any and all left over wrong residue.

The Hurt and Pain Courts Judgment

And now it's time for the final transformation of the nature, spirit, attitude, mood, and personality of the hurt person. That final change will be noticeable and recognizable in and through the spirit they will be speaking out of, making a final relationship choice and decision out of, and making a final conclusion and judgment as to what will happen next with what they feel or once felt for you. Any hurt and pain-filled person who have you in their court of hurt and pain will take on and have the nature, spirit, and the personality of a persecutor, prosecutor, witness, jury, and judge. Satan will lead the person you have hurt or use you into focusing on what you said or done that caused the relationship to break down as well as the matters you have handled, the choices and decisions you made, your mistakes, what acts, actions, and deeds that you have committed that brought you into their court of hurt, pain, and brokenness.

That person who said they loved you, cared for you, had compassion and concern for you, and wanted to be with you till death said they believed in you, would support you, be there for you, etc. Whatever they said to you and whatever you said to them that would bring you into the relationship you had with them, they are the same person Satan have filled their heart, mind, thoughts, thinking, way of thinking with unforgiveness, bitterness, anger, resentment, retaliation, self-will, self-effort, with "I never said or done that to you, and treated you that way" attitude, selfishness, self-centeredness, self-righteousness, and self-justification. He is prompting, persuading, and pushing them to use all of it as a weapon formed and used to kill, steal, and destroy not just your relationship, but there is also a secret weapon that is also formed against you. The weapon formed to take you out was devised and has been kept hidden in a special hidden-motive, hidden-agenda-sealed indictment.

CHAPTER TWENTY-THREE

In the Court with Fate and Faith

The Fate Processor

One of the most dangerous and damaging places to be or to find yourself in is the court of hurt and pain, and fate is the judge or fate is the processor that is processing what is taking place in the hurt and pain proceedings. The moment when you walk into a hurt and pain-filled circumstance, situation, or confrontation, the fight between fate and your faith will begin. The spirit of fate will do its best to gain total control, so it can deceptively pull out of your hurt and pain that which is damaging, deadly, dangerous, and self-destructive enough for it to process for the hurt person. With the very lives, love, and relationship of both persons weighing in the balance, the spirit of fate will work at trying to overpower, overtake, overthrow, and heavily take over, take down, take out or totally tilt the scales of relationship justice into its favor.

What God has shown me was, that day, even though my motives and intentions was clear, clean, and pure in the course of me trying to hold a conversation and communicate how I was feeling about some important matters that was hurting the person I had hurt, me, and us, in the right spirit, with the right tone of voice, and for all of the right reason(s), she wasn't where I was. Satan had somehow distracted me and my thinking, way of thinking, thoughts, and train of thought and detoured my conversation and then delayed what I was wanting to communicate with her on and then derailed my mentality, and finally, my *power of choice* was denied, and my right reasoning was detained.

Not only was I hurt, but now my mind-set, mental frame of mind, mental state of mind, and mental frame of mind was also being held hostage, hindered, and bombarded with hurt. As all of this was unfolding, Satan and all of his imps and demon spirits started assaulting, attacking, and assassinating that whole moment with unseen, unexpected, uncertain, unplanned, unknown, unfair, undetected, unaware, unsure, unexplainable, unforgettable, unthinkable, and unbelievable generational curses that they knew would kill, steal, and destroy our relationship.

The door for the distracting happened when the person I was talking to went into a selfish protective mode and begin to reject, resist, and refuse me and what I was trying to share. The very moment when Satan was able to pull, push, persuade, seduce, trick, force, lead, and trap her thinking, way of thinking, thoughts, and train of thought long enough to get them over into a selfish mode, that would end up being the place where her thought and thinking processes would come out of. As she began thinking and feeling her selfishness was in danger of being overthrown, tested, tried, threatened, tormented, and tortured, her self-centeredness kicked in automatically and provided the detour, and then her self-righteousness then kicked in automatically and provided the delay, and then her self-righteousness finally kicked in automatically and provided the derailing for the whole moment, conversation, and communication.

This whole demonic and satanic assault, attack, and assassination process was quick, automatic, systematic, and strategic. Neither one of us really didn't have time to think about what was happening. It was like that ball rolling down a steep hill. Before we knew it, our three worst enemies showed up for the party, and they are your feelings, your emotions, and your desires. If and when all three of these are powered by selfishness, self-centeredness, self-righteousness, and by self-justification, all of that person's power to discern, detect, and do right reasoning is disconnected.

Caught in the Counterfeit

God created faith and Satan's counterfeit to what God created is fate. Fate is a spirit and that force that lives, dwell, and abide in the unseen, unexpected, he unplanned, unknown, unfair, unaware, undetected, and unsure. Fate is a unclean spirit that you cannot see with your human eyes nor can you defeat and defend yourself from its attacks and assaults with human or carnal means. Satan is working behind the scenes following behind faith, and when he gets a chance to challenge faith, he will do so. There are a lot of times when what looked like faith is really fate that is trying to take over and take down faith.

It is important that you do not get caught and then get caught up in the counterfeit. It will take you having the knowledge I am sharing with you and the spiritual gift of discerning of spirits in order to protect yourself. You can be moving along in the function and flow of your life and relationship and thinking you are following faith, and all along you are following fate. Just as you have faith principles, procedures, and processes, you also have fate principles, processes, and procedures. Fate's best friends are fear, doubt, worry, stress, and unbelief.

Faith's best friend(s) are hope, belief, trust, and confidence. At times you think and feel you are fighting fate when all along it is your faith you are fighting with and against. You can also think you are fighting with the weapons of faith, and the reality is you are using fate weapons. It is important that you don't allow yourself to get caught and caught up in what you see, but be sure you know the difference. Fate is always trying to make a quick switch with faith and go undetected when it does so.

Each time there is a fate manifestation, it will consistently bring about an unforgettable, unexplainable, unthinkable, and unbelievable vicious cycles of a development of events that's beyond a person's control, regarded and determined by a supernatural power. Once again, it is important for you to know you can't see fate itself, and you can't physically touch fate because it is a demon spirit. Fate is a foul spirit, and it is a foe of faith. You can be in a faith fight and you can be in a fate fight and not even know it or be aware of it. The moment when your faith is about to cross the finish line, fate will often find a way to step in and steal that victory from you. If and when fate is successful in stepping in, it will then overpower and overtake your faith finish line, and you will not even know it.

The message that fate will be consistent in sending will be, when you are on the path with it and you are in the same place and time with it, whatever negative, dangerous, destructive, deadly, damaging, destitute, demoralizing, hurtful, painful, and brokenness-filled circumstances, situations, and confrontations that Satan have seduced, tricked, trapped, deceived, bamboozled, and enticed you to be involved in, near or around, that exist at that moment the final end results have already been dictated, decided, and determined and is destined to happen, turn out, or act in a particular way.

I can assure you the fate end results will not be in your favor. Fate can be the final processor of your hurt, pain, and brokenness, and you will never know it. When this happens, Satan has already assigned and attached what is destined to happen to your hurt, pain, and brokenness and how the circumstance, situation, confrontation, matter and moment will turn out and the particular way they all will cause you to act.

You can have faith-filled, driven, and motivated methods, mind-set, motives, and mentality, and you can have fate-filled, driven, and motivated methods, mind-set, motives, and mentality. Satan knows how to disguise fate, and he knows how and when to deceptively try to draw and drive you into being deceived by fate. The weapons of choice for fate is fear, family inherited generational curses, doubt, worry, stress, and unbelief. When fate is the force that has set the atmosphere negatives exist in that place and the end results has already have been assigned and attached. Whatever end results Satan have assigned and attached to your hurt, pain, and brokenness will inevitably happen.

God is the force that powers faith, and he is force that is behind, in the middle, and at the end of faith. SATAN is the force that powers fate, and he and his core of demon spirits are the forces that are behind, in the middle, and at the end of every fate manifestation. The inevitable is always assigned to fate-filled events, matters, memories, and moments. One of the most dangerous and deadly places for a person to be at and one of the most damaging and self-destructive points for anyone to be in and at will be to be in the same space with a person who have fate-filled feelings, fate-filled emotions, and fate-filled desires. The only thing that can and will come out of that place will be the inevitable.

When we are talking about a fate processor, we are talking about a spirit that has the power and the authority to prepare, treat, convert, and translate the development of events beyond a person's control, that's destined to happen, turn out, or act in a particular way, regarded and determined by a supernatural power. I'm now going to breakdown and reveal to you the strategies, deceits, wiles, trickeries, schemes and devices fate will use when it is the processor of your pain.

(1) Fate prepare happens when the power and the authority in the development of events that is beyond human control, regarded as supernatural power that is destined to happen, turn out, or act in a particular way that is so power-packed it have pushed, placed, and positioned the person's pain, personality, integrity, and intellect in its proper condition or readiness that is unstable, unreliable, and uncertain.

(2) Fate treat happens or occur as the power and the authority in the development of events that is beyond human control, regarded as supernatural power that is destined to happen, turn out, or act in a particular way is yoked, in a stronghold, in bondage links and connects with the person's pain, causing, creating the atmosphere, and contributing to that hurt person acting or behaving toward another person in a specified way.

(3) Fate convert happens consistently when the power and the authority in the development of events that is beyond human control, regarded as supernatural power that is destined to happen, turn out, or act in a particular way manifest in the person's pain, bringing about a modifying in the person's character, conduct, conversations, communication, mood, and attitude so that they all will serve a devastating demonic-attached and assigned different function.

(4) Fate translate can only take place when the development of events that is beyond human control, regarded as supernatural power that is destined to happen, turn out, or act in a particular way, tutor, train, and teach the person's pain, feelings, emotions, and desires how to change their form, condition, nature, etc., from being more than just dangerous, destructive, deadly, and damaging but into also being so highly volatile that it dictate,

dominate, and determine how the person behave and what kind of behavior patterns they can and will have and demonstrate.

Fate is a spirit that carries out the process of hindering, holding hostage, and hurting a person and their life, ability, and willingness to forgive, their ability to release themselves from the bondage of their past hurt, pain, brokenness, disappointments, discouragements, frustrations, fears, doubts, worries, and stresses, etc. This spirit knows how to use the person that has been hurt, that you have hurt in preparing their hurt-filled, pain-filled, and brokenness-filled case against you.

That same foul spirit is behind the scenes, pulling, pushing, persuading, drawing, driving, leading, suggesting, influencing, and forcing the person that is hurt into how they should behave toward you and how to deal with you in a specific or certain way. Not only so, but that same wicked, highly volatile spirit is also the one who has tutored, trained, and taught the person who is feeling hurt, pain, and brokenness in how to change their personality, intellect, character, conduct, conversation, communication, attitude, point of view, their opinion of you, thoughts of you, thinking and way of thinking when it comes to you, etc., into a different perspective so that the good things that person said about you can be used in a different, judgmental, harsh, cruel, and condemning way.

The spirit of fate is the one that have seduced, tricked, trapped, enticed, and entangled that person's loving, caring, concerned, and compassionate heart into a belief, view, different system and method of perceiving and seeing you. Fate have tutored, trained, and taught that person how to hide their heart, hide their open mind, hide their feelings, hide their emotional attachment, and hide their desires from you so it can pimp, prostitute, and use that person's hurt, pain-filled, brokenness-filled memory as a weapon formed against you.

Fate have taken down, taken over, and taken out the person who has been battered, beaten, bruised, molested, raped, abandoned, rejected, left destitute, violated, mistreated, disrespected, demoralized, tormented, tortured, taken advantage of, etc. That same spirit has taken down, taken over, and taken out the person who is hurt power of choice, their right reasoning ability capacity and capability, and fate has the person's mind, mind-set, thinking, way of thinking, thoughts, train of thought, and mentality locked into remembering all of the negative former things that took place in your relationship with them and considering the negative things of old that they have been harboring and hiding.

Fate was strategic also in how it went about taking down, taking over, and taking control of that hurt, pain-filled, broken person's mental state of mind, mental condition/conditioning, and mental frame of mind so the person you hurt would not see it, know it, or recognize it. After being successful at doing so, fate would dominate, manipulate, and control their personal feelings, emotional attachment to you, and their desire to see you, touch you, hold you, listen to you, hear you, help you, reach out and come to you, and their power of choice in a way and to a degree that the person who once said they loved you, cared about you, needed and wanted to be with you always and forever is now having their dominated, manipulated, and controlled fate-filled feelings, fate-filled emotions, and fate-filled desires along with their mood and their attitude also being fate-filled, processing the problem(s) that both of you have had.

After doing so, that hurt person who have and is being used to cause, create the atmosphere, and contribute to your repentant heart and spirit, love, care, compassion, and concern for them being deceptively drawn and driven into the court of hurt and pain where fate and all of its imps and cohort foul demon spirits will be and is the judge, jury, and executioner. Fate will be the spirit or force that will ultimately dictate how the misunderstanding-filled meeting, corrupt, confrontational, condemning conversations, and miscommunication will happen, occur, or take place.

Fate have already assigned and attached a decided and determined beforehand, long before what happened between you and that person took place end. It is an assigned and attached end result and a end ruling that is dangerous, destructive, devastating and damaging. When you are in the court of hurt and pain, your voice, opinions, feelings for that person that's hurt, emotional attachment to that person, and your desire to see reconciliation take place between you and that person and have been overruled long before you committed the act, action, deed, said, done, and handled matters the way you wrongly did and made.

Long before you made the bad and wrong choices and decisions you made that affected and effected the person whose fate is using and have used to bring you into its unseen and unknown court, you and that person, your life, your love for each other, your relationship that you both have worked hard to build, and everything else that you both have challenged, confronted, compromised, and changed personally for and on behalf of your relationship—all of it is being judged and condemned because of, due to, and by the development of events beyond you and the hurt person control that was destined to happen, turn out, or act in a particular way, regarded and determined by a supernatural power you now know is called fate.

Facts about the Fate Court

Not only are you now made aware and have knowledge when it comes to the spirit of fate, but you also need to know there is also a fate court that you and the person you have hurt never knew of or heard of. Why? There are some important facts that you need to know when it comes to a fate court.

1. It exists in the unseen, unknown, unnoticed, and undetected.
2. When manifested, it will always bring about the unexpected, unplanned, unfair, unaware, uncertain, and unsure.
3. Its finished works will always leave everyone that was in the moment with it with an unforgettable, unexplainable, unthinkable, and unbelievable feeling and thoughts.
4. It is manifested whenever someone opens the door for it to come in. It cannot invite itself in, and it cannot overpower, overtake, and overthrow your will and your power of choice unless you allow it to.
5. It gains control whenever there is a breakdown of communication, understanding, when bad behavior and behavior patterns is being demonstrated, when any type of negatives have the freedom and power to dominate, manipulate, and control a matter, moment, memory, circumstance, situation, and confrontation.
6. It gains control whenever the atmosphere and environment is changed and is charged with hurt-hindering hostile feelings, emotions, and desires.
7. It gains control whenever people bring selfish or negative hidden agendas and hidden motives into a positive atmosphere.
8. It gains control when the atmosphere is clouded with chaos and confusion.

It's another World

The other fact that you have to know and be aware of is being in the fate court is like being in another world. In fact, the fate court is another world within itself, and it resides and hides in the invisible and manifests itself in the visible. The only noticeable indications would be when a positive and a good atmosphere, conversation, communication, conduct, etc., suddenly changes or turn into a negative or hostile one. Someone have to open the door for it to come in.

Satan and his principality or despotism called fate is a spirit that rule, reign, assault, attack, and send assassination assignments from the unseen, unexpected, unplanned, unknown, unfair, uncertain, unaware, undetected, and unsure place or point in and through inherited generational curses. He does so the moment when a person yield, submit, and surrender to something he have suggested or influenced, that one or both persons willingly or unwillingly accept, adopt, and apply. In doing so, they open the door for Satan to send the development of events beyond you and the hurt person's control and beyond human control that was destined to happen, turn out, or act in a particular way, regarded and determined by a supernatural power.

Satanic fate lives, abide, reign, rule, dominate, manipulate, control, suggest, influence, assault, attack, assassinate, activate, enlivened, and alerted generational curses, bad things that happen to good people, right that goes wrong, wrong that looks right but goes wrong, right that looks wrong from another world. It's a supernatural world where world rulers of our present world's darkness have total presence, power, control, and authority. It's another world where the only thing that exists, functions, flows, and floats in the atmosphere is a strong, powerful, overpowering, overtaking development of events that is beyond your control, fare beyond the person(s) you are in a relationship with control and far beyond any human control; that is destined to happen or occur, turn out, or act in a particular way, regarded by and determined by a supernatural power. I suggest you wake up and you wise up. Never leave room for fate-suggested and influenced compromises.

Fate fact: One of the most important facts you need to know is by having fate as the processor of your pain, it can and will only end up producing, preparing, presenting, and positioning you for a continuous vicious cycle of a development of events that is beyond human control, regarded and determined by a supernatural power that is destined to happen, turn out, or act in a particular way.

Fate-Versus-Faith Pain Processor

When faith is the processor of your pain, what ends up happening or taking place is you and the person you are in a relationship with, the person that is hurt, have a strong belief or trust in the existence of God, strong religious feelings or beliefs, and a system of religious beliefs have the power and the authority to prepare, treat, convert, and translate your pain, hurt, and brokenness.

You both yield, submit, and surrender to having the assurance, confirmation, title deed of the things we hope for, being the proof of things you do not see, and the conviction of their reality, faith perceiving as real fact what is not revealed to the senses (Hebrews 11:1) have the power and the authority to prepare, treat, convert, and translate our pain. Now let me break it down a little further.

A. Faith prepare: When faith has the power and the authority to prepare your pain, faith makes your pain ready for the right activity, purpose, and use. You will have the assurance, confirmation, title deed of the things you hope for, being the proof of things you do not see and the conviction of their reality, faith perceiving as real fact what is not revealed to the senses that your pain can, will, and is being made ready for something that it will be doing, something that you expect to happen. Your pain is being made ready for the use in its God-given, purposed-by-divine design cause, reason, and fulfilled purpose.

B. Faith treat: When faith has the power and authority to treat your pain, what takes place is the assurance, confirmation, title deed of the things you hope for, being the proof of things you do not see and the conviction of their reality, faith perceiving as real fact what is not revealed to the senses, that your pain will be dealt with so you can begin to think about it in a different way or in a particular way.

That different way or particular way will be you beginning to allow and give your pain the freedom to prosper in the right way.

C. Faith convert: When your faith have the power and the authority to convert your pain, faith establishes, strengthens, and settles you while you are feeling the pain that you feel, in having the assurance, confirmation, title deed of the things we hope for, being the proof of things you do not see and the conviction of their reality, faith perceiving as real fact what is not revealed to the senses when it comes to your pain that God will change your pain into a different function and flow so that it can be used in a different way.

Faith will change your pain from the fate method, system, process, principles, and procedures your pain used to follow and transform. Change the nature and attraction of your pain to a different system, method, process, principles, and procedures that is productive, and your pain can prepare and present you the person with a different behavior and behavior pattern system, method, process, principles, and procedures.

D. Faith translate: When faith have the power and the authority to translate your pain, faith will change the form, condition, and nature of your pain and move it from one place and position to another. As this is happening, there will be the assurance, confirmation, title deed of the things you hope for, being the proof of things you do not see and the conviction of their reality, faith perceiving as real fact what is not revealed to the senses can and will still unveil and unfold your pain and reveal the (a) particular condition, character, or mode that your pain is in; (b) the particular mode of being of your pain and reveal (c) the character and quality of that your pain is having.

Once faith have been freed to reveal, expose, challenge, and confront how your pain has been functioning, faith will change how your pain has been flowing by moving it from flowing and being in a dangerous, deadly, destructive, and damaging state and condition inside of your heart and move it to the state and condition in your heart where the pain is functioning and flowing in a planned, purpose-filled, prosperous, productive, and successful mode.

Faith fact number 1: Having faith as the processor of your pain will let God's presence in, and the processing is done in and through God's power, and that pain is transformed and changed into a place of power.

Faith fact number 2: The other important thing you need to know is having faith as the processor of your pain can and will only end up producing, preparing, presenting, and positioning you for the assurance, confirmation, title deed of the things you hope for, being the proof of things you do not see and the conviction of their reality, faith perceiving as real fact what is not revealed to the senses.

CHAPTER TWENTY-FOUR

Fate Flowing 3M

Fate and Faith Flowing

There are times in our life and in our relationships when we inadvertently end up thinking about, remembering, and relieving moments and memories that bring about former, old, and past hurt, pain, and brokenness that remind us where we have been and what we have been through. And without knowing it, we begin to react, have reactionary responses, or respond out of that moment and out of that memory. It all started when we were just having a thought, and that thought led to you thinking, and that thinking opened up the door for your mind being linked, connected, and locked into the remembering and reliving of matters, moments, and memories.

Mental Memories, Moments, and Matters

When we get into a specific place mentally and we get into a specific mental mind-set, we can somehow feel the spirit of that matter, that moment, and that memory. And when we do so, we end up being emotionally enticed, entangled, entrapped, yoked, bound, and emotionally limited to all three. With our emotions running real high due to being emotionally enticed, entangled, entrapped, yoked, bound, and limited because of and due to us taking an unplanned and unexpected walk down memory lane, we are drawn, driven, pushed, pulled, persuaded, and forced into having desires that aggravate and agitate our right rational reasons and can easily stir up a spirit of revenge.

It's happened, and it is happening; and we are caught up in the moment, and we are caught in and with the memory. Our mind, thoughts, and thinking have got us to that place and point and into that moment and into that memory. We don't know what triggered it, and the only thing we know is we are trapped in that moment with that memory and with that matter. It seemed so real, and it felt so present even though it was something that had to do with and come from the past.

Our train of thought and our way of thinking are and have been seduced into falling into a trance or a stare into the atmosphere. We can hear people talking, and we can hear what they are saying. But instead of responding, we end up wrongly reacting, and we end up delivering a harsh, rude, disrespectful, anger-filled, condemning, and judgmental relived reactionary response. Everything you are saying and doing is coming not out of you being consciously aware, but it's almost like you are speaking, responding, reacting, and having reactionary responses that are being delivered out of your unconscious state, condition, and from an unconscious frame of mind. Your mood and attitude have changed from a positive to a negative one. Your mind-set and your mentality have also changed or have been altered. But you are not really sure when it was, why it was, how it was changed, and what changed them.

Something from your past has showed up and has become your present and could very well end up dominating, manipulating, and controlling your future. All of the hurt, pain, brokenness, and what you had to suffer and go through just to survive until you could overcome that matter and that moment in your life is being replayed. Your mental state of mind, mental condition, and your mental frame of mind is processing it all.

And without you being consciously aware, your tone of voice, and how you are answering questions you can hear but really don't clearly understand or can articulate and analyze correctly what's being said, you start to reject, resist, refuse, rebuke, and refute in a retaliatory argumentative manner the words, conversation, reasons, cares, and concerns of the one that's talking. Which in turn bait you into refuting the person who is talking, refuting their returned arguments, refuting their theories and reasons. All of which your past hurt, your past pain and your past experiences are interpreting. You are now saying whatever comes to your mind, and you are doing whatever your urges, tendencies, intuitions, inclinations, and instincts are forcefully, like a quiet storm, pulling, pushing, persuading, drawing, driving, and forcing you into saying and doing.

Your past hurt, pain, brokenness, and past experiences is interpreting what the person who is in a conflicting conversation with you as someone who is trying to bring you hurt, pain, brokenness, hinder you, belittle you, walk all over you, take advantage of you, treat your kindness like it is your weakness, and take you for granted. Why? It's all because there are broken lines of communication. Everything you are reliving from your past moments and past memories that involved you being battered, abandoned, violated, molested, abused, left destitute, rejected, disrespected, etc., feels like it is happening right now, but in all actuality, it's not happening.

Yet the moment, the memory, and the matter seem like and feel like it is so real. While you were talking to that person, your mind just slipped, eased, transitioned, or stepped over into another place, time, and moment that you really didn't want it to or thought you would not ever have to remember and relive ever again in your life. After coming out and regaining your consciousness and after regaining your right reasoning mind, your reality and the room is filled with a lot of emotion, hurt, pain, chaos, and confusion. What happened?

You and that person was just talking and holding what you thought and felt was a good conversation, and both of you were laughing and talking. And all of a sudden, the atmosphere changed, and things were happening on their own, and words were just coming out of you. It's like you couldn't stop what was flowing out of you. You even tried to stop, but the urged flow was stronger. How did what happen just happen? You remember holding a good, peaceful conversation where there was good and right communication and understanding. The next thing you know, fingers are being pointed at you, and the person who is in the room with you is accusing you of saying and doing something your really don't remember you said or done. You can see the hurt and pain on their face, and you can hear the brokenness in their voice, but what they are saying you said and done is really not you.

Fact: The scenario I just described above is how fate is at work behind the scenes. What that spirit has done is get you into *fate flowing* or into proceeding smoothly or easily, facile, long, smooth, graceful, and without sudden interruption or change of direction into the development of events that is beyond human control, regarded as supernatural power that is destined to happen, turn out, or act in a particular way. Fate is using mental memories, mental moments, and mental matters as a way of bringing your mind, mind-set, mental state of being, mental condition, and mental frame of mind into the fate flow.

This a consistent and constant strategic maneuver satanic fate uses as a weapon and as a way to get you to open up the doors of your life, heart, and relationship so he can sneak in or come in and kill, steal, and destroy something. This method is also the one he uses to set someone up for failure and a fall or to get someone into selfishness, self-centeredness, self-righteousness, and over into self-justification, into self-willed, self-performance, and over into self-effort.

Faith Flowing 3M

Faith flowing and flowing in faith is the direct opposite of fate flowing. They are not on the same path, and they will never end up at the same place and point. Whenever we are in the right flow, all of the right things can, will, and should happen for us. The person whom satanic fate is or had used to lure you into the court of hurt and pain is someone who was in the fate flow. They had been hiding or harboring some hidden negative unspoken grievances, resentments, and things they never told you about until the day you were bullied and badgered through and with the things they said, done, the way they handled a matter, or through the use of them making a choice and decision that wasn't mutually agreed upon.

Fate used that person to badger, bully, and bait your already-breached and compromised character, conduct, conversation, and way of communication.

Flowing in faith is defined as proceeding smoothly or easily, facile, long, smooth, graceful, and without sudden interruption or change of direction into the assurance, confirmation, title deed of the things we hope for, being the proof of things we do not see, and the conviction of their reality, faith perceiving as real fact what is not revealed to the senses. Flowing in faith happens when you yield, submit, and surrender to following faith, following the faith flow, following the flow of faith and flowing and following faith.

Faith flowing is also defined as the assurance, confirmation, title deed of the things we hope for, being the proof of things we do not see, and the conviction of their reality, faith perceiving as real fact what is not revealed to the senses that is proceeding smoothly or easily, facile, long, smooth, graceful, and without sudden interruption or change of direction. This type of flowing is the best one to be involved in and it will keep you out of the court of hurt and pain. Faith flowing involves you and that person holding, encouraging, and motivating conversations that end up being driven and powered by words of faith or by faith words. Functioning in, flowing in, and following fate will lead you away from facts and from the truth. Fate is that spirit that was and is behind the judgments that we, out of hurt, pain, and brokenness, pass upon each other. Fate cannot and will not help and heal and can only continue to hinder and hurt.

CHAPTER TWENTY-FIVE

Record of Your Wrong

One of the hardest things to conceive in your mind and to believe is the same person you have shared and spend some time out of your life with and had shared dreams, hopes, desires, like passions, and had seen God do so many great and wonderful things in your relationship is the same person who has been keeping a record of all of the wrong. They mentally recorded and remembered and at the right time, place, and moment everything you have ever said and done in your relationship with them. They will recall every detail. We all are just mere human beings, and none of us are perfect. From time to time, we all say and do things we don't really mean. We all, at one time or another, may handle things in a way that offend or hurt the person you are in a relationship with.

And no matter who we are, we, without really trying to do so, may make a choice(s) and a decision(s) for all of the right reasons, and when we do, the final results may, at the time, hurt and hinder the person you are in a relationship with. What do we do in times like that? We do what the Bible tells us to do, and that is to be clothed with humility and go to that person with a humble heart. Out of a heartfelt, sincere, repentant heart, we ask them to forgive us. Once we do so, we are released from the guilt of that wrong no matter if the person you are seeking and is asking for forgiveness from doesn't forgive you.

God have forgiven you before you committed the wrong. In fact, God has forgiven you for any past, present, and future wrong you will ever do. This is what the message of grace is all about. Receiving forgiveness and the power to forgive has been provided in the finished works of Jesus Christ when he died on the cross. None of us are perfect, and we all have flaws, weaknesses, and inadequacies as human beings. But when you have caused someone some hurt, pain, brokenness, and it was something they never expected or thought you would say or do, that hurt, pain, and brokenness becomes a lot greater, and it is felt in a deeper place within that person.

When the person you are in a relationship with has experienced some kind of hurt, pain, and brokenness, and it is something that you knew would bring those kind of feelings or you didn't know would bring about what they had experienced, that something you said or done, that act, action, and deed would end up bringing that person you are in a relationship with hurt, pain, and brokenness that caught them off guard and left them stunned, in shock, in disbelief. They are left in a place, in a frame of mind, in a state of mind, in a state of being where they are consistently touched with the feelings of that moment, and they are consistently reliving the memory of what happened just like it was happening to them all over again.

Some of us are strong enough to handle the hurtful, painful, broken-filled memory and moment flashbacks. Some of us know when and how to go to God and ask him to give us his strength in the place where hurt, pain, and brokenness came out of being shocked, stunned, caught off guard, and hit with something that we never expected from the person we love and have been in a relationship with. All hurt, pain, and brokenness are bad, and at the time, they are the worst that we can ever feel. But in my opinion, the worst kind of hurt, pain, and brokenness is felt and experienced when the person we have been in a relationship say, do, commit an act, action, deed, make a choice and a decision or handle a matter in a way that you never, in your wildest dream, would have expected them to.

It is a something that is uncharacteristic of them, and there were no hints or previews of the hurt, pain, and brokenness coming. There were no visible warning signs and there were no promptings indicating what was about to happen was coming. And in that moment and at that time, when you were suddenly and without warning, hit with the unforgettable, unexplainable unthinkable, unbelievable, unseen, unexpected, unplanned, unknown, unfair, uncertain, unaware, undeniable, and unsure, the person you were in a relationship with had done a selfish thing. They had opened the door for and had caused, created the atmosphere, and had contributed to the hurt, pain, and brokenness that you really feel that is really deep down within you.

You hurt in places you never thought, felt, or knew you could hurt in. You feel pain deep down within you in places where you didn't know pain could be felt, and the brokenness you feel really breaks you. As the three are flowing from a place that is deep down within you, the only thing you can do is cry uncontrollably. When you are the one who has caused, created the atmosphere, and had contributed to the person you are in a relationship with being hit, shocked, stunned, taken by surprise, faced with reality, and having to find a way to deal with a deep wounding unbelievable, unforgettable, unthinkable, unexplainable, undeniable, unseen, unexpected, unplanned, unknown, and unfair hurt, pain, brokenness, abuse, neglect, being battered, rejection, being depressed, raped, molested, used, etc., that was the same that they had been through in their past, the person will have an even more difficult time getting past it, especially if they are not spiritually strong enough.

At times, even those who are, have been and is spiritually strong will still have a tough time dealing with a wrong that was done to them that came right out of the book of their past. This is especially true when they did not expect, believe, know, was a aware of, had knowledge of, had planned, prepared and positioned themselves for, had a clue, had a thought or feeling, saw warning signs that you was about to and would be the one who would draw, pull, push, persuade, force them into remembering and reliving something they never wanted to remember and relive.

For that person to have to remember and relive a moment, memory, flashback or a going back through something that you or they had finally got over, got past, worked hard to get over, had got delivered, cleansed and purged, healed or made whole from and had finally received the right closure from and had closed your heart and mind to happening again, would be much harder to overcome.

The person who is the recipient of the above will end up saying things like, "I never thought, felt, or expected you would be the one to do that to me." They will shake their head in disbelief and have a blank look on their face and will have a stunned, shocked stare on their face, and they will say, "I never thought and I can't believe you would be the one that would say or do that to me especially when you know what I have been through in my past." The hurt, pain, and brokenness are a lot deeper; and the hurt, pain, and brokenness the person feels is up close and personal. The sting and excruciating pain they feel is not like any they had experienced before.

Stunning, shocking, unbelievable, unforgettable, unseen, unexpected, unplanned, unknown, unfair, unaware, and unsure hurt, pain, and brokenness brought about from someone you never expected, thought, believed, or felt is, for many, much harder to get over and get past. If the person whom Satan had targeted for this kind of relived personal past pain, past hurt, and past brokenness, being battered, abused, neglected, rejected, abandoned, belittled, put down, let down, disappointed, discouraged, frustrated, etc., is still being, have not been, is not really seeking nor wanting, is running from, don't believe in being delivered, cleansed, purged, healed, and made whole, when they come face-to-face, have to deal with the reality, have to go through all over again, have to wake up and go through their day, have to relive all over again something happening from their past, they end up being more deeply and emotionally devastated, deeply and emotionally damaged, deeply and emotionally discouraged and downtrodden, and they can end up in a depressed mental state and depressed mental frame of mind.

They have to deal with Satan being the mastermind demon spirit that's working behind the scenes of it all. He is at work reviving, restoring, renewing, refreshing, and forcing the person to relive the matter, the moment, and the memory from the past that is now made manifest in the present, bringing with it the same old past feelings and emotional tormenting, torturing, and trauma they had ran from, swept under the carpet, dealt, confronted, overtaken, or overpowered. The emotional effect and emotional affect is different from the first time, and it is much deeper. Why? It's because you had opened yourself up to believe again, trust again, love again, give again, and believe that you could, would, and can be in a good and healthy relationship.

Once again, you opened up and gave all that you had to the person and to the relationship, and you really wanted it to work. For some reason(s) unknown to you, the same thing(s) you dealt with in your past, this new person, years later, have done the unbelievable, unforgettable, unthinkable, unseen, undeniable, unexpected, unplanned, unknown, and unfair to you. What do you do, where do you go, and who do you turn to? Your heart is saying forgive him and let God have it and let him help you, but your head is still shocked and stunned. The hurt, pain, brokenness and your shocked, stunned, and bruised body is saying he hurt you. Keep a record of this wrong. Don't you let it go. Get your revenge. Make that person pay. They need to feel what you felt.

Your heart, your head, and your hurt are all at war, fighting against one another and then fighting and standing with one another. Your brokenness, feeling betrayed, being battered and bruised won't let you release love, you know, an unconditional love. The pain you feel pierces in places within you in an indescribable way and with so much power that you struggle to feel God's presence, and you feel pressured. Because of the pain to not forgive and to never forget, you never expected the person you are in a new relationship with to be the one to let what happened to you be at their hand. You never would have thought in a million years that person would say and do something that is right out of your past.

I'm Just a Hostage

What do you do when you are a hostage to your own hurt? What do you do when you are a prisoner to a past pain relieved again in your present? What do you do when you are bound because of the brokenness you feel? Where is your place of refuge? Where is the place and at what point does God give you the strength to release the moment and memory and matter you don't want to relive so that you will be restored? How do you fight against the feelings of fear, and what do you use to fight against the feelings of fear that will bring you a win? You can hear, see, and feel the person who brought you into this quiet storm of emotionalism apologizing out of a humble heart clothed with humility and out of a repentant, remorseful, and regret-filled heart, mind, and spirit.

You know it's all real, and you know what you are supposed to do and have to do is right, but the deep wounding hurt you feel is keeping you a hostage. The deep hurt is hindering you from forgiving so that reconciliation can take place. Only God can teach you how to love that person again, and only God can teach you and show you how to live with that person again and be at peace with it. The question is how do you go about releasing the person who wronged you from the record of their wrong? Your hurt, pain, brokenness, being battered, bruised, abused, neglected, rejected, abandoned, belittled in a derogatory manner/way, and shamed is keeping you holding on to what happened.

And you are also still holding on to those relived thoughts, relived moments, relived feelings, relived emotions, and relived memories of how you felt and what you felt. You can still feel yourself holding on to being angry, upset, disappointed, frustrated, discouraged, damaged, shocked, and stunned and being consistently halt between two opinions. And your feelings, emotions, and desires are constantly being in a double-minded state and condition. Your love, care, concern, and compassion for that person is in a state of chaos and confusion because of the deep wounding pain their wrong act, action, deed, choice, and decision has caused and brought you.

Fate-Filled Witnesses

There you are standing in the presence of someone you never thought would be working hard at tearing you down and not building you up. At first, it all seems so surreal and a little cold and chilling. No matter what you say, nothing can stop the person you really wanted to reach out to, draw close to you, and show that person your remorse-filled, regret-filled, repentant heart. You want them to know how you really feel, but they are not the person you felt or wanted to be close to. All of the wrong things that you had ever said and done over the course of your relationship are being dragged out from a place called forgiveness and Satan is using the hurt person as a weapon formed against you.

He knows that person is the one weapon he knows, if formed against you in the right place, at the right time, and at the right moment, who can gain a win and a victory over the both of you. He is using the person you hurt to bring up all of the wrong you have ever committed because he knows that person is the closest person to you, and his ultimate plan is to take down and take out both of you. As you are listening to the person you hurt recalling the record of your wrongdoings, they, with a vicious and malicious intent, start bringing up out of the archives of their heart and mind each one of them as if they just took place. The reality hit that they are not going to let you talk. When you look at their facial expression as they are talking, they are exhibiting that of a person who is locked into what they are saying, and they can't get out.

One record of your wrong after another is being brought up. Wrongdoings that the person you hurt said they had forgiven you, and you thought both of you had worked it out and worked past that wrong. Where is the record keeper? Who are these witnesses that have been recording your wrong? Where is the record keeper, the one who has been in hiding and has been secretly recording your faults, weaknesses, failures, flaws, mistakes, errors in judgment, generational sin curses that came out of your faith fights and out of your human frailties?

The prosecutor is fate, and the witnesses that will be called are fate witnesses. Each one of those fate witnesses have been secretly recording and remembering every wrong that you have ever committed against the person who is accusing you of hurting them in the first degree. Fate had them believing that you had a malicious intent when you hurt them, and he had the person you hurt believing that they have you where they want you, which is in their court of hurt and pain. Satan had the person you hurt believing they have the right to read from the list of wrongs you have ever committed against them.

The person you hurt is in a mental frame of mind and mental state of mind where they do not care, and they have been pulled, pushed, persuaded, forced, drawn, and driven into an I-got-you mentality. With their feelings and emotions being wide open and with hurt, pain, brokenness, anguish, frustration, disappointment, and deep feeling of disappointment, everything the person you have hurt had been holding back, and everything they had been keeping inside of themselves that they have always wanted to say to you, at that moment when the record of your wrong is being read, comes out of them just like an erupting volcano.

The witnesses who are reading the record of your wrongs are called fate feelings, fate emotions, and fate desires. When we take a closer look at these three recorders of your wrong keepers, we see three powerful expressive parts or pieces of who you are out of control, and they are seemingly unstoppable. It's a moment that you, in no way whatsoever, would have helped cause, create the atmosphere, nor contributed to. There is nothing that you can say or do that could and would stop the record of all of your wrongs being read. The same person who was for you is now tricked and deceived into being against you.

Fate Feelings

Fate feelings are defined and described as your awareness and the ability to experience physical sensation that comes out of the power supposed to determine the outcome of the final events, which are death and destruction. In other words, your awareness to physical sensation and your ability to experience physical sensation is under a satanic and demonic power that has already determined the outcome and the final events of those expressed awareness to physical sensation. The final outcome and the final events of your expressed ability to experience physical sensation, which are death and destruction, have already been determined as well

It is a physical sensation and awareness to physical sensation that comes from events or that comes from hurtful, painful, brokenness-filled event(s), matters, moments, and memories that an outward display or show of expression has already been assigned and attached. In other words, how the person is going to outwardly shows or demonstrates the physical hurt-filled, pain-filled, brokenness-filled sensations and their awareness to the physical hurtful, painful, and brokenness that came as a result of what has happened to them, and what they have been through has already been determined.

Let Me Paint the Fate Feelings Picture

Long before you and the person you hurt met and had decided to get into a relationship and long before you and that person made selfish, self-centered, self-righteous, self-justified, self-willed, self-effort mistakes, Satan knew he could and would get the both of you to use accusations and assumptions that would eventually hurt the both of you. Fate, that unseen, unexpected, unplanned, unknown, unfair, unaware, undetected, and unsure foe, was behind the scenes, making sure he brought about unbelievable, unexplainable, unthinkable, and unforgettable *final* events that he had already determined long before you and that person met that would bring death and destruction to your relationship.

And when the mission was carried out successfully and the weapons formed prospered and the tongues that rose against the relationship went un-condemned, he knew he had won. Satan would use your already known to himself inherited generational curses, the final negative relationship event(s) and your already-determined final relationship ending event(s) that he knew would bring death and destruction to your relationship. And he took away your awareness to physical sensation and took away your ability to experience physical sensation, or he made you feel numb when the wrong was committed against you. When you entered into that, "feeling numb" state, condition, or frame of mind, because of being shocked, stunned, or caught off guard at what happened and at what was being said or done, Satan would then use your feelings to record the wrong that was done to you.

CHAPTER TWENTY-SIX

I'm Done

More to This Life

Today I watched in silence as people passed me by, and I strained to see if there was something hidden in their eyes, but they all looked at me as if to say life just goes on. The old familiar story told in different ways makes the most of your own journey from the cradle to the grave. Dream your dreams tomorrow because life must go on today.

Deep down within, in the deepest parts of the core of his being, he hears there's more to life than living and dying, more than just trying to make it through the day, more to this life more than these eyes alone can see, and there's more than this life alone can be. Tonight he lies in silence, staring into space, and looking for ways to make tomorrow better than today. But in the morning light, it looks the same. In the spirit of being contented, he says to himself, "Life just goes on." Over the years, he has learned the true meaning of what it means to be a man. It haven't been an easy journey for him learning how to be a husband, father, provider, and learning how to be a strong man who has turned negative experiences into positive encounters.

Soul-Searching

In spite of all that he has been through, he still takes care of his family, he takes care of his work, and every Sunday morning, he takes his place at the church. Somehow he still feels the need to search, but life just goes on. His soul-searching has led him to ask the question, "Where do we start to find every part of what makes this life complete?" The answer became clear to him one day as he was praying. If we turn our eyes to Jesus, we'll find that life's true beginning is there at the cross where he died.

More to this life—that's what he hears deep down within, and that's what his heart, mind, soul, and spirit echoes. No matter what he has accomplished, achieved, and accumulated, he kept hearing that small still voice saying there's more to your life… there's more to her life… there's more to your relationship… more than living and dying… more than just trying to make it through the day.

That's the way he feels, and that's the way she feels. Both of them are in search of something deeper, more rewarding, and fulfilling when it comes to their relationship. What do you do when the only thing you can hear within yourself is more? What do you do when you can never be satisfied with where you are, what you have, and where you are in your life? What do you do when you still sense and feel that void inside of you and everything you have said and done to try and fill it up only have made that void deeper than deep? He says to himself, "There is more to me, more to you, and more to us. There is more to our life, to our love, and to our relationship. How do I, we and us get to the more?"

Poetically so, Their Love Song

He never thought the things that brought them together would be the very things that would cause, create the atmosphere, and contribute to them becoming distant and far apart. She was happy with the things they had, but he couldn't, didn't, and wouldn't ever be able to come to that point in his life and with his relationship. She was complacent, contented, in a comfort zone, and had made a lot of compromises that really didn't help make things better in their relationship. He said he would love her always and forever until the twelfth of never. She said he would always be his one and only fairy-tale guy, and now they find themselves in a place they never thought, imagined, or dreamed of in their wildest of dreams.

They have found themselves sharing the same space and just staring at each other in the face. They both are thinking and trying to figure out what went wrong with her fairy tale and what went wrong with his fantasy and what exactly went wrong with their relationship. Everything felt so good, felt so right, but things went so wrong. She feels she is right; he think she is wrong. He thinks he's right she feels he is wrong. Somebody please tell me what did they bring into their relationship that really didn't belong. She couldn't believe he… and he couldn't believe she would ever… you know. They both couldn't believe they would ever… Tell me, baby. What are we going to do when you still have someone who's into you? He feels like screaming. She just wants to shout. What have their relationship really been all about? She feels like she just wanted to cry, and he looked at her and wondered why.

Tell me, baby, how and when do we just kiss and say goodbye. God in heaven, please tell us, did we really try? He says yes. She says no. They both really don't know how and when to let go. She wants to try, and find a new beginning. He feels like it's over. There will be no one winning. He's holding on to the memories they made. She let go of the moments that he promised would never fade. She just wants to turn and walk away. He came back because he felt everything would be okay. Tell me, baby, should we go out into the rain? Maybe just being there would help ease and wash away our pain.

Lord, please tell us why we grew apart, and, Lord, please tell us what to do with our broken heart. Please show us where we went wrong. Our love is just another sad love song. She says she can't feel him. He just can't find her. She says, "Just hold me." He says, "Just let me go." Where do they go from here? They really don't know. He's just staring; she's just standing. Maybe they are believing what happened to them is just deceiving. He never meant to… She never intended to… They never should have… Tell me, baby, what we are going to say when all of our unfinished dreams never come our way. He won't be there, and she won't be here. Both will, in their own time, shed a tear.

While trying to fight their fear, God in heaven knows that was a very tough year. Can't go by how things appear. He just wanted her to hear. She just needed him to listen… He just wanted… He was her fairy tale, and she was his fantasy. They had a bond. What about their connection? They lived their love and they lived their life with words unspoken. It's not just another love song. It's love with a song.

I Made A Vow

Time have passed since the first day they met, got into a relationship, and started to build their home, their family, and their life together. Like any relationship, theirs had its share of ups and downs, good times and tough times, happy days and days when there was sadness. But through all of their days and through all of their times, they survived, and they made it through them all.

They had vowed early in their relationship that they would stay together no matter what, and divorce and letting go would never be an option for them. But as the years would go by and the challenges would come, both of them started to change for all of the wrong reasons and not for the better. There were things they never took the time to confront, and it was those things that end up tearing their love apart. They both wanted and needed more out of their life, their love, out of each other, and more out of their relationship. That's what brought them to where they are. They are not really sure if they should let go or if they should hold on. Both have come to realize that there really is more to life than just living and dying, and there is more to life than just existing in your own life and just existing in your relationship.

They were brought together for all of the right reasons, but one day, all of the wrong things started to happen in their relationship. There were things that neither one of them never expected nor planned. The end of their relationship started when they both begin to question their relationship. She remembered telling him she was leaving, and when he asked why, she said it's because "you don't hold me anymore."

She would go on to tell him if he would just hold her like he used to and hold her more than he held on to the things she had said and done wrong and to all of the things she didn't say or do that he wanted and needed her to say and do. She would want to be with him. Because her heart still belonged to him, she would go on to tell him she would be loving him even though she wouldn't be sleeping very well. She would continue by telling him that she would still be loving him until its cold in hell.

He would tell her he would never let her go, and he would hold her if she would let go of their life and the way it used to be. He would hold her if she would embrace their life as it is and the way it can be. If she did so, they would find a new relationship beginning, and they would finally find themselves winning. He would go on to say to her he had never been so much in love before. Her love had made a big difference in his life. And every day he would wake up to her, and loving her gave him something new that he had never had before. He would tell her that her touch really meant so much to him.

And for the things that have happened to them and the mistakes he had made to suggest, he really don't care about her and that he is not a least bit really into her. That's just what fate and people say. He would finally look at her and say to her, "Don't you know they're never there when I am loving you and showing you I care?"

What Are We Going to Do?

With tears in her eyes, she would say to him her heart will never have a song if he is not there. He would look at her. With his voice quivering, he would tell her his moments would not have a melody if she wasn't there. They both would whisper to themselves, saying their memories won't have any meaning if they weren't there to help make them. What are we going to do when all we can and will end up doing is earnestly remembering former things and have to consider the things of old? That was the question they both heard in the quiet whispers of their "I remember when."

They both came into their fairy-tale fantasy relationship encounter looking for a new thing, something that neither one of them have ever had in a love and relationship. They both entered into a covenant fairy-tale fantasy relationship, believing, hoping, and trusting all of the good, great, awesome relationship things they both have never had would begin to spring forth. Every day they were together, they were looking for and expecting those good, real, and right new fairy-tale fantasy relationship things to spring forth. And when they didn't do so as they both felt, thought, believed, and expected them to, they felt so much frustration, disappointment, and discouragement that they made some big relationship mistakes.

You see, what you really have to grasp a hold of and not try to do the wrong thing is to try to wrap your mind around all of this. Your mind is too carnal-driven and motivated to understand what God is saying to you in what these two people are trying to show and tell you. The truth be told, your mind of the flesh with its carnal thoughts and purposes is so hostile to God that it does not want to yield, submit, and surrender itself to the fairy-tale fantasy relationship standards, principles, processes, and procedures that God can and will give to help enhance and help that which he have joined together.

You can't wrap your mind around any of this because your mind cannot, will not, and have not been drawn, driven, pulled, pushed, persuaded, forced, led into being entangled and entrapped into accepting, adopting, and applying God's relationship laws, rules, regulations, and conditions. Indeed, it has not. As a matter of fact, it is your trying to understand with your carnal mind and you listening to carnal-minded relationship wisdom, knowledge, and understanding that have gotten you and your relationship into the trouble that it is in.

When you have listened to and you are being led, seduced, tricked, and trapped and you are deceived into functioning, flowing, following, abiding by and within the boundaries and limitations of carnal-minded relationship words, images, ideas, instructions, inspirations, information, insights, ingenuities, and creativity, you will end up living the life of someone who is in a carnal relationship. You will have the urge, tendency, inclination, intuition, and the instinct to forever be catering to your appetites and impulses that stem, and they are a product of and is produced, prepared, and presented out of a carnal relationship nature.

No one could have told them they would one day be sitting in a room staring at each other, wondering what happened to their relationship and to their lives. No one could have told them that they were going to go through the things they went through. Because she made a covenant relationship with her Boaz, her prince charming, the man of her dreams, her fairy-tale guy. Looking back on the first day he saw her, he still found himself back at the place that he had always been, even in spite of what have brought them together in that room. She is still his fantasy woman, the woman he loves and his heart craves for.

And the thought of him not seeing her, touching her, and someone else loving her is more than he can take. In the quiet whispers of his heart, down where real meets reality and on the other side of where time never ends and just below and to the right of "I do love you still." And you know, just over there and a little beyond "I do need you... still." He can still see her and him living just a little, laughing just a little, really taking life easy. Just fulfilling and satisfying and sharing and caring and pleasing and being the eternal, until the twelfth of never twin flames with the same twin fires.

As she once again looks over at him and as always, you know, as usual, she can still feel his heart. She can still sense his sensitivity. She can still desire the things that made him her fairy tale that he has so freely given like no man ever have in her life. She can still see herself standing by him, standing with him, and helping him fulfill that which have encompassed and envisioned his soul. In the quiet whispers of her soul down where two hearts met and just below the point where two dreams became one and far over there where time cannot and will not place boundaries and limits on their love, she finds herself in her "I remember when's."

She remembers when he first touched her dreams, and she remembers when he first made love to her heart. She will never forget when and how he loved all of her, and there was that day when... And she will never ever forget the day when he said... yes, he said that and when he did, oh, she replays the moment when he did.

Just like a twin flame is supposed to do, he did it. He brought to life that twin fire, that twin flame inside of her that no man has ever done before. It happened, he happened, they happened, that fire and desire for life, love, relationship, always and forever, until death do they part. It really, really happened. And when it did, it came rushing into her and flowing out of her like nothing she have ever experienced or had encountered before... his passion and her passionate pursuits and purpose just burst forth like a thirst-quenching river of water.

You don't understand. She happened, they happened, their life together happened, their everlasting love happened, their dreams, hopes, and desires, well, yes, they were beginning to happen. But something else happened while they were happening. And that is what has brought them together in the same place sharing the same space.

Here We Are, Tell Me

He thinks he is right; she feels he is wrong. She thinks she is right, and he just feels like she was so wrong. All they can do is stare each other in the face, wishing wanting and needing. She says no, and he says yes. She wanted to go, and he is trying not to stay. He walked out the door... She walked in through the door. He wanted to see her, and she wanted him to touch her. He needed her to hold him, and she just wanted to help him. Here they are just two fairy-tale and fantasy relationship travelers, trying to find, trying to discover, trying to be.

He wants to hold on to... and she just wants to let go of. She says they are too different. He keeps trying to show her where they are the same. How in the midnight hour he screams and shouts and calls her name. She then whispers, "Baby, you are not the blame." Inside of themselves they both say, "Our love is not a game." He looks at her, and the only thing he could say was, "Tell me, baby, tell me what went wrong." With a love we know just didn't fit, our love did... do... still belong. She would walk over to him, and with all of the love that she have for him, she would say, "There you go, honey, letting me listen to your, our heart song."

She would gently stroke his face, wiping away his tears. Doing what she has always done, take away his fears. Reminding him of his faith in a God he had come to know in a very real way. Reassuring him that they are going to be okay because God, well, he is in their room today. Before what happened to them ever happened, He had already made a way. For him she prays both night and day. And before she could whisper another word, he passionately places his finger gently on her lips, looks into her eyes, and in a childlike way, he asks her, "Tell me it's me you want. Please tell me I want to come home."

"My home is in your heart and my home is wherever your heart is." Hey, baby, tell me what are we going to do. I can't live without and I can't see myself going through life without you. Tell me, my sweet fantasy. Is it so wrong for me to love you and desire you and yearn for your love like I do, because I'm so still into you? Looking into his heart and soul like she has always done, she whispers so that only his heart and soul can hear her say, "no, no, no honey that could never be wrong." And then he finally says to her "tell me, baby what are we going to do about this, you know, this that has happened to you, me, and us?"

Mama Told Me

When I was younger, I used to dream a lot about how you would love me and you would write me poetry and want to be with me and be there for me, to love me, hold me, and protect me. I would never feel or be alone, and I would really be happy. Well, my mama told me you might one day wander far, but she never told me you would not physically wander from my presence, but something inside of you would wander. A priceless part of you that I would one day realize I desperately needed, wanted, valued, and treasured.

She never warned me that the dreams and visions you have, the passionate pursuits you would lock into, and the things that you needed and wanted out me when it came to those dreams and visions would own your heart. And so I'm sitting here in this room with you, and I'm saying if you have to go away, I will be waiting for you to call. I will be waiting to hear your voice. I will do for you what you have always done for me. I will be there to save you and swim through the stormy seas. I will cry with you, be happy with you, pray for and with you, encourage and support you, believe in you, cry for you, and love you unconditionally.

That is what I have come to recognize and realize that you done for me, your fantasy. And if you have to go away, I will put your accomplishments and the things that you achieved right next to the things you have acquired and accumulated, which is right close to the picture of you and me and us that I love so much. I'll pretend that you are still at home because the door of my heart will always be open for you.

I never wanted things to be this way, and there are some things I regret I didn't say or do right. But it wasn't because I didn't love you, and it wasn't because I didn't care.

Mama Used to Say

When I was growing up, I always wanted things to happen for me really fast. I couldn't wait until I was old enough to leave home, and I would be grown and on my own. Every day I used to count the days when I could walk out the door and follow my dreams, follow my passion, and follow after my fantasy. I just felt like my life was out there somewhere, and it was up to me to find it. My mama used to say, "Take your time, son. Don't be in a hurry." She would tell me how hard it would be to have a family, be a provider, and be a parent and be a person.

But at the time, I was young; and most of the time, I really didn't know what to say. But there was this feeling I had that moved me in silence anyway. As the days of my life would go on, I would slowly make a change. Somewhere deep down within me, I heard a calling from a boundless love; and the moment when I saw you, love had lit a fire deep down within my fantasy. And you, well, you were, are the flame that has forever burned into the darkest times in my life. I know God had sent and placed you in the life of and for an eternity traveler like myself. I live in a place where time never ends and where every day never begins. I know we both really and truly deserve each other's love, and the day I met you, I was saved by your love.

I can't imagine ever leaving you now, and nothing short of death is ever going to stop me from loving, needing, and wanting you. All my love I gladly give to you because all your love I know you gave gladly to me. Just tell me, why do we have to hurt each other? You know, making each other cry, and we really don't know exactly why. We let our differences stop us from connecting on where we are the same. He says to her, I feel more, I want more… That's all I can hear inside of me is more… There has to be more to you, more to me, more to us, and more to our lives, love, and relationship.

She Said within Herself

As she stood there listening and really hearing what he was saying, she did what the woman with the issue of blood did (Matthew 9:21). It was a powerful faith move. "She said within herself…" And what she had said within herself was exactly what she did. She needed something, and she knew she could have it. This was the moment when she could and should do what she didn't do before. "She said within herself." I just need to touch his heart. Lord, please let me touch his heart in a way that I never have. And she began to tell him, "At times, the woman deep down inside of me wanders far from home, and in my mind, I live a life that chills me to the bone. My heart is sometimes just running for the arms I see that's stretched out, that I just feel I have to reach."

And then I ask myself, "Who is that stranger my longing seeks?" I don't know, and I didn't know. But what I did scares me through and through. Because I knew I had a man at home. It's you who needs me to be true. I never meant to hurt you, I never meant to hurt myself, and I never meant to hurt us.

Late at night, I would sit and cry, and I would just say within myself, "Oh, faithless heart, you are consistently tempting me to the core. But you can't have a hold on me, so in Jesus name, don't come around here anymore." She said within herself, "Oh, faithless heart, flee and don't ever come near me, playing games with my head. Playing mind games that only I can see." She told him that day, when God opened the eyes of my heart and I began to see, the only thing I could do was to "say within myself."

Heart Song

They both just sat there in silence after saying what they both had to say and after both really listening and hearing each other's heart. They realized both of their hearts still had a song that both of their spirits, souls, feelings, emotions, and desires knew and would often begin to sing and hum from a place that was deep down within them. From within a place where only they knew of and from a place that only their love for each other knew and had the directions to. Her heart would sing of its love for his heart, and his heart would sing of its love for her heart. And when it did, the melody was so sweet, and how magical those moments would be.

There's no doubt he is her fairy-tale romantic man, and no one will ever question the fact that she is his fulfilled fantasy. She was always bringing out the best in him, and he was always making sure she knew and felt she was so very important, and she always mattered. How they got to the place that brought them to this point where they both at times felt like they were done with their relationship, done with loving each other, done with wanting to see and be with each other, only time and God know the real story.

Yes, it's them, and they just sat in the same room sitting in silence. He knows there has to be, had to be more to their life, their love, and their relationship than just existing in it and trying to make it through the days of their lives. She know they have to start somewhere in order to find what is the one thing they need that can and will help make their life and relationship complete. He just knows there have to be more to this life, his life, their life than living and dying, much more, more than just trying to find ways to make it through their tests, trials, tribulations, temptations, days, and nights.

Her heart song says more, and his heart song says much, much more. They are at the right place for God to show them how to get on the right path. If they would just look to him and let him be their guiding light. He spent most of his days looking for ways to get more out of his life. She had become too complacent, too contented, and in a comfort zone, and she made compromises with her journey from her cradle to grave. She had her family, she had her husband, she had her children, she had her church, and she had her job, and that was her world and her life.

He spent a lot of time alone searching for more... more than just accepting, adopting, and applying, just trying to make it through this life and its processes, principles, and procedures. He was looking for that which would make his life, their life, and their relationship fulfilling, rewarding, prosperous, productive, successful, and complete. He had a heart song, she had a heart song, and they had a heart song. They had a heart that had its own song. Gentle is the melody... sweet is the sound.

CHAPTER TWENTY-SEVEN

Dissecting Divorce

Why does it hurt so much when people have to get divorced? Is it because of the things they may or may not end up with? Getting out of any kind of relationship is the same as getting a divorce from it. You don't have to be married in order to get a divorce. Whenever there is a complete separation or dissolving of a relationship of any kind and for any reason, it can and will bring heartache and pain. Divorce is not about two people going their separate ways. Nor is it about two people and their differences, who did wrong and who is wrong or right.

It is about getting disconnected from something or someone that you really believed in. Basically, what happens is both people end up having to sit back and watch their fairy-tale and fantasy dreams, hopes, and desires go up in smoke. Both people will walk away with nothing or very little that they expected to get or gain. Both are left with the reality that they are going to have to start all over again. I'm not talking about a person who gets involved with another person while they are still in a relationship, and once they get out of one relationship, they just move on over into the next. I'm talking about two people who really love and care about their relationship and the person they are in a relationship with. The reality that it is over and both will have to find a way to regroup and restart their lives all over again is not easy at times.

All of us, when we get into a relationship of any kind, invest our thoughts, feelings, emotions, desires, dreams, hopes, time, energy, and expectations into that relationship. Those investments are ones that are deep-rooted, and they are personal and private. No matter who we are, we all want a prosperous, productive, and successful return on our relationship investments. It takes a lot of time and energy to pour into something or someone that you really are not 100 percent sure you will get the right return out of them.

It takes a lot to believe in a person and it takes a lot sometimes to open yourself up to someone and give yourself to someone especially after being hurt and having to fight through past pain and past brokenness. There is more than one way to divorce a person, and there is more than one way to disconnect yourself from them. In most cases, the spirit of divorce had already taken place long before one or more of the persons in that relationship made it a civil matter.

Power thought number 1: But just think for a minute if all of us would take what we have heard or personally know about divorce and apply our knowledge to divorcing our past hurt, past pain, past brokenness, divorce being battered, abused, neglected, abandoned, rejected, violated, molested, taken advantage, being taken for granted, raped, demoralized, and put down, etc. And just imagine if both people would take the same approach, mind, mind-set, thoughts, train of thought, thinking, way of thinking, mental state of mind, mental frame of mind, spirit, attitude, and mentality they exhibit when they are going through a divorce and apply all of that being angry, bitter, resentful, mean, hard-hearted, vengeful, etc., energy and apply it to assaulting, attacking, and assassinating all of the things in your past that slipped into your present and have hindered, held, or stopped you from having an awesome and incredible fairy-tale and fantasy relationship future.

If we took the same approach to divorcing the bad and negative circumstances, situations, confrontations, matters, moments, and memories that Satan uses to keep us yoked, in a stronghold, enslaved, in bondage, bound, and limited by that we do when we are divorcing another human being that we are in a relationship with, God would really get all of the glory out of our relationships, and the devil wouldn't get what he has been given every time a relationship is divorced and disconnected for whatever reason or reasons.

Power thought number 2: Just think where we would be in our relationships and how powerless Satan would be if we divorced all of our dangerous, destructive, deadly, depressed, damaging feelings, emotions, and desires that can, will, and have only enticed, entangled, and entrapped us into the wrong type of relationship urges, tendencies, inclinations, intuitions, and instincts. The spirit of jealousy, envy, being territorial, controlling, and possessive would be destroyed and defeated, and those who have lost their lives and lost their will to win as a result of being tortured, tormented, taken down, and taken out because of those self-destructive spirits would still be alive today.

That is not what we do. We continue to look at the other person as our enemy instead of looking at the spirit of divorce as our enemy. Now I'm not talking about nor would I ever suggest, imply, nor endorse someone who is or was in an abusive, volatile, and dangerous relationship to continue therein. No, you are to get out quick, fast, and in a hurry. Run! Get away. Run for your life and run for the life of those who love you, look up to you, and need you in their life. Run for the life of your children. Run, run, run!

Divorce is the legal dissolution of a marriage by a court or other competent body. It is to legally dissolve ones marriage with someone. It is also a complete separation between two things.

The point I am making is just for a moment. Think where we would be in our fairy-tale and fantasy relationship experience(s) and encounter(s) if we spiritually, physically, mentally, and emotionally disconnected, dissolved, separated, and divorced ourselves from bad, wrong, and negative relationship standards, principles, processes, procedures, and practices that are generationally cursed.

Different Perspective Relationship Thought

Where would your relationship be if you became your own attorney and went about with a personal vengeance, disconnecting, dissolving, and making sure you separated yourself from hand-me-down, demonically suggested and influenced cursed and tainted relationship behavior, learned behavior, and behavior patterns that open the door for you to be pulled, pushed, persuaded, drawn, driven, and forced into causing, creating the atmosphere, and contributing to you being targeted for relationship torture and tormenting thoughts, train of thought, thinking, and way of thinking.

For as he thinks in his heart, so is he. As one who reckons,
he says to you, eat and drink. Yet his heart is not with
*you but is grudging the cost. (*Proverbs 23:7)

What are you thinking about when it comes to your relationship that you should not be thinking about that you find yourself without any type of restraints and control, thinking about that is not good or healthy? Satan always wants to find ways to get us to disconnect, dissolve, and separate ourselves from our relationships and from the person who we are in a relationship with. For just a moment, indulge me by setting your mind on cruise control and flow and follow me into these thoughts that I hope can and will make you think. Just think what would happen

(A) if you were to disconnect, dissolve, and separate yourself from any and all humanly tainted, tutored, trained, taught, driven, and motivated relationship self-performance, self-willed and self-effort acts, actions, and deeds. Where would your relationship(s) be right now?

(B) If you were to dissolve, disannul, disconnect, and separate yourselves from any and all relationship boundaries and limitations that restrict your relationship from functioning, flowing, and following faith, hope, belief, and confidence-filled relationship mental state of mind, mental conditioning, and mental frame of mind relationship rules, relationship regulations, and relationship guidelines.

(C) If you were to dissolve, disannul, disconnect, and separate yourself and your relationship from being complacent, contented, in a comfort zone, and compromising with relationship images, ideas, insights, ingenuity, information, inspirations, and instructions that is satanically sent and is designed to distract, detour, detain, delay, and deny you the right to have a safe, stable, and secure mind-set and mentality relationship character, conduct, conversations, and communications.

(D) If you were to dissolve, disannul, disconnect, and separate yourselves from any and all relationship confessions and professions that lead you into procrastinating, hesitating, questioning, and second-guessing the relationship and second-guessing the God who has brought you into that relationship because he knows it is a healthy, rewarding, and fulfilling relationship that will eventually lead you into your relationship land that is flowing with milk and honey.

(E) If you were to dissolve, disannul, disconnect, and separate yourselves from any and all relationship principles, processes, and procedures that have a form of God likeness but deny the power thereof that can and will keep you seduced, tricked, trapped, and deceived into making bad and wrong relationship choices and decisions that dominate, manipulate, and control your relationship power of choice.

(F) If you were to dissolve, disannul, disconnect, and separate yourselves from any and all feeling-, emotion-, and desire-driven and motivated relationship practices, principles, processes, and procedures that is constantly and consistently being a distraction to your relationship. They also hinder, hold up, and get in the way of you getting onto the path that will bring it to the place where it is being prosperous, productive, and successful and thus fulfilling its purpose by divine design destiny.

I could go on and on, but I won't because I know you get what I'm sharing here. We have to stop divorcing the things that are important in our relationships because doing so will only bring the relationship itself to a place where it can and will end up being dissolved, disannulled, and disconnected. That is not God's perfect will for our relationships.

The spirit of divorce takes place in our relationship long before the final act of being in a divorced relationship occurs. Throughout our relationship, we start the divorcing process and begin to accept, adopt, and apply the divorce principles and procedures when the person we are in relationship with began to say and do things that we don't like and that hurt us, bring us pain, heartache, and brokenness of any kind and to any degree.

If we don't get the right relationship prescription from the right relationship doctor, who is Jesus, and apply it in the right relationship doses, that which he prescribes personally for us, our relationships will not work, and our relationships will get sick and remain sick. And as a direct result, eventually, something that we value and treasure in that relationship will die, and that death or dying of something will have a powerfully profound effect and affect upon and in that relationship as a whole. Jesus is the author and finisher of relationships.

The truth is, God has a vision for your relationship, and Satan has a counterfeit, different, and twisted vision for your relationship. The most common occurrence when it comes to relationships is the persons in their relationship start out functioning, flowing, and following the vision God has for their relationship; and when they experience and encounter an unseen, undetected, unexpected, unplanned, and unknown matter, moment, memory, circumstance, situation, and confrontation that was not in the fairy-tale and fantasy relationship and marital handbook, that person or persons not really knowing how to handle that occurrence begin to do three things.

- They seek out the advice of others they confide in, people they look up to, and have placed them in the role of their relationship expert.
- They engage in and indulge in and follow their wrong reasoned tutored, trained, and taught relationship urges, tendencies, intuitions, inclinations, and instincts that are initiated out of fear impulses. The persons have a wrong reaction, wrong response, and a wrong reactionary response and take matters into their own hands.
- They seek out and run to the real relationship deliverer and healer who know how to accurately diagnose what is going on and what is wrong in a relationship. He knows what the right prescription is that will deliver, cleanse, purge, heal, and make that relationship whole.

This final choice, number 3 is usually the last one most will turn to. For some reason that is satanically designed, most people conduct themselves as if they do not believe Jesus is a mender of broken people with broken lives and broken spirits. They conduct themselves in a way and in manner that strongly suggest they do not believe he is the mender of broken relationships. Running to Jesus should never be the last option or any other numerical option. Running to him when we have relationship matter, issue, or challenge should be our first reaction, response, and reactionary response.

God created and is the creator of relationships, and he knows how to fix them and make them whole. I want to say it again, God has a vision for your relationship, and Satan has a wicked, dangerous, selfish, self-centered, self-righteous, self-justified, and self-destructive vision for you, your life, and your relationship. I would encourage you to disconnect, dissolve, disannul, and separate yourself, your life, your love, and your relationship from the devious, defiling, demoralizing, delusional, deceptive, and deceiving vision he have for you, your life, and for your relationships.

Divorcing Visions

You cannot and will not win if and when you open yourself and your relationship up to functioning, flowing, and following the vision satanic fate have for you and your relationship. Your relationship will have to suffer through all kinds of unreal, unfair, uncertain, unaware, and unsure tests, trials, tribulations, and temptations that will, in the end, leave you with aggravating and agitating, frustrating, distasteful, discouraging, disappointing, and depressing relationship occurrences that will forever end up being unforgettable, unexplainable, unthinkable, and absolutely an unbelievable vicious cycle of relationship experiences and encounters.

All of which will forever change your life and change the way you see, perceive, and handle every relationship you will ever get into. The questions I have for you are the following:

1) Do you know the vision God have for your relationship?
2) Do you have a clear, accurate vision God have for you, your life, your love, and your relationship that is not humanly tainted and contaminated, influenced, or suggested? *Fact A:* Please understand this. If you do not have a clear, concise, and accurate vision God has for you and your life, then you cannot and will not have a clear, concise, and accurate vision God have for you in a relationship. *Fact B:* Your covenant relationship(s) are supposed to help you and help your relationship fulfill their highest God-given calling, purpose, and destiny. *Fact C:* God did not allow you to get into a relationship he created for you so that you can take control of it and say, do, handle, and make whatever kinds of relationship choices and

decisions you selfishly want to make. He did not give you the right and the power and the authority to define and designate a relationship he created for you for whatever you selfishly want and need it to do. He created the relationship you are in solely for the purpose of helping you reach your full relationship potential, be prosperous, productive, and successful and fulfill your personal and private relationship destiny. He did not give you His best for the satisfying of what you feel is your relationship entitlement.

3) Do you know and have the vision for your relationship that God have established and set in place? It is one that you have *not* seen or perceived, but you have processed in and through that relationship your personal feelings, emotions, and desires. *Fact A:* When you have an unhealthy vision for your life, love, and relationship, the opposite of what Proverbs 29:18 says will happen. What will begin to happen is some part of you, your life and what you really need or want or can give and recognize, realize, and receive in that relationship will begin to perish, die, and fade away right before your eyes. *Fact B:* The vision you have for your relationship have to have the *redemptive revelation of God* in it, powering it, working through it, and working for it. That is the only way to stop your life, love, and relationship(s) from perishing and having to be disconnected, dissolved, and disannulled. *Fact C:* When you have unhealthy feelings, emotions, and desires, they will lead you to having and demonstrating an unhealthy behavior, behavior patterns, conduct, conversations, and communications.

It is important that we continually be constant and be consistent in and with disconnecting, dissolving, and disannulling the relationship visions that others in relationships have tutored, trained, and taught us to accept, adopt, apply, strengthen, settle, and establish our relationships in. The vision God has for someone else's relationship is not always the same one he has for you. On the other hand, the vision Satan has for you, your life, your love, and your relationship is always the same as the one he has given to someone else.

And if you function, flow, and follow the relationship advice they are or have given you, whatever is happening or have happened in their relationship will eventually manifest itself in your relationship. You see, there are a lot of things the people you think and feel have good, healthy, and wholesome relationships have going on in their relationship or have had happen to them and to their relationship that they keep secret and hidden from human view. They have not and will not tell you their whole relationship mistake truths.

The people we often listen to and take relationship advice from do not always tell us everything or the whole truth about their relationships. Why? It is because it is human nature for us to protect, value, and treasure what we have. Most relationship people are walking around in and with a relationship protective mode, mind-set, and mentality. Anything they share concerning their relationship is filtered and processed through their relationship-sharing perception. We have to make it a daily practice and priority to make sure we disconnect, dissolve, disannul, and separate ourselves and our minds with all of its learning capacity and capabilities from visions that have no redemptive revelation of God in them.

CHAPTER TWENTY-EIGHT

Unfinished Dreams

Power thought number 3: The main reason why divorce really hurt so badly is because both people feel, believe, and know they will end up having to walk away with unfinished dreams. Her reality is she is divorcing her fairy tale, and his reality is he is divorcing his fantasy, and their reality is they are both divorcing their dreams. Your reason for getting into that relationship with him or her was because you actually believed that you and that person could and would work together, and in doing so, you would make all of yours and her dreams come true. The formula for a prosperous, productive, and successful relationship is

Faith-filled, driven, and motivated fairy tale + faith-filled, driven and motivated fantasy = fulfilled dreams

Please note that I said faith-filled, faith-driven, and faith-motivated. The fairy-tale and the fantasy dream and desire you have must be pure, holy, clean, clear, concise, and accurate if it is to do what it is to do. Just think about that one dream and desire you have had all of your life and that one dream and desire have helped you make it through all of the challenges, changes, circumstances, situations, confrontations, tests, trials, tribulations, and temptations that you have had to endure through.

You knew deep down within, with a blessed assurance, that one dream and desire you had was real and so right, that if and when it was fulfilled, you would have the life and the lifestyle that you knew really belonged to you. Your motive with your vision, dream, and desire have never been to impress people or to elevate and turn you into someone who thinks they are better than others or to make you a snooty, arrogant, and selfish person.

The only thing you were trying to do and wanting to do with your dream, desire, and vision was to better yourself and to be all that God created you to be, have all that he said you could have, go and do everything that he said, and, more important, you just want to fulfill your God-given, prophesied purpose and destiny. This is the right relationship mode, mind-set, and mentality you should always be in and stay in. As your life begins to unveil, it started to unfold in a way that you did not expect nor want it to.

You found yourself under all kinds of unseen, unexpected, unplanned, unknown, undetected relationship and personal assaults, attacks, circumstances, situations, confrontations, and matters of the heart that you felt and knew were unfair, left you feeling uncertain, showed up unannounced, and you were unaware they were going to show up, thus leaving you unsure of what will happen next and what your life, love, and relationships would really end up being like. But you held on to your faith in God, and with patience, you persevered through all of the not so good days and through the hurt, pain, and broken-filled days and moments that showed up in your life. It wasn't and had not been easy for you, but God has always been there to help you, hold you, and give you his strength to make it through your weakest and darkest moments. You learned how to be full of joy, exult and triumph in your troubles and rejoice in your sufferings, knowing that pressure and affliction and hardship produce patient and unswerving endurance (Romans 5:3).

God was there to help you make it through all of the unforgettable, unexplainable, unthinkable, and unbelievable times and moments in your life, and he helped you to see, know, and understand that by you exercising and staying on the path called endurance (fortitude) even in those times when you felt overwhelming feelings of frustration, discouragement, disappointments and you wanted to quit and give in and give up. God wouldn't let you, and he sent those you knew and didn't know to hold you up.

He was developing maturity of character, approved faith, and tried integrity and character that produces the habit of joyful and confident hope. God was there letting you know that having the right kind and type of hope never disappoints or deludes or shames you. The journeys you have had when it comes to relationships have not been to your personal and private expectations.

Some have been just good, some bad, and some just downright ugly. But you held on and kept believing in spite of the hurt, pain, brokenness, etc. You wouldn't give up on your vision, your dream, your hope, and your desire. There have been a lot of lonely nights, and there have been some nights when you have had to cry yourself to sleep. All kinds of things were said and done to you, and some were intentional and, but you still held on and kept believing, hoping against hope. You see, nobody knows... They just don't know.

And one day you meet that one person whom you feel is right for you. All of the signs point in the right relationship direction. You see that person as your fairy-tale and fantasy relationship person. So you open yourself up and allow yourself to get into that relationship. Things were really good for a long time, nothing outside of the usual or normal relationship things. You and that person really connected, and you were seeing the visions, dreams, hopes, and desires you have always had finally coming true. What a happy time and a happy moment in your life.

Running the Relationship Race

For the first time, in your life you were feeling like you were with the right person, and being with that person gave you everything you have never had in a relationship. You could see and sense you were about to accomplish, achieve, acquire, and accumulate the things you always wanted, even needed. Every moment, when you would wake up and enter into running in your relationship race you, can now see it was worth it. You can now see that all of the relationship challenges and things you had to confront and change when it came to yourself and all of the other relationship adjustments you have had to make that nobody but you and God know about were well worth it. It's the last relationship hurdle before the final sprint to the relationship finish line.

You are ready, and you feel you are prepared for the final sprint. Once you and this relationship you are in cross that relationship finish line, everything that the both of you have ever needed, wanted, desired, envisioned, prayed, trusted, and believed God for, sacrificed for, and endured through would become a reality. Everything that you and your fairy-tale guy and your fantasy sweetheart have planned, prepared, and positioned yourselves for would finally be, become, and end up being yours and her reality.

Maybe you are on the path, or you are and were close to and about to get on the right relationship path, and no one could have or did prepare you for what would happen next in your relationship. Out of seemingly nowhere, you or that person you are in a relationship with opened the door for what seemed right but was wrong. And before you knew it, the unseen, unexpected, unplanned, unknown, unfair, uncertain, unaware, unsure, uncertain, and undetected showed up in your day, your life, your love, and your relationship.

It was an unforgettable, unexplainable, unthinkable, and unbelievable moment in your life, in his life, and in your relationship. Your fantasy woman and you her fairy-tale man would never cross that relationship finish line. And that is what have brought the both of you into that room, into that space, and into that place that you are in spiritually, physically, mentally, emotionally, and financially. It is what have caused and contributed to bringing you and her into the same mood, mind, mind-set, mental mode, and mentality. Both of you are hurt, and the both of you are halt between two opinions.

She Whispers "It's true"

It's true. There is so much going through you, and there is so much going through the person that you shared that good relationship with. As you look back and listen again to what Mama said and what some other people said, you know, they warned you of what could and sometimes would happen in a relationship. Well, you can hear Mama and even your closest friends telling you about your fairy-tale guy, but they never took the time to tell you that you and him would argue, fuss, cuss, and feel all kinds of feelings and emotions. She never told you there would be days when you would cry and scream. She never said that maybe someday, one day he'd say goodbye.

She quietly whispers under her breath, "Why didn't she tell me the wrong feelings I had that at the time I really felt was right, would, and could wipe my world away ended up ravaging the promises my stronger heart once made." She continues, "I was there for him, and I thought he would be there for me, but he never came to save me. He lets me stand alone out in the wilderness and cold. Since that day, our life, my life, our days, our relationship, my heart, and our home have never been the same. Something has happened with us, and I'm not sure. I don't know how to undo what I've done.

Mama, you see, she never told me that one day my head would be filled with scattered pictures of him; and as I walked through the memories we made in my heart, those memories and scattered pictures would remind me of you, the man whose picture I treasured so much that I kept it by our bed. The thought of me waking up and you are not there really causes my mind to wander. I often found myself checking through the moments I had with you, and it's obvious that you are the one who made those memories with me. It's true, my memories and moments have a way of connecting me to the simple things I noticed about you. Simple things like remembering the shoes size you wear, waking up and seeing how you would lay in the spot you used to sleep in.

I never thought this day would come when I wouldn't know just who this man is that I'm looking at in this room. There was a time when we were so connected, and I could feel you, and I knew you. And the mere fact that you would be near and close kept me and my heart excitedly waiting for you to arrive, but now it's hard for me to accept how I felt, how I came to feel you were a stranger in my house. There was a time in my life, in our relationship where I knew you would know my heart, but now you're not the same, I am not the same, and we are not the same.

It took a while for me to figure out that there's no way with all of what we had shared and with all of the moments when he demonstrated he really cared; that man that I last saw standing where the man I had came to love, respect, and adore standing can't be who he say he is. He's just got to be someone else. You see, my fairy-tale man, guy, well, I know he wouldn't say and do things that would hurt me. He wouldn't reject and resist me like this man I'm in this room did. My fairy-tale guy, the one that I love and have shared so many wonderful, fulfilling, happy, unforgettable, unexplainable, unthinkable, and just unbelievable moments and memories with, well, deep down within my heart and soul, I know he would adore me. He wouldn't ignore me.

Mama, it's true. It's so very true. You told me, and I wish you were here now. Maybe you can tell me because I'm not sure who he is. Every day he is here in this place, and in this same space with me I can see his shadow, and I can sense his sensitivity, but he is not leaving me any room to enter in so that I can find myself in him. I miss his kisses and it hurt to hear his goodbyes because they are with the words of a stranger, you know, someone else. So many times I would just sit in the room where we shared and made so many precious moments and memories. If these walls could speak right now of things they remembered. If these hallowed halls of my heart could speak because of the hurt that's inside of me right now, well, they wouldn't have nothing good to tell.

No one had to say we were changed, and nothing else we live through would ever be the same. Even though I know the truth, my truth, I still ask myself, "What could it be? Is there someone he met trying to be me? Could she be so heartless that she would be trying to take my place?" I wish he would look me in the face and tell me I'm wrong. I know I wasn't there when he needed me, but have I changed so drastically? And now I can't feel and find his heart, the heart that I had come to love falling into. I wish I knew what was in his mind just like I know he loves me as no other could.

I remember the day he surprised me, I found it hard to believe he was leaving me a note saying he's gone for good. That day when he left me, well, our home, it wasn't the same ole place. It's really, really true. My mama used to tell me about having lovesick blues, and at the time, I really didn't understand what she was talking about. I used to laugh at her, and I just figured she was doing what she was always doing, you know, talking old days talk. She told me one day I would understand, and you know she was right.

Today, as I sit here in this room with my fairy-tale guy, faced with the reality of having unfinished dreams, my heart and soul is filled, singing, and echoing broken heart blues. I just want, you know, I just wish things would be like they once were. When I was having a tough day and I was not really myself, well, he would do what he has always done, and that was put his magic touch to my tough days. Lord, is my fairy-tale relationship romance over? If so, my life must now begin without the man I will always love and call my fairy-tale man. Oh, Lord, please tell me what am I going to do with my unfinished dreams? And, Lord, you know all things, and you know how things are going to turn out with me, him, and our relationship. Please tell me why me, why us, and please tell me why this?

CHAPTER TWENTY-NINE

Tear My Heart Apart

He Can Only Say, "It's So Very True"

This is my truth, and this is my reality. It's so very true. I can see it, and I now understand it. We both have hurt each other. I have hurt her, and now I'm sitting here in this room no longer living life in paradise and no fantasy being fulfilled. My real true friends, well, they told me I would one day be faced with that one relationship challenge that I would either have to conform to or confront. It's so very true. I left her a note, telling her I was gone for good, but what she didn't know was I was staying down the street with a friend of mine, and every day I would watch her come and go. I would make sure she was doing all right, and there were those days when I would just sit in my car and watch her, and I would break down and cry.

Why? Because I really missed her so much, and I never thought we would ever be in the place we are. I do love her, and there is nothing or no one who can erase or remove that. You see, I woke up one morning, and I realized I was without her once again. I knew then that I didn't want our dreams to just fly away, and I knew there were some things I really didn't say that I needed to say. When I felt like I couldn't and wouldn't be able to find my way back into her heart, I left her that note, knowing deep down inside I really didn't want to be without her.

I think we both, well, I got lost in the quiet storms that were raging in my life. I wanted more out of my life, more out of my relationship, and I expected more out of me that what I was seeing and getting. Somehow in the midst of what we were going through, we both lost what we had found in each other. I know we, I mean, I let her down. I wasn't there to save her, and I allowed myself to become a stranger in her heart. Everything that I had worked so hard to build and establish with us personally and with our relationship, I one day stopped maintaining that which I had worked hard to build and establish. I started focusing on and eventually other distractions, and before I knew it, I was living in and out of the voids that were within me.

As I sit here in this room with her and I look across at her, I know I do love her… still… I realize she's my weakness, and she really changed my world and my life. The only thing I ever wanted from the first day I met her and we had our first conversation was for her to share my world and be a part of my life. I wanted her to know that from the first day I saw her, I knew she was all I wanted, and she was absolutely everything I needed. I know there were some things I said and done that I really didn't mean to say and do, and I know I made my mistakes along the way. But there is one thing I know wasn't a mistake, and that was the moment and the day when I gave her all of my heart. I'm so deep into her, and my soul sets anywhere she is.

They always told me I dreamed the dreams of a foolish dreamer, but I don't care because my reality is that she's still my heartbeat, and her love is like a river flowing right through me. Her love is washing me, watering and quenching my thirst for her and her love. You see, it's so very, very true. She is my fantasy, and I only want and wanted her to share my life and my world with me. I have never had any woman in my life that I ever wanted to say what I'm about to say to her and that is, "You're my dream and my joy, and my heart belongs to you."

One day when I was really missing her, I sat down and wrote her a letter; and in that letter, I wrote down all of the reason(s) why I needed her. After each thing I wrote, I end up writing, "I need you in my world. I came here today to tell you I'll give you whatever it is you really want, and I'll give you anything and everything you wanted from me that I have never given you. I'm through doing things the way I have done them. Whatever it is you want you can have it. That place you have always wanted to be in my life and in my heart, it's yours."

I'm sitting here in this same space with her, and and I want to go over to where you are, gently hold you close to me, and say, "Listen, I want you right here in my world, right here in my life, right here in my soul." I'm so happy to be near her once again, that I want the world to know that I need her. I heard her heart when she apologized, and I believed her. And if she will let me back into her heart, I promise her I'll never deceive her.

Lord, I pray that this is not our end because if it is, you know I can't and won't be able to move on because of all of the memories we have made. Lord, I won't be able to carry our memories. Oh, those memories, sweet, sweet memories of days gone by. Lord, I don't want to cry. Please don't let this be our goodbye.

Her memories, our memories, sweet memories—it's so very true. They make me sad, and no matter where I go and no matter how hard I try to lose them, I find a path that takes me back to her. Somewhere deep in my heart, I know I would never be able to shake the memories, sweet, sweet memories of the love we shared that we will never share again. I realized she needs me, and I also realizes I need her so desperately, and it hurts for me to think that I would have to live with the memories, our moments, and with the things we both made matter. And when I would do so, it would be without her, the one who made the memories and moments matter the most.

I know a man is not supposed to cry, but I know I wouldn't be able to dry those tears from my eyes. Why, you ask? It's because I love her. I will love her no matter what she does, and I hope you, the reader of this book, understand this relationship, our relationship, and understand me. Every word I say is so very true because I love her, and even though I'm sitting right here in the same room with her, I'm thinking of her. I have spent all of the time we spent together, trying to be more of a man for her, and I didn't and don't have much to offer her, but I tried to let her know no matter what, she and I, well, we, are going to make it through.

Some men need a lot of women in and out of their life just for their passions to feel alive, but I'm not that kind of man, and the note I left her, well, it wasn't because I was running into the arms of another woman. I know, I know. I want only her because God in heaven knows I love her with all my heart and soul. In the quiet whispers of my heart, the only thing I can say is, "I love you... I need you... I want you...

This just can't be the end." What you don't know is when I first met her, she left me mesmerized. How can this be happening to us? We still haven't… and… you see, we had planned to… Oh, Lord, please don't let us walk away with unfinished dreams.

Just Tear My Heart Apart

One of my friends told me love is a game, and you don't play to win. You play to survive. Another friend told me, "The same girl that makes you laugh is the same girl that will make you cry." And there was another friend who said, "I just ought to forget about you." I told them all I tried, but I couldn't because when I met you, there was something different about you. I told them I remember the day when you smiled at me, and then you reached out your hand, and you helped me get to where I am today. And then I told my friends I broke a promise I made you when I told you I wouldn't ever leave you, and I wouldn't ever grieve you. I know they are trying to help me, but I don't understand how they can just say things they know really tear my heart apart.

I remember that day when I was trying to reach out for you, reach for you, and you kept resisting, rejecting, and refusing to listen to me and hear me and let me share my heart. I really couldn't take it, and I said to myself, "What's the use of me trying to win? Just play hard to survive." I realized that day, love and loving someone ain't easy, and I don't like to lose, and I'm not trying to lose. I didn't want to spend my time waiting on you because sometimes I would get lonely for loving you. I didn't know when and if you would ever start thinking about me again and not what I had done to hurt you.

My friends, they just didn't know that sometimes I would get lonely, and I never thought I would miss her, but I just couldn't hide the feeling. I still love her, and I'm sitting in this room, thinking how I have been filled with so much emptiness and how I have missed you so bad. I realized every time when I wasn't near and with you that you were the best thing I ever had. I wish I could take back all of the wrong I have done, and I wish saying I'm so sorry for all the wrong I've done would be enough. You are my truth, and you are my reality. You are the only one I need. I wish you would just come across this room to me and hold me like you used to.

If she's not going to do so, is it something I'm going to have to get used to? When I wasn't near her, I would think back on how she used to make me feel like I was her fairy-tale man. I remember how I felt when I was feeling and hearing her show and share her love for me. Now I'm trying and have to deal with the thought of someone else holding, kissing, and loving her. It's not something I want to see happen. Over and over I asked myself, "How can anything I loved and cared for so good, so real, and so right end up to be so wrong?" The more I try to figure it out I realize I really don't understand that.

From the first day we met, I knew all I would ever want to do would be to live my whole life long with her. It's important for me to tell her what's happening to us is not just something that happened because our relationship is not just something that just happened. Our love and life together isn't, can't, and won't be an insignificant something that some would say just happened. And I know for sure she's not just someone that has happened to me and to us that would bring us into this same place. We just can't let it—what happened to us—just end up being one of the unexplainable things we are going to have to get used to. Before I go, before we go, I got to let her know I will give her anything. Lord, please tell me how would anything that's so good end up to be so wrong? Please tell me why me, why us, and why this? I don't understand it.

Here We Are

Well, here we are! I hope you now understand that they were brought to this point and place in their relationship so they could see all of the things that went wrong in their relationship, your relationship, and in your marriage. I also hope you can clearly see that there is and always will be a force that is working behind the scenes of every relationship. It is up to you and me and the people we are in relationships with to decide and determine who and what that force is.

When things go wrong in your relationship and you are not sure what's happening and why, just remember the following:

(1) God allows what's happening in your relationship and marriage because he wants to show you something about yourself first and then show you something about your relationship. God very seldom show you something about the person you are

in a relationship with unless that person is a batterer, abusive, violent, etc., or they pose some kind of danger to you.

(2) God will take the bad and wrong that's happened in your relationship and in your life, and he turns it around in your favor and turns it around so he can get the glory out of it.

(3) God is not the author of negative and bad things happening to good relationships and to good people, but he will use it to tutor, teach, train, grow, develop, and mature you.

(4) God wants to show you what you and the person you are in a relationship have brought, and you are still bringing into your relationship and into your life that is wrong. It can be the wrong things and the wrong person and people that you have opened yourself and your relationship and life up to.

But the most important thing God wants you to see and understand is how important it is for you to spend time divorcing all of the wrong things that have taken place in your fairy-tale and in his fantasy relationship and not spend time trying to find ways or make excuses and have reasons to divorce a person. Your heart has never been the problem when it comes to your relationship. It's your mind. That's where the real problem is.

This story that I have shared with you is true, and a lot of it is about you… Yes, you, the reader of this book. The heart of the person he once knew and came to love, need, and want, he didn't know anymore even though she still had a hold on his heart. The woman who have helped bring them into the place and into the position they are in, were in, when it came to their relationship, he couldn't, wouldn't, and didn't find that same person when he looked for her in his heart.

She used to be there, and he used to know how to reach her when he spoke and shared his heart with her. She is not the same person that he met and was drawn into her love, and in his heart, he's really not sure who she is anymore. Day after day, he would walk into their home, and she would be there waiting for him and glad to see him. They would laugh, talk, share, cry, and pray together, and he always kept his heart and mind open to her and for her. He was always loving, giving, caring, concerned, and compassionate. She knew his heart, passion, dreams, hopes, desires, needs, and wants.

But when things went wrong in their relationship, the person she once knew wasn't the same person who would be walking into the doors of their home, her home. Her fairy-tale man became someone she didn't know anymore. In the end, she wanted him to be happy, and he wanted her to be happy as well. They both recognized and really and truly realized these three truths, and they are the following:

❖ There's a stranger in her house.
❖ There's a stranger in his heart.
❖ There's a stranger in their relationship.

No matter what has occurred in your life and regardless as to what Satan has tried to do to you in the relationships you have been in, God is there for you, and he is reaching out to you right now. He will mend your broken heart, mend your broken spirit, pick up the pieces of your broken life, and mend your broken life. He will deliver, cleanse, purge, heal, and make you and your relationship whole. His name is Jesus, and he is a mender of broken lives and broken people. He is always there for you, and he loves you. He sees and knows the hurt, pain, and brokenness that you have suffered in that relationship. He knows you have been battered, beaten, bruised, molested, abandoned, rejected, demoralized, put down, walked over, taken advantage, taken for granted, raped, etc.

He see and know all about your hurt, pain, and brokenness that came as a result of the last person you were in a relationship with or how someone who was and is close to you hurt you. And as a result, you are having a hard time opening up and giving love and receiving love again. You are having a hard time trusting and believing again in anyone. I want you to know that Jesus will teach you and show you how to love, give, and receive again. He is calling you to himself. Yield, submit, and surrender to his love.

Thank you for reading this book.
I would like to hear from you. Please e-mail me at
<u>write2reachplays@yahoo.com</u>

"SHOW ME HOW TO LOVE AGAIN"

I heard that love could take all my hurt away, but love to me was just another word for endless pain. My life before was wrong, but then you came along. Since you came, my life has changed. I'm now ready for love. Show me how to love again, for my heart is yearning desperately for love. Show me how to give again. Teach me how to receive again. I need you to show me how to love. I was lonely and confused. My heart was torn in two. Nothing seemed to ease the pain, nothing, Lord, but you. Now there's you.

"SHOW ME HOW TO LOVE AGAIN"

CHAPTER THIRTY

Breaking the Relationship Curse

1. **RECOGNIZE THE RELATIONSHIP CURSE.** In order to be free and stay free, you have to admit you have a relationship problem. That sounds simple, but we live in a day and age of denial. No matter what has happened to us in our lives and in our relationships, each of us are responsible for the relationship choices and decisions we make. If you really want to be free, you will accept that responsibility.

2. **BREAK THE RELATIONSHIP CURSE.** As we apply God's Word and power to our relationships and lives and as we choose to walk in righteousness and obedience to God, the chains of relationship bondage will be broken. There are three steps to breaking a relationship generational curse.

   (1) Give your life to Jesus. The blood of Jesus removes our sin.

   (2) Fight the battle with spiritual weapons (such as the Word of God and the armor of God).

   (3) Regain control over the power of your will. When Jesus shed his blood, he bought back our willpower. Through the blood of Jesus, we can say no.

3. **REVERSE THE CURSE.** There are three keys you can use to reverse the curse and live in victory.

   (1) Recognize your enemy. We battle not with flesh and blood. Our enemy is Satan, and the battle is spiritual.

   (2) Forgive people whom you have been in a relationship and have hurt you.

(3) Treat causes, not symptoms (for example, insecurity, jealousy, or fear).

4. **RELEASE THE POWER OF LOVE.** To become people whose lives and relationships are transformed by the love of God, we must not only get rid of what holds us relationship captive and keeps us in relationship bondage, but we must also be filled up with love—for God, for ourselves, for our relationships, and for others. Unconditional love will release blessing. To know more of the love of God in your life, love those who you were, are in a relationship with who have hurt you, those in your relationships who have opposed you, and those who, in your relationships, have sinned against you.

5. **DEVELOP A GODLY ATTITUDE.** A good attitude toward your relationship does not make everything go perfectly all the time. Matthew 5:45 tells us that God sends the rain on the just and the unjust. But our relationship attitude determines whether the rain will water the seeds of our harvest or wash those seeds away. Get serious about where you are going with God by getting your relationship attitude lined up with his Word, having faith, and trusting in him.

6. **ALIGN YOUR WORDS WITH GOD'S WORDS.** Your words give evidence of your faith, and they should reflect God's good purposes for you. Exchange your negative relationship words for positive relationship words. Exchange your negative relationship thoughts for positive relationship thoughts, and exchange your negative relationship actions for positive relationship actions.

7. **ACCEPT GOD'S ACCEPTANCE.** Jesus didn't come to condemn or punish us nor our relationships. He came to give us hope that our lives and relationships can be really different. We don't have to live under the burdens of relationship pain, hurt, shame, or sorrow. All the power in heaven is available to you to set you free from every relationship chain that binds you. Corrie ten Boom said, "There is no pit so deep that God's love is not deeper still."

8. **WALK IN OBEDIENCE.** In order to break free from the relationship curses and walk in relationship freedom, you must learn to walk in relationship obedience to God's ways. We don't

have to be perfect in our relationships, but our hearts need to be surrendered and pliable toward God. We need to be moving forward in the things of God every day of our lives. Today's decisions we make in our lives and in our relationships determine our lives and relationship tomorrow. There is a relationship miracle on the other side of your relationship obedience.

CHAPTER THIRTY-ONE

Power Thought to Remember

The cure for a compare-and-compete curse spirit, a compare-and-compete conspiracy theory spirit, a generational curse and for a generational relationship curse has always been repentance. When Israel turned from idols to serve the living God, the curse was broken, and God saved them (Judges 3:9, 15; 1 Samuel 12:10–11) Yes, God promised to visit Israel's sin upon the third and fourth generations, but in the very next verse He promised that He would show "love to a thousand [generations] of those who love me and keep my commandments" (Exodus 20:6). In other words, God's grace lasts a thousand times longer than His wrath.

For the Christian who is in a relationship and who is worried about a generational curse and about a generational relationship curse, the answer is salvation through Jesus Christ. Covenant with someone who is a Christian just like yourself and who will believe and stand with you on the things you will stand for and against. A Christian is a new creation (2 Corinthians 5:17). How can a child of God still be under God's curse (Romans 8:1)? The cure for a generational curse and a generational relationship curse is for both people in the relationship to express and exercise repentance of the relationship sin in question, faith in Christ, and a life consecrated to the Lord (Romans 12:1–2).

Not only is Jesus a mender of broken people with broken lives, broken spirits, broken hearts, broken dreams, broken will, etc. But he is also the mender of broken relationships, and he is the *master* curse breaker. He wants to make you the person and the one you are in a relationship with and your relationship whole, fulfilling, and rewarding.